D1376580

WITHDRAWN

David Pugh

Collected Papers

II

PHAENOMENOLOGICA

COLLECTION PUBLIÉE SOUS LE PATRONAGE DES CENTRES
D'ARCHIVES-HUSSERL

15

ALFRED SCHUTZ

Collected Papers

II

Comité de rédaction de la collection:
Président: H. L. Van Breda (Louvain);
Membres: M. Farber (Philadelphia), E. Fink (Fribourg en Brisgau),
J. Hyppolite (Paris)†, L. Landgrebe (Cologne), M. Merleau-Ponty (Paris)†,
P. Ricœur (Paris), K. H. Volkmann-Schluck (Cologne), J. Wahl (Paris);
Secrétaire: J. Taminiaux (Louvain).

ALFRED SCHUTZ

Collected Papers

II

Studies in Social Theory

EDITED AND INTRODUCED BY

ARVID BRODERSEN

MARTINUS NIJHOFF / THE HAGUE

Photomechanical reprint 1971

First printing 1964
Second printing 1968
Third printing 1971

© Copyright 1971 by Martinus Nijhoff, The Hague, Netherlands
All rights reserved, including the right to translate or to
reproduce this book or parts thereof in any form

PRINTED IN THE NETHERLANDS
ISBN 90 247 0248 8

CONTENTS

Part II | Applied Theory

EDITOR'S NOTE

The present volume, the second of Alfred Schutz's *Collected Papers*, contains works in sociology from the period 1940–1959 and – in one case – from the year 1932, selected according to a table of organization drafted by the author shortly before his death. In the last weeks of his life Schutz made plans to have the numerous papers of his "American period" collected and published in English, in book form. The material was to be included in three volumes: one volume, for which he chose the title: *The Problem of Social Reality*, the present volume of *Studies in Social Theory*, and one of *Studies in Phenomenological Philosophy*. He left few instructions regarding the two latter volumes, apart from a provisional listing of items to be included, but still had time to give some thought to such editorial details as the subdivisions of *The Problem of Social Reality*, their sequence and the sequence of chapters within each section. That was all. The rest had to be entrusted to others.

In his Preface to Volume I, Father H. L. Van Breda has recalled the main data of Alfred Schutz's life and intellectual development, evoking the memory also of his personality as a man and a scholar. Readers of the present volume will find these pages (Vol. I, pp. VI–XIII) as well as the Introduction by Maurice Natanson (Vol. I, pp. XXV–XLVII) helpful toward a deeper understanding of Schutz's mind and work.

As far as *Studies in Social Theory* is concerned, the selection and organization of its material generally conform with the table of contents drafted by the author. The only major exception is the introductory piece, "The Social World and the Theory of Social Action," which for reasons presently to be explained, was included, although it had not been listed by the author. All the present papers are, as the title of the volume indicates, studies in social theory. They are grouped according to the general categories of pure and applied theory, the former comprising the first three sections of the book. The sequence in which the material is presented within the two main parts is, by and large, in the chronological order of original publication.

A few remarks first concerning the volume as a whole. The title "Applied Theory" may appear somewhat misleading if the key phrase of *Part II* is read as meaning the use of insight for merely practical ends. These studies are not concerned with "social engineering" or "how to solve social problems." They are, as was their author in all his works, concerned with the use of theory for a more adequate interpretation of social reality. Their accent is on understanding rather than operation. Yet the clues they find to the inner meanings of human conduct lead closer to a sensible way of approaching its problems than any treatise on "techniques and methods of problem-solving" could ever do. The man who wrote pieces such as the essay on "Equality" and the related one on "The Stranger" and on "The Homecomer" with its touch of self-reflection is a man of wisdom in human affairs no less than in scholarly thought and inquiry.

On the origin and nature of the theory which in the hands of Alfred Schutz became his instrument of interpreting the human life-world there is no need to elaborate here. It is enough to say that while the title refers to it as "social theory," this does not place it exclusively within the field of sociology in the conventional academic sense of the term. One lesson which Schutz learned early in life and continued teaching to the end was the necessity for basing any social theory upon a foundation of philosophy. From the beginning he found the basis for his own philosophy in Husserl more than anywhere else, but also in Bergson, William James, Georg Simmel, Max Scheler, and others.

Against this background the term "applied theory" describes the character of the present *Studies* in yet another sense – as exercises in the application of philosophic thought to the interpretation of society. The result is not a philosophy of society, far less a social metaphysics; it is a sociology informed by an art of envisioning and conceptualizing the social world as a whole. Schutz developed the unique art of interpretation, with which he was able to conquer new ground of his own, by a creatively combined application of two master tools: phenomenological analysis and the general sociological methodology of Max Weber.

With the exception of the second paper: "The Dimensions of the Social World" – an English adaptation of a chapter from Schutz's early book: *Der sinnhafte Aufbau der sozialen Welt* [1] and the paper "Don Quixote and the Problem of Reality" which was published in a Spanish translation [2] – all the papers in the present volume were originally published in English.

The following notes provide the bibliographical data of each paper and in addition some further explanation concerning the nature and history of the two first sections of the volume.

Part I

Pure Theory

Part I. 1. "The Social World and the Theory of Social Action." First published in *Social Research*, Vol. 27, No. 2, Summer 1960 pp. 203–221, this essay represents the last section, about one third of a longer paper, written in New York in the summer of 1940, the author's first work after his arrival from Austria. The paper was mainly devoted to a critical review of Talcott Parsons': *The Structure of Social Action* (1937), a work which Schutz had studied with the keenest interest. He originally intended to have the entire paper published as his first contribution to scholarly debate in America. However, he changed his mind when he realized that a critical piece such as this would scarcely be understood nor its constructive aspects appreciated unless readers were acquainted with the position in philosophy and social theory on which it was based.

Schutz never returned to this particular subject. However, reading through the manuscript twenty years later, the editor was struck by the fact that the final section of the paper stands apart from the rest, being simply a statement of Schutz's own sociological thinking without critical or polemical reference to

[1] Wien, Springer Verlag 1932, 2nd edition, 1960.
[2] *Dianoia*, Anuario de Filosofia, 1955.

any other author. Here are in brief his basic ideas of a theory of social action, conceived from his familiarity with the masters of modern sociology such as Weber, Simmel, and Scheler, as well as with the philosophers whose work he considered most relevant to such a theory – Bergson and, above all, Husserl. It is this final part of the paper which is here reproduced. The text is identical with that of the manuscript, except for slight bibliographical amplifications and the insertion of two minor passages and a single major one from the preceding sections (enclosed within brackets), the deletion of occasional punctuation changes and paragraph divisions. The title was supplied by the editor.

Part I. 2. "The Dimensions of the Social World." The inclusion of a central piece from *Der sinnhafte Aufbau der sozialen Welt*, a work containing the essence of Schutz's thought during the formative period of his life, is appropriate and indeed necessary for reasons beyond those of intellectual history. The book was published in Vienna in 1932. It was at once enthusiastically received by those especially interested in the subject matter and seemed obviously destined to become a work of major influence among social science scholars in general. But Schutz and his work had to suffer the fate so tragically typical of that period of European culture: the rising wave of barbarism, soon to engulf the entire continent, drove him into exile and for many years to come destroyed the intellectual community where the book had been conceived and where alone it could have made its immediate impact upon the contemporary mind. Only after many a long year did it finally resume its career as one of the very few high-ranking contributions to modern social theory. A new edition, identical with the first, was published in Vienna in 1960 [1]. So far no English translation is available, although *Der sinnhafte Aufbau der sozialen Welt* still remains the foundation upon which most of Schutz's subsequent work rests – written in the United States and almost all of it published in English.

For all its variety of subject matter, this later production – papers and articles printed in learned journals – shows a rigorously disciplined inner consistency and perseverance in the pursuit of the author's early vision. Thus, the book and the numerous subsequent papers are, in a sense, variations on a

[1] Springer Verlag, 2nd edition, 1960.

grand theme. Taken together they form a unity which, though highly diversified, possesses the beauty and force of a well-rounded system of thought. The student who wants to understand the system as a whole must take into account both halves of Schutz's work, the early book which set the theme as well as the later papers elaborating and enriching it from the many new sources he discovered, especially in American social thought. The selection from the book therefore has its rightful place in the present volume. Pending the appearance of an English translation of the whole, [1] it will at least give readers to whom the original work is inaccessible an opportunity to acquaint themselves with a central part of it.

It was Schutz's original intention to include in this volume a condensed restatement of the analysis of "The Dimensions of the Social World, The World of Contemporaries, Predecessors, and Successors" (*Der sinnhafte Aufbau der sozialen Welt, Vierter Abschnitt: Strukturanalyse der Sozialwelt. Soziale Umwelt, Mitwelt, Vorwelt*) omitting those parts of the investigation tangential to the central theme or those already adequately treated in his papers. Unfortunately Schutz could not carry out this plan himself. Professor Thomas Luckmann undertook the difficult task of doing so.

The systematic unity of Schutz's production, superficially obscured by its diversification and fragmentation (in "papers") during the American period, would have become abundantly clear had he lived to complete the project which most urgently occupied him during the final phase of his life. This was to be a major volume presenting in fully organized form and elaborate detail the main body of his social theory. He had to leave it unfinished. But he managed, virtually with his last strength, to work out an extremely detailed system of organization, showing the conceptual structure of the whole, and to write several large, though fragmentary parts of what was to be the text of the book. This material, comprising several hundred pages of typescript (some of it second draft and almost ready for print) and handwritten notes, was in large part written in German, and Schutz intended to publish his new book first in the language of

---

[1] A partial translation was recently prepared for private circulation by Professor Dorion Cairns.

Der sinnhafte Aufbau der sozialen Welt, to which in a sense it was to be a second or companion volume. [1]

Part I. 3. "The Problem of Rationality in the Social World." Presented at the Interdepartmental Conference at Harvard University, 1942; published in *Economica*, New Series, Vol. X, No. 38, May 1943, pp. 130–149. In this paper the original English spelling has been adjusted to conform with the American usage which prevails throughout the volume.

Part II

Studies in Applied Theory

"The Stranger." Read before the General Seminar of the Graduate Faculty of the New School for Social Research.
Published in *The American Journal of Sociology*, Vol. XLIX, No. 6, May 1944, pp. 499–507.

"The Homecomer." Read before the General Seminar of the Graduate Faculty of the New School for Social Research, December 6, 1944.
Published in *The American Journal of Sociology*. Vol. L. No. 4, December 1945, pp. 363–376.

"The Well-Informed Citizen: An Essay on the Social Distribution of Knowledge." Read before the General Seminar of the Graduate Faculty of the New School for Social Research, March 20, 1946.
Published in *Social Research*, Vol. 13, No. 4, December 1946, pp. 463–478.

"Don Quixote and the Problem of Reality." Read before the General Seminar of the Graduate Faculty of the New School for Social Research, December 16, 1953.
Published in Spanish (translation by Professor and Mrs. Luis Recasens-Siches) in *Dianoia*, Yearbook of the Department of Philosophy, University of Mexico, 1954.

"Making Music Together: A Study in Social Relationship." Read

---

[1] Professor Thomas Luckmann is attempting at present to integrate this material into the precisely developed conceptual structure for the book. It is hoped to have this work published as a separate volume.

before the General Seminar of the Graduate Faculty of the
New School for Social Research.

Published in *Social Research*, Vol. 18, No. 1, March 1951,
pp. 76–97.

"Mozart and the Philosophers." Read before the General
Seminar of the Graduate Faculty of the New School for
Social Research, January 1956.

Published in *Social Research*, Vol. 23, No. 2, Summer 1956,
pp. 219–242.

"Santayana on Society and Government." Read before the
General Seminar of the Graduate Faculty of the New School
for Social Research, January 9, 1952.

Published in *Social Research*, Vol. 19, No. 2, 1952 pp. 220–246,
with this note by the editors: "In this paper the presentation
of Santayana's thought follows as closely as possible his own
wording, as it is the conviction of the author that this
procedure best assures the correct rendering of the philosopher's ideas. The permission of Charles Scribner's Sons to use
Santayana's text in this way is gratefully acknowledged."

"Equality and the Meaning Structure of the Social World."
Presented at the Fifteenth Symposium of the Conference on
Science, Philosophy and Religion, Columbia University,
1955.

Published as Chapter III (pp. 33–78) of *Aspects of Human
Equality*, Edited by Lyman Bryson, Clarence H. Faust,
Louis Finkelstein and R. M. MacIver, Harper & Brothers,
New York 1957.

"Some Equivocations of the Notion of Responsibility." Extension
of oral comments made at the meeting on "Determinism and
Freedom in the Age of Modern Science," New York University,
February 1957.

Published in *Determinism and Freedom*, Edited by Sidney
Hook, New York University Press, New York 1958, pp.
206–208.

"Tiresias, or our Knowledge of Future Events."
First draft written in 1942; second draft 1943; final version
1958. Read before the Department of Philosophy of Columbia
University, March 1958.

Published in *Social Research*, Vol. 26, No. 1, Spring 1959, pp. 71–89. The last contribution submitted by the living author himself.

Grateful acknowledgment is made to the editors and publishers of these journals and books for permission to republish these papers.

I wish to express my thanks to Professors Father Van Breda, Dorion Cairns, Thomas Luckmann, Maurice Natanson, Drs. Arthur Goddard and J. Taminiaux. In different ways they have all contributed to the preparation of this volume. Mrs. Ilse Schutz, who with deep devotion and meticulous care always helped her husband preparing his manuscripts for print, continues her selfless service also to the posthumous publications of his works. Readers and friends of Alfred Schutz owe her a special gratitude.

ARVID BRODERSEN

PART I

Pure Theory

THE SOCIAL WORLD AND THE
THEORY OF SOCIAL ACTION

At first sight it is not easily understandable why the subjective point of view should be preferred in the social sciences. Why address ourselves always to this mysterious and not too interesting tyrant of the social sciences, called the subjectivity of the actor? Why not honestly describe in honestly objective terms what really happens, and that means speaking our own language, the language of qualified and scientifically trained observers of the social world? And if it be objected that these terms are but artificial conventions created by our "will and pleasure," and that therefore we cannot utilize them for real insight into the meaning which social acts have for those who act, but only for our interpretation, we could answer that it is precisely this building up of a system of conventions and an honest description of the world which *is* and is alone the task of scientific thought; that we scientists are no less sovereign in our system of interpretation than the actor is free in setting up his system of goals and plans; that we social scientists in particular have but to follow the pattern of natural sciences, which have performed with the very methods we should abandon the most wonderful work of all time; and, finally, that it is the essence of science to be objective, valid not only for me, or for me and you and a few others, but for everyone, and that scientific propositions do not refer to my private world but to the one and unitary life-world common to us all.

The last part of this thesis is incontestably true; but doubtless even a fundamental point of view can be imagined, according to which social sciences have to follow the pattern of natural sciences and to adopt their methods. Pushed to its logical conclusion it leads to the method of behaviorism. To criticize this principle

is not within the scope of the present study. We restrict ourselves to the remark that radical behaviorism stands and falls
with the basic assumption that there is no possibility of proving
the intelligence of "the fellow-man." It is highly probable that
he is an intelligent human being, but that is a "weak fact" not
capable of verification (Russell, similarly Carnap).

Yet, it is not then quite understandable why an intelligent individual should write books for others or even meet others in
congresses where it is reciprocally proved that the intelligence of
the Other is a questionable fact. It is even less understandable
that the same authors who are convinced that no verification is
possible for the intelligence of other human beings have such
confidence in the principle of verifiability itself, which can be
realized only through cooperation with others by mutual control.
Furthermore they feel no inhibition about starting all their deliberations with the dogma that language exists, that speech
reactions and verbal reports are legitimate methods of behavioristic psychology, that propositions in a given language are able to
make sense, without considering that language, speech, verbal
report, proposition, and sense already presuppose intelligent alter
egos, capable of understanding the language, of interpreting the
proposition, and of verifying the sense.[1] But the phenomena of
understanding and interpreting themselves cannot be explained
as pure behavior, provided we do not recur to the subterfuge of a
"covert behavior" which evades a description in behavioristic
terms.[2]

These few critical remarks, however, do not hit the center of
our problem. Behaviorism as well as every other objective scheme
of reference in the social sciences has, of course, as its chief purpose, to explain with scientifically correct methods what really
happens in the social world of our everyday life. It is, of course,
neither the goal nor the meaning of any scientific theory to design
and to describe a fictitious world having no reference whatsoever
to our common-sense experience and being therefore without any
practical interest for us. The fathers of behaviorism had no other

[1] John B. Watson, *Psychology, from the Standpoint of a Behaviorist*, 3rd ed.,
Philadelphia, 1929, pp. 38 ff.
[2] The foregoing remarks are only partially true for the so-called behavioristic
position of the great philosopher and sociologist G. H. Mead (*Mind, Self and Society*,
for example, pp. 2 ff.).

purpose than that of describing and explaining real human acts within a real human world. But the fallacy of this theory consists in the substitution of a fictional world for social reality by promulgating methodological principles as appropriate for the social sciences which, though proved true in other fields, prove a failure in the realm of intersubjectivity.

But behaviorism is only one form of objectivism in the social sciences, though the most radical one. The student of the social world does not find himself placed before the inexorable alternative either of accepting the strictest subjective point of view, and, therefore, of studying the motives and thoughts in the mind of the actor; or of restricting himself to the description of the overt behavior and of admitting the behavioristic tenet of the inaccessibility of the Other's mind and even of the unverifiability of the Other's intelligence. There is rather a basic attitude conceivable – and, in fact, several of the most successful social scientists have adopted it – which accepts naively the social world with all the alter egos and institutions in it as a meaningful universe, meaningful namely for the observer whose only scientific task consists in describing and explaining his and his co-observers' experiences of it.

To be sure, those scientists admit that phenomena such as nation, government, market, price, religion, art, science refer to activities of other intelligent human beings for whom they constitute the world of their social life; they admit furthermore that alter egos have created this world by their activities and that they orient their further activities to its existence. Nevertheless, so they pretend, we are not obliged to go back to the subjective activities of those alter egos and to their correlates in their minds in order to give a description and explanation of the facts of this social world. Social scientists, they contend, may and should restrict themselves to telling what this world means to them, neglecting what it means to the actors within this social world. Let us collect the facts of this social world, as our scientific experience may present them in a reliable form, let us describe and analyze these facts, let us group them under pertinent categories and study the regularities in their shape and development which then will emerge, and we shall arrive at a system of the social sciences, discovering the basic principles and the analytical laws of the social world. Having once reached this point, the social sciences may confidently leave the subjective analyses to psychologists, philosophers, metaphysicists, or whatever else you like to call idle people bothering with such problems. And, the defender of such a position may add, is it not this scientific ideal which the most advanced social sciences are about to realize? Look at modern economics! The great progress of this science dates exactly from the decision of some advanced spirits to study curves of demand and supply and to discuss equations of prices and costs instead of striving hard and in vain to penetrate the mystery of subjective wants and subjective values.

Doubtless such a position is not only possible but even accepted by the majority of social scientists. Doubtless on a certain level real scientific work may be performed and has been performed without entering into the problems of subjectivity. We can go far ahead in the study of social phenomena, such as social institutions of all kinds, social relations, and even social groups, without leaving the basic frame of reference, which can be formulated as follows: what does all this mean for us, the scientific observer? We can develop and apply a refined system of abstraction for this purpose which intentionally eliminates the actor in the social world, with all his subjective points of view, and we can even do so without coming into conflict with the experiences derived from social reality. Masters in this technique – and there are many of them in all fields of social research – will always guard against leaving the consistent level within which this technique may be adopted and they will therefore confine their problems adequately.

All this does not alter the fact that this type of social science does not deal directly and immediately with the social life-world, common to us all, but with skillfully and expediently chosen idealizations and formalizations of the social world which are not repugnant to its facts. Nor does it make the less indispensable reference to the subjective point of view on other levels of abstraction if the original problem under consideration is modified. But then – and that is an important point – this reference to the subjective point of view always *can* be performed and should be performed. As the social world under any aspect whatsoever remains a very complicated cosmos of human activities, we can always go back to the "forgotten man" of the social sciences, to the actor in the social world whose doing and feeling lies at the bottom of the whole system. We, then, try to understand him in that doing and feeling and the state of mind which induced him to adopt specific attitudes towards his social environment.

In such a case the answer to the question "What does this social world mean for me the observer?" requires as a prerequisite the answering of the quite different questions "What does this social world mean for the observed actor within this world and what did he mean by his acting within it?" In putting our questions thus we no longer naively accept the social world and its current idealizations and formalizations as ready-made and meaningful beyond all question, but we undertake to study the process of idealizing and formalizing as such, the genesis of the meaning which social phenomena have for us as well as for the actors, the mechanism of the activity by which human beings understand one another and themselves. We are always free, and sometimes obliged, to do so.

This possibility of studying the social world under different points of view reveals the fundamental importance of the formula of Professor Znaniecki, [that all social phenomena can be described under one of the following four schemes of reference: social personality; social act; social group; social relations]. Each social phenomenon may be studied under the scheme of reference of social relationship or social groups (or, may we be allowed to add, social institutions) but with equal legitimacy under the scheme of social acts or social persons. The first group of schemes of reference is the objective one: such a scheme will do good service if applied exclusively to problems belonging to the sphere of objective phenomena for whose explanation its specific idealizations and formalizations have been designed, provided, however, that they do not contain any inconsistent element or elements incompatible with the other schemes (the subjective) and with our common-sense experience of the social world in general. Mutatis mutandis the same thesis is valid for the subjective schemes.[3]

[3] To be as precise as possible: on the level of what we have just called objective schemes the dichotomy of subjective and objective points of view does not even become visible. It emerges only within the basic assumption that the social world *may* be referred to activities of individual human beings and to the meaning those indi-

In other words, the scientific observer's decision to study the social world under an objective or subjective frame of reference circumscribes from the beginning the section of the social world (or, at least, the aspect of such a section) which is capable of being studied under the scheme chosen once and for all. The basic postulate of the methodology of social science, therefore, must be the following: choose the scheme of reference adequate to the problem you are interested in, consider its limits and possibilities, make its terms compatible and consistent with one another, and having once accepted it, stick to it! If, on the other hand, the ramifications of your problem lead you in the progress of your work to the acceptance of other schemes of reference and interpretation, do not forget that with the change in the scheme all terms in the formerly used scheme necessarily undergo a shift of meaning. To preserve the consistency of your thought you have to see to it that the "subscript" of all the terms and concepts you use is the same!

This is the real meaning of the so often misunderstood postulate of "purity of method." It is harder than it seems to comply with it. Most of the fallacies in the social sciences can be reduced to a mergence of subjective and objective points of view which, unnoticed by the scientist, arose in the process of transgressing from one level to the other in the continuation of the scientific work. These are the dangers that the mixing up of subjective and objective points of view would involve in the concrete work of social scientists. But for a theory of action the subjective point of view must be retained in its fullest strength, in default of which such a theory loses its basic foundations, namely its reference to the social world of everyday life and experience. The safeguarding of the subjective point of view is the only but sufficient guarantee that the world of social reality will not be replaced by a fictional non-existing world constructed by the scientific observer.

To make this matter clearer let us forget for a moment that we are social scientists observing the social world with a detached and disinterested mind. Let us see how each of us interprets the social world, common to us all, in which he lives and acts just as a man

viduals bestow on their social life-world. But precisely this basic assumption which alone makes the problem of subjectivity in the social sciences accessible is that of modern sociology.

among fellow-men, a world which he conceives as a field of his possible action and orientation, organized around his person under the specific scheme of his plans and the relevances deriving from them, but mindful, too, that the same social world is the field of other people's possible action and from their point of view organized around them in an analogous manner.

This world is always given to me from the first as an organized one. I was, so to speak, born into this organized social world and I grew up in it. Through learning and education, through experiences and experiments of all kinds, I acquire a certain ill-defined knowledge of this world and its institutions. Above all I am interested in the objects of this world in so far as they determine my own orientation, as they further or hinder the realization of my own plans, as they constitute an element of my situation, which I have to accept or to modify, as they are the source of my happiness or uneasiness – in a word, in so far as they mean anything to me. This meaning to me implies that I am not satisfied with the pure knowledge of the existence of such objects; I have to understand them, and this means I have to be able to interpret them as possible relevant elements for possible acts or reactions I might perform within the scope of my life plans.

But from the beginning this orientation through understanding occurs in cooperation with other human beings: this world has meaning not only for me but also for you and you and everyone. My experience of the world justifies and corrects itself by the experience of the others with whom I am interrelated by common knowledge, common work, and common suffering. The world, interpreted as the possible field of action for us all: that is the first and most primitive principle of organization of my knowledge of the exterior world in general. Afterwards I discriminate between natural things, which may be defined as things essentially given to me and you and everyone, such as they are, independent of any human interference, and on the other hand, social things, which are understandable only as products of human activity, my own or others' (the term "thing" used in both cases in its broadest sense, covering not only corporeal objects, but also "ideal" – mental – ones).

Concerning natural things my "understanding" is limited to the insight into their existence, variations, developments, in so far as all these elements are compatible with all my experiences and those of others within the natural world in general and with the basic assumptions about the structure of this world we all accept by common agreement. Within these limits prediction (though only of likelihood) is possible for us all. This thing here, is, in my opinion and in the opinion of us all, a wild apple tree. This implies that it will bear blossoms in spring, leaves in summer, fruits in fall, and become bare in winter. If we want to have a better view, we may climb to its top; if we need relaxation in the summer, we may rest in its shade; if we are hungry in the fall, we may taste its fruits. All these possibilities are independent of any human agency; the cycle of natural events revolves without our interference.[4]

If I want to do so, there is no objection to calling this organized knowledge of natural facts an "understanding" of them. But used in this larger sense the term "understanding" means nothing else than the reducibility of known and tested facts to other known and tested facts. If I consult an expert in the physiology of plants in order to learn what is really behind the aforenamed cycle in vegetative life, he will refer me to the chemistry of chlorophyl or to the morphological structure of cells; in short he will "explain" the facts by reducing them to others, which have a greater generality and which have been tested in a broader field.

Quite another "understanding" is peculiar to social things (this term embracing also human acts). In this case it is not sufficient to refer the fact under consideration to other facts or things. I cannot understand a social thing without reducing it to the human activity which has created it and, beyond it, without referring this human activity to the motives out of which it springs. I do not understand a tool without knowing the purpose for which it was designed, a sign or a symbol without knowing what it stands for, an institution if I am unfamiliar with its goals, a work of art if I neglect the intentions of the artist which it realizes.

[The present writer thinks that only a theory of motives can deepen an analysis of the act, provided that the subjective point of view is kept in its strictest and unmodified sense. He has tried

---

[4] Of course the interpretation of natural things as products of the agency of another intelligence (though not a human one) is always an overt possibility. The life of the tree is then the result of the activities of a demon or of a dryad, etc.

elsewhere [5] to sketch the outline of such a theory and hopes to be allowed to repeat here some of its outstanding features.

His starting point was a distinction between action and behavior. The distinguishing characteristic of action is precisely that it is determined by a project which precedes it in time. Action then is behavior in accordance with a plan of projected behavior; and the project is neither more nor less than the action itself conceived and decided upon in the future perfect tense. Thus the project is the primary and fundamental meaning of the action. But this is an over-simplification, which can be used only as a first approach. The meaning attributed to an experience varies according to one's whole attitude at the moment of reflection. When an action is completed, its original meaning as given in the project will be modified in the light of what has been actually carried out, and it is then open to an indefinite number of reflections which can ascribe meaning to it in the past tense.

The simplest complex of meaning in terms of which an action is interpreted by the actor is its motives. But this term is equivocal and covers two different categories which have to be well distinguished: the in-order-to motive and the because motive.[6] The former refers to the future and is identical with the object or purpose for the realization of which the action itself is a means: it is a "terminus ad quem." The latter refers to the past and may be called its reason or cause: it is a "terminus a quo." Thus the action is determined by the project including the in-order-to motive. The project is the intended act imagined as already accomplished, the in-order-to motive is the future state of affairs to be realized by the projected action, and the project itself is determined by the because motive. The complexes of meaning which constitute the in-order-to motive and the because motive respectively differ from one another in that the first is an integral part of the action itself, whereas the latter requires a special act of reflection in the pluperfect tense, which will be carried out by the actor only if there are sufficient pragmatic reasons for him to do so.

[5] Alfred Schutz, *Der sinnhafte Aufbau der sozialen Welt*, Vienna, 1932; 2nd ed., 1960, pp. 93–105.
[6] I borrow some English terms from the excellent study A. Stonier and Karl Bode published about my theory under the title "A New Approach to the Methodology of the Social Sciences," in *Economica*, November 1937, pp. 406–24.

It must be added that neither the claims of in-order-to motives nor the claims of because motives are chosen at random by the actor performing a concrete act. On the contrary, they are organized in great subjective systems. The in-order-to motives are integrated into subjective systems of planning: life plan, plans for work and leisure, plans for the "next time," time table for today, necessity of the hour, and so on. The because motives are grouped into systems which are treated in the American literature (W. James, G. H. Mead, Znaniecki, Allport, Parsons) correctly under the caption of (social) personality. The self's manifold experiences of its own basic attitudes in the past as they are condensed in the form of principles, maxims, habits, but also tastes, affects, and so on are the elements for building up the systems which can be personified. The latter is a very complicated problem requiring most earnest deliberation.]

Above all, I cannot understand other people's acts without knowing the in-order-to or the because motives of such acts. To be sure, there are manifold degrees of understanding. I must not (even more, I cannot) grasp the full ramifications of other people's motives, with their horizons of individual life plans, their background of individual experiences, their references to the unique situation by which they are determined. As we said before, such an ideal understanding would presuppose the full identity of my stream of thought with that of the alter ego, and that would mean an identity of both our selves. It suffices, therefore, that I can reduce the Other's act to its typical motives, including their reference to typical situations, typical ends, typical means, etc.

On the other hand, there are also different degrees of my knowledge of the actor himself, degrees of intimacy and anonymity. I may reduce the product of human activity to the agency of an alter ego with whom I share present time and present space, and then it may occur that this other individual is an intimate friend of mine or a passenger I meet for the first time and will never meet again. It is not necessary even that I know the actor personally in order to have an approach to his motives. I can, for instance, understand the acts of a foreign statesman and discuss his motives without having ever met him or even without having seen a picture of him. The same is true for individuals who have motives of Caesar as well as of the cave-man who left no other testimony of his existence than the firestone hatchet exhibited in the showcase of the museum. But it is not even necessary to reduce human acts to a more or less well known individual actor. To understand them it is sufficient to find typical motives of typical actors which explain the act as a typical one arising out of a typical situation. There is a certain conformity in the acts and motives of priests, soldiers, servants, farmers everywhere and at every time. Moreover, there are acts of such a general type that it is sufficient to reduce them to "somebody's" typical motives for making them understandable.

All this must be carefully investigated as an essential part of the theory of social action.[7] Summing up, we come to the conclusion that social things are only understandable if they can be reduced to human activities; and human activities are only made understandable by showing their in-order-to or because motives. The deeper reason for this fact is that as I naively live within the social world I am able to understand other people's acts only if I can imagine that I myself would perform analogous acts if I were in the same situation, directed by the same because motives, or oriented by the same in-order-to motives – all these terms understood in the restricted sense of the "typical" analogy, the "typical" sameness, as explained before.

That this assertion is true can be demonstrated by an analysis of the social action in the more precise sense of this term, namely of an action which involves the attitudes and actions of others and is oriented to them in its course.[8] As yet we have dealt in this study only with action as such without entering into the analysis of the modification which the general scheme undergoes with the introduction of social elements proper: mutual correlation and intersubjective adjustment. We have, therefore, observed the attitude of an isolated actor without making any distinction as to whether this actor is occupied with the handling of a tool or acting with others and for others, motivated by others and motivating them.

[7] An attempt was made by the present writer in his book *Der sinnhafte Aufbau* ... (cited above, note 5).

[8] Max Weber, *Wirtschaft und Gesellschaft*, Tübingen 1922; new ed., 1956. Parts of this important work are available in English translation in H. H. Gerth and C. Wright Mills, eds., *From Max Weber: Essays in Sociology*, New York, 1946; other parts translated by A. M. Henderson and Talcott Parsons under the title *The Theory of Social and Economic Organization*, New York, 1947.

This topic is very complicated to analyze and we have to restrict ourselves to sketching its outlines. It can be proved that all
social relations as they are understood by me, a human being
living naively in the social world which is centered around myself,
have their prototype in the social relation connecting myself with
an individual alter ego with whom I am sharing space and time.
My social act, then, is oriented not only to the physical existence
of this alter ego but to the Other's act which I expect to provoke
by my own action. I can, therefore, say that the Other's reaction
is the in-order-to motive of my own act. The prototype of all
social relationship is an intersubjective connection of motives. If I
imagine, projecting my act, that you will understand my act and
that this understanding will induce you to react, on your part,
in a certain way, I anticipate that the in-order-to motives of my
own acting will become because motives of your reaction, and
vice-versa.

Let us take a very simple example. I ask you a question. The
in-order-to motive of my act is not only the expectation that you
will understand my question, but also to get your answer; or more
precisely, I reckon *that* you will answer, leaving undecided what
the content of your answer may be. *Modo futuri exacti* I anticipate in projecting my own act that you will have answered my
question in some way or other, and this means I think there is
a fair chance that the understanding of my question will become
a because motive for your answer, which I expect. The question,
so we can say, is the because motive of the answer, as the answer
is the in-order-to motive of the question. This interrelationship
between my own and your motives is a well tested experience of
mine, though, perhaps, I have never had explicit knowledge of
the complicated interior mechanism of it. But I myself had felt
on innumerable occasions induced to react to another's act, which
I had interpreted as a question addressed to me, with a kind of
behavior of which the in-order-to motive was my expectation
that the Other, the questioner, might interpret my behavior as
an answer. Over against this experience I know that I have succeeded frequently in provoking another person's answer by my
own act called questioning, and so on. Therefore I feel I have a
fair chance of getting your answer when I shall have once realized
my action of questioning.

This short and incomplete analysis of a rather trivial example shows the great complications inherent in the problem of the social act, but also gives an idea of the extension of the field to be explored by a theory of action worthy of its name. We do not intend to enter further into this topic here but we must draw some conclusions from our example concerning the role of the subjective point of view for the actor in the social world.

The social world in which I live as one connected with others through manifold relations is for me an object to be interpreted as meaningful. It makes sense to me, but by the same token I am sure it makes sense to others too. I suppose, furthermore, that my acts oriented to others will be understood by them in an analogous manner as I understand the acts of others oriented to me. More or less naively I presuppose the existence of a common scheme of reference for both my own acts and the acts of others. I am interested above all not in the overt behavior of others, not in their performance of gestures and bodily movements, but in their intentions, and that means in the in-order-to motives for the sake of which, and in the because motives based on which, they act as they do.

Convinced that they want to express something by their act or that their act has a specific position within the common frame of reference, I try to catch the meaning which the act in question has, particularly for my co-actors in the social world, and, until presented with counter-evidence, I presume that this meaning for them, the actors, corresponds to the meaning their act has for me. As I have to orient my own social acts to the because motives of the other's social acts oriented to me, I must always find out their in-order-to motives and disentangle the texture of social interrelationship by interpreting other people's acts from the subjective point of view of the actor. That is the great difference between the attitude of a man who lives amidst manifold social interrelations in which he is interested as a party and the pure observer who is disinterested in the outcome of a social situation in which he does not participate and which he studies with a detached mind.

There is another reason why man living naively among others in the social world tries above all to find out the motives of his co-actors. Motives are never isolated elements but grouped in great and consistent systems of hierarchical order. Having grasped a sufficient number of elements of such a system, I have a fair chance of completing the empty positions of the system by correct conjectures. Basing my assumption on the inner logical structure of such a motive system, I am able to make, with great likelihood of proving them right, inferences concerning those parts which remain hidden. But, of course, all this presupposes interpretation from the subjective point of view, i.e., answering the question "What does all this mean for the actor?"

This practical attitude is adopted by us all in so far as we not only observe a social situation which does not touch us but are actors and reactors within the social world, and this is precisely the reason why the subjective point of view must be accepted by the social sciences too. Only this methodological principle gives us the necessary guarantee that we are dealing in fact with the real social life-world of us all, which, even as an object of theoretical research, remains a system of reciprocal social relations, all of them built up by mutual subjective interpretations of the actors within it.

But if the principle of safeguarding the subjective point of view in the social sciences were even admitted, how is it possible to deal scientifically – and that means in objective conceptual terms – with such subjective phenomena? The greatest difficulty lies, first of all, in the specific attitude the scientific observer has adopted towards the social world. As a scientist – not as a man among other men, which he is too – he is not a party in social interrelationship. He does not participate in the living stream of mutual testing of the in-order-to motives of his own acts by the reactions of others, and vice-versa. Strictly speaking, as a pure observer of the social world, the social scientist does not act. In so far as he "acts scientifically" (publishing papers, discussing problems with others, teaching) his activity is performed *within* the social world: he acts as man among other men, dealing with science, but he no longer has, then, the specific attitude of a scientific observer. This attitude is characterized by the fact that it is performed in complete aloofness. To become a social scientist the observer must make up his mind to step out of the social world, to drop any practical interest in it, and to restrict his in-order-to motives to the honest description and explanation of the social world which he observes.

But how should this job be performed? Not being able to communicate directly with the actors within the social world, he is unable to verify directly the data he has obtained about them from the different sources of information open to him within the social world. To be sure, he himself has, as a man among others, direct human experiences of the social world. In that capacity he can send out questionnaires, hear witnesses, establish test-cases. From these sources and others he gathers data which he will later use, once retired into the solitude of the theoretician. But his theoretical task as such begins with the building up of a conceptual scheme under which his information about the social world may be grouped.

It is one of the outstanding features of modern social science to have described the device the social scientists use in building up their conceptual scheme, and it is the great merit of [Durkheim, Pareto, Marshall, Veblen, and] above all Max Weber, to have developed this technique in all its fullness and clarity. This technique consists in replacing the human beings which the social scientist observes as actors on the social stage by puppets created by himself, in other words, in constructing ideal types of actors. This is done in the following way.

The scientist observes certain events within the social world as caused by human activity and he begins to establish a type of such events. Afterwards he coordinates with these typical acts typical because motives and in-order-to motives which he assumes as invariable in the mind of an imaginary actor. Thus he constructs a personal ideal type, which means the model of an actor whom he imagines as gifted with a consciousness. But it is a consciousness restricted in its content only to all those elements necessary for the performance of the typical acts under consideration. These elements it contains completely, but nothing beyond them. He imputes to it constant in-order-to motives corresponding to the goals which are realized within the social world by the acts under consideration; furthermore he ascribes to it constant because motives of such a structure that they may serve as a basis for the system of the presupposed constant in-order-to motives; finally he bestows on the ideal type such segments of life plans and such stocks of experiences as are necessary for the imaginary horizons and backgrounds of the puppet actor. The social scientist places these constructed types in a setting which contains all the elements of the situation in the social world relevant for the performance of the typical act under inquiry. Moreover, he associates with him other personal ideal types with motives apt to provoke typical reactions to the first ideal type's typical act.

So he arrives at a model of the social world, or better at a reconstruction of it. It contains all the relevant elements of the social event chosen as a typical one by the scientist for further examination. And it is a model which complies perfectly with the postulate of the subjective point of view. For from the first the puppet type is imagined as having the same specific knowledge of the situation – including means and conditions – which a real actor would have in the real social world; from the first the subjective motives of a real actor performing a typical act are implanted as constant elements of the specious consciousness of the personal ideal type; and it is the destiny of the personal ideal type to play the role the actor in the social world would have to adopt in order to perform the typical act. And as the type is constructed in such a way that it performs exclusively typical acts, the objective and subjective elements in the formation of unit-acts coincide.

On the other hand, the formation of the type, the choice of the typical event, and the elements considered as typical are conceptual terms which can be discussed objectively and which are open to criticism and verification. They are not formed by social scientists at random without check or restraint; the laws of their formation are very rigid and the scope of arbitrariness of the social scientist is much narrower than seems at first sight. We are unable to enter into this problem within this study. But briefly we will summarize what was brought out elsewhere.[9]

1) *Postulate of relevance*. The formation of ideal types must comply with the principle of relevance, which means that the problem once chosen by the social scientist creates a scheme of reference and constitutes the limits of the scope within which relevant ideal types might be formed.

---

[9] I have sketched some of the principles ruling the formation of ideal types in "The Problem of Rationality in the Social World." See *infra*.

2) *Postulate of adequacy.* It may be formulated as follows: each term used in a scientific system referring to human action must be so constructed that a human act performed within the life-world by an individual actor in the way indicated by the typical construction would be reasonable and understandable for the actor himself as well as for his fellow-man.

3) *Postulate of logical consistency.* The system of ideal types must remain in full compatibility with the principles of formal logic.

4) *Postulate of compatibility.* The system of ideal types must contain only scientifically verifiable assumptions, which have to be fully compatible with the whole of our scientific knowledge.

These postulates give the necessary guarantees that social sciences do in fact deal with the real social world, the one and unitary life-world of us all, and not with a strange fancy-world independent of and without connection to this everyday life-world. To go further into the details of the typifying method seems to me one of the most important tasks of a theory of action.

THE DIMENSIONS OF THE SOCIAL WORLD *

I. INTRODUCTION

Elsewhere [1] we were concerned with fundamental aspects of
the question how man can comprehend his fellow-men. We
analyzed man's subjective experiences of the Other and found in
them the basis for his understanding of the Other's subjective
processes of consciousness. The very assumption of the existence
of the Other, however, introduces the dimension of intersubjectivity. The world is experienced by the Self as being inhabited
by other Selves, as being a world for others and of others. As we
had occasion to point out, intersubjective reality is by no means
homogeneous. The social world in which man finds himself
exhibits a complex structure; fellow-men appear to the Self
under different aspects, to which correspond different cognitive
styles by which the Self perceives and apprehends the Other's
thoughts, motives, and actions. In the present investigation it
will be our main task to describe the origin of the differentiated
structures of social reality as well as to reveal the principles
underlying its unity and coherence.

It must be stressed that careful description of the processes
which enable one man to understand another's thoughts and
actions is a prerequisite for the methodology of the empirical
social sciences. The question how a *scientific* interpretation of
human action is possible can be resolved only if an adequate

---

* From: *Der sinnhafte Aufbau der sozialen Welt*, Vienna, 1932; 2nd ed. 1960
(Sektion IV: Strukturanalyse der Sozialwelt, Soziale Umwelt, Mitwelt, Vorwelt,
English adaptation by Professor Thomas Luckmann.)

[1] *Op. cit.*, III, pp. 106–153; cf. also "Le problème de l'intersubjectivité transcen-
dentale chez Husserl," in *Husserl*, Cahiers de Royaumont, Paris, 1959, pp. 334–365;
and "Sartre's Theory of the Alter Ego," *Collected Papers I*, pp. 180 f.

answer is first given to the question how man, in the natural attitude of daily life and common sense, can understand another's action at all.

It is evident that in the routine of everyday life one does not interpret the actions of one's fellow-man in accordance with scientific rules of procedure and scholarly canons of objectivity. Such naive and pre-scientific interpretations, however, constitute the subject matter of the social sciences. In contrast to the physical scientist, the social scientist confronts a reality whose structure originates in subjective common-sense constructs and typifications. Hence, an account of the way in which these constructs and typifications are constituted is a step which must precede the discussion of the nature of scientific constructs proper and of the procedures by which the social sciences interpret social reality. The construction of the categories and models of the social sciences is founded on the pre-scientific common-sense experience of social reality.[2]

Description of the constitution of social reality in the natural attitude of daily life calls for a method which is neither the method of the empirical social sciences nor the method of common sense. To the social scientist the conscious processes of other men are cognitive constructs arrived at through processes of typification and selected by the criteria of relevance inherent in the scientific problem at hand. On the other hand, in everyday life, as I share experiences with my fellow-men and pursue the ordinary pragmatic motives in acting upon them, I find the constructs ready-made and I take it for granted that I can grasp the motives of my fellow-men and understand their actions adequately for all practical purposes. I am highly unlikely to turn my attention to the various strata of meaning upon which my comprehension of their conduct is·based. In order to explicate the structure of the social world, however, it is necessary to direct attention to those experiences in which another man's consciousness becomes accessible, for they are the foundation of the constructs by which his motives and actions are interpreted. It is precisely these experiences which, for different

[2] Cf. "Common-Sense and Scientific Interpretation of Human Action," in *Collected Papers I*, pp. 3–47; also "Concept and Theory Formation in the Social Sciences," *ibid.*, pp. 48 f.

reasons, continue to be taken for granted in everyday life as well as in the social sciences.[3]

The world of daily life is not a private world. It is common to me and my fellow-men. Other men whom I experience in this world do not appear to me in identical perspectives. They present themselves to me under different aspects and my relations with them have different degrees of intimacy and anonymity. The modifications which determine my relations to others and my experiences of them are a central factor in the constitution of the several domains within the social world. The social world contains a domain characterized by the immediacy of my experience of others. Human beings in this domain are my fellow-men; they share with me a common sector of space and time; the world which surrounds us is the same and *my* conscious processes are an element of this world for him just as much as *his* conscious processes are an element of this world for me. But my social world contains more than experiences of fellow-men given directly in a common vivid present. It contains a domain of social reality which is not experienced by me directly, here and now, but which is contemporaneous with my life and which I can therefore bring within reach of my direct experience. This domain is thus not at the moment part of the world within my reach, in consequence of my present situation. The social world not within the reach of my present direct experience contains, however, a domain which I directly experienced before and which I can, at least in principle, restore to direct experience. The immediate world of my fellow-men thus shades into the larger world of my contemporaries. While I do not experience my contemporaries in the vivid present of a face-to-face relation, they are potentially my future fellow-men. Their conscious processes are not given to me in direct evidence; yet I have some knowledge of them, since I can impute to contemporaries typical motives with a high degree of likelihood. I can act upon them as I can act upon fellow-men, and I stand to them in typical social relations.

Beyond this region of Others with whom I coexist in time and who may come to share with me a common sector of time and space, i.e., beyond the world of contemporaries and fellow-men

[3] For a more detailed discussion, see again, *Op. cit., eod. loc.*; and *idem*, pp 207–259.

with its internal modifications of immediacy and vividness, there are regions of social reality which are neither actually nor potentially accessible to direct experience. They transcend not only my present situation but also my life. There is the world of my predecessors, i.e., a world of Others of whom I may have knowledge and whose actions may influence my own life, but upon whom I cannot act in any manner. There is the world of my successors, i.e., a world of Others of whom I have only vague and inadequate knowledge, but upon whom I can exert some influence through my own actions.

Obviously, just as other men are fellow-men, contemporaries, predecessors and successors to me, I am a fellow-man, contemporary, predecessor and successor to other men. In the sequel we shall undertake a detailed description of these structures of social reality and analyze their originary constitution. We will devote much attention to the key domain, that is, the social world which coexists with me in time, the world of my contemporaries. Within it those sectors in which contemporaries become accessible to me in direct experience will be of special interest, since, as we will attempt to show, all other domains of social reality receive their originary legitimation in the direct experience of fellow-men.

II. SOCIAL REALITY WITHIN REACH OF DIRECT EXPERIENCE

1) The face-to-face situation and the "pure" we-relation

I experience a fellow-man directly if and when he shares with me a common sector of time and space. The sharing of a common sector of time implies a genuine simultaneity of our two streams of consciousness: my fellow-man and I grow older together. The sharing of a common sector of space implies that my fellow-man appears to me in person as he himself and none other. His body appears to me as a unified field of expressions, that is, of concrete symptoms through which his conscious life manifests itself to me vividly. This temporal and spatial immediacy are essential characteristics of the face-to-face situation. The specific style and the structure of social relations and of social interaction which occur in face-to-face situations are decisively influenced by these characteristics.

We shall first consider the way in which a face-to-face situation becomes constituted. In order to become aware of such a situation, I must consciously pay attention to a fellow-man, to a human being confronting me in person. We shall term this awareness *Thou-orientation*. Since a face-to-face situation presupposes this orientation, we shall now describe the features of the latter.

The Thou-orientation is the general form in which any particular fellow-man is experienced in person. The very fact that I recognize something within the reach of my direct experience as a living, conscious human being constitutes the Thou-orientation. In order to preclude misunderstandings, it must be emphasized that the Thou-orientation is not a judgement by analogy. Becoming aware of a human being confronting me does not depend upon an imputation of life and consciousness to an object in my surroundings by an act of reflective thought. The Thou-orientation is a prepredicative experience of a fellow being. In this experience I grasp the existence of a fellow-man in the actuality of a particular person who must be present here and now. The Thou-orientation presupposes the presence of the fellow-man in temporal and spatial immediacy. The essential feature of the Thou-orientation is the recognition that a fellow-man *is* before me; the orientation does not presuppose that I know what are precisely the particular characteristics of that fellow-man. The formal concept of the Thou-orientation refers to the "pure" experience of another Self as a human being, alive and conscious, while the specific content of that consciousness remains undefined. Of course, I never have such a "pure" experience of another Self. I always confront a particular fellow-man, living his particular life and having his own particular thoughts. The Thou-orientation is therefore not "pure" in fact but is always actualized in different degrees of concreteness and specificity.

The Thou-orientation is either one-sided or reciprocal. It is onesided if I turn to you, but you ignore my presence. It is reciprocal if I am oriented to you, and you, in turn, take my existence into account. In that case a social relation becomes constituted. We shall define this relation formally as the "pure"

We-relation, knowing fully that in fact a We-relation is always filled with "content," that is, that the "pure" We-relation, in anology to the "pure" Thou-orientation, is actualized in different degrees of concreteness and specificity. An illustration may help to clarify this point. If you and I observe a bird in flight my "bird-flight observations" are a sequence of experiences in my own mind just as your "bird-flight observations" are experiences in your mind. Neither you nor I, nor any other person, can say whether my experiences are identical with yours since no one can have direct access to another man's mind. Nevertheless, while I cannot know the specific and exact content of your consciousness, I do know that you are a living human being, endowed with consciousness. I do know that, whatever your experiences during the flight of the bird, they were contemporaneous with mine. Furthermore, I may have observed movements of your body and expressions of your face during these moments, interpreting them as indications of your attentiveness to the bird's flight. Therefore, I may coordinate the event "bird-flight" not only with phases of my own consciousness but also with "corresponding" phases of your consciousness. Since we are growing older together during the flight of the bird, and since I have evidence, in my own observations, that you were paying attention to the same event, I may say that *we* saw a bird in flight.

I am born into a world which is inhabited by others who will confront me in face-to-face situations. My experiences of particular fellow-men as well as my knowledge that there are other human beings – only some of whom I have experienced directly as fellow-men – originate in this a priori given by my birth. Scheler [4] rightly maintains that the We-experience forms the basis of the individual's experience of the world in general. The difficult question of the *transcendental* constitution of this experience and of the experience of the alter ego cannot be pursued here. By assuming the *mundane* existence of other Selves we may turn to the description of the origin of experiences of fellow-men in the We-relation.

I "participate" in the conscious life of another Self only when I am engaged in a concrete We-relation, face to face with a

[4] *Die Wissensformen und die Gesellschaft*, Leipzig, 1926, II. "Erkenntnis und Arbeit," p. 475f.

fellow-man. If you speak to me, for example, I understand the objective sign-meaning of the words. But, since I "participate" in the step-by-step constitution of your speaking experiences in the contemporaneity of the We-relation, I may also apprehend the subjective configuration of meaning in which the words stand for you. But the process by which I apprehend the subjective configuration of meaning in which my fellow-man's experiences stand for him must not be confused with the We-relation proper. The words of my fellow-man are primarily signs in an objective context of meaning. They are also indications for the subjective context in which any experience, including speaking, stands for him. But the process by which I apprehend his conscious life is necessarily a process in my own conscious life. It is I who interpret the words as signs in an objective meaning context and as indications of his subjective intentions. The very fact that I can do so, however, presupposes my experience of the other Self as a fellow-man who shares experiences with me in the ongoing community of space and time; it presupposes the "pure" We-relation.

The stream of concrete experiences which fills the We-relation with "content" bears a strong similarity to the manifold and continuous stream of my own consciousness. There is one fundamental difference. My own stream of consciousness is interior, it is "pure" duration. The We-relation, however, consists not only in the community of time, that is, in the synchronization of two interior streams of duration; it consists also in the community of space, that is, the bodily and thus exterior presence of a fellow-man face to face with me. Hence, the experience of a fellow-man in a We-relation is, strictly speaking, also "mediate": I apprehend his conscious life by interpreting his bodily expressions as indications of subjectively meaningful processes. Yet, among all self-transcending experiences the We-relation most closely resembles the inward temporality of my stream of consciousness. In that sense we may say that I experience my fellow-man "directly" in a We-relation.

My experience of the fellow-man is direct as long as I am straightforwardly engaged *in* the We-relation, that is, as long as I participate in the common stream of *our* experiences. If I think and reflect *about* our experience, this directness is broken. I must interrupt my straightforward engagement in the We-relation. In a manner of speaking, I must step outside the face-to-face situation. While I was engaged in the We-relation, I was busy attending to you; in order to think about it, I must break off the immediate rapport between us. Before I can reflect about our common experience its vivid phases, in which we were jointly engaged, must have come to a stop. Straightforward engagement in the We-relation is possible only in the ongoing experiences of a face-to-face situation, while reflection is ex post facto. It begins after the concrete We-relation has come to an end.

The retrospective grasp of past common experiences may be clear and distinct or confused and unsharp. The more I am involved in reflecting upon the common experience, the less directly do I live it and the remoter is the living, concrete human being who is my partner in the We-relation. The fellow-man whom I experience directly while I am busily engaged in our common experience becomes a mere object of my thought as I begin to reflect about us.

2) *Social relations in the face-to-face situation*

The foregoing description of the pure We-relation will provide a useful basis for the analysis of the We-relation as a concrete social relation in face-to-face situations. We found that the pure We-relation is constituted in the reciprocal Thou-orientation; that the latter, in its pure form, consists in the mere awareness of the existence of a fellow-man before me; and that it consequently does not necessarily involve a grasp of the specific traits of that fellow-man. In a concrete social relation, however, this is precisely what is involved.

Obviously, the extent of my knowledge of the traits which characterize my partners in different social relations varies considerably. In the pure We-relation I apprehend only the existence of a fellow-man and the fact that he is confronting me. For a concrete social relation to become established, however, I must also know how he is oriented to me. In face-to-face situations I gain knowledge of this specific aspect of my partner's conscious life by observing the concrete manifestations of his subjective experiences in the common stream of the We-relation.

Hence, we may say that concrete social relations in face-to-face situations are founded upon the pure We-relation. Not only is the latter logically prior to the former in the sense that it contains the essential features of any such social relation; the grasp of the specific traits of the partner which is an element of concrete social relations presupposes the community of space and time which characterizes the pure We-relation. The pure We-relation may be thus also considered as a formal concept designating the structure of concrete social relations in the face-to-face situation.

This point becomes clear if one considers the fact that no specific *"pure"* experiences correspond to the pure We-relation. The participant in an ongoing We-relation apprehends this relation only in the shared experiences which refer, by necessity, to the specific partner confronting him. The essential features of the pure We-relation can be seen in reflection, after the concrete We-relation has come to an end; they are experienced only in the variety of its actualizations.

Having discussed the connection between the pure We-relation and the concrete We-relation, we must now describe the various actualizations of the latter and show how it differs from all other social relations. The experiences which go on concretely in the We-relation are differentiated in several ways. I do not experience partners in all We-relations with equal intensity, nor am I equally intimate with them. Furthermore, my partners appear to me in different perspectives which exercise a certain amount of constraint upon my experiences of the partner. Finally, in the We-relation I may be turned attentively to my partner's experiences, i.e., to his conscious processes and subjective motivations, or I may be only remotely interested in these, concentrating instead on his overt acts and expressions. The concrete actualizations of the We-relation are determined by these factors; within the temporal and spatial immediacy given by the face-to-face situation these factors bestow a higher or lower degree of "directness" upon the experiences in the We-relation. An example may illustrate this point.

Both sexual intercourse and a casual conversation are instances of the We-relation in which the partners are face-to-face. Yet what a difference in the degree of directness which characterizes the experiences in these relations! Very different depth-levels of the conscious life of the partners are involved. Intensity and degree of intimacy vary radically. But not only *my* experiences *in* these relations differ in all the aforementioned aspects. We may say that differences in the "degree of directness" are characteristics of the We-relation proper.

With the discussion of the relative directness of social relations we touch upon a problem of basic significance for the understanding of the constitution of social reality and subjective experience. We shall be obliged to take up this problem again when describing the transition from the direct experience of fellow-men in face-to-face situations to the experience of social reality transcending this situation. At present we must hold to the analysis of the characteristics peculiar to social relations in the face-to-face situation.

We found earlier that in the face-to-face situation the conscious life of my fellow-man becomes accessible to me by a maximum of vivid indications. Since he is confronting me in person, the range of symptoms by which I apprehend his consciousness includes much more than what he is communicating to me purposefully. I observe his movements, gestures and facial expressions, I hear the intonation and the rhythm of his utterances. Each phase of my consciousness is co-ordinated with a phase of my partner's. Since I perceive the continuous manifestations of my partner's conscious life I am continuously attuned to it. One highly important consequence of this state of affairs is the fact that my partner is given to me more vividly and, in a sense, more "directly" than I apprehend myself. Since I "know" my past, I "know" myself in infinitely greater detail than anyone else. Yet this is knowledge in retrospect, in reflection; it is not direct and vivid experience. Hence, while I am straightforwardly engaged in the business of life, my own self is not present to me in an equally wide range of symptoms as is a fellow-man whom I confront in the Here and Now of a concrete We-relation.

In the face-to-face situation I have immediate experience of my fellow-man. But as I confront my fellow-man, I bring into each concrete situation a stock of preconstituted knowledge which includes a network of typifications of human individuals in general, of typical human motivations, goals, and action patterns. It also includes knowledge of expressive and interpretive schemes, of objective sign-systems and, in particular, of the vernacular language. In addition to such general knowledge I have more specific information about particular kinds and groups of men, of their motivations and actions. If I formerly had direct experience of this particular fellow-man now confronting me, I may, of course, fall back upon the highly specialized information sedimented in these experiences. In the ongoing experiences of the We-relation I check and revise my previous knowledge about my partner and accumulate new knowledge about him. Thereby my general stock of knowledge also undergoes a continuous modification. My experience of a fellow-man in the We-relations thus stands in a multiple context of meaning: it is experience of a human being, it is experience of a typical actor on the social scene, it is experience of this particular fellow-man, and it is experience of this particular fellow-man in this particular situation, Here and Now.

As I look at you in the community of space and time I have direct evidence that you are oriented to me, that is, that you experience what I say and do, not only in an objective context of meaning but also as manifestations of my conscious life. I know that the same goes for you, and that you refer your experiences of me back to what you grasp of my experiences of you. In the community of space and time our experiences of each other are not only coordinated but also reciprocally determined by continuous cross-reference. I experience myself through you, and you experience yourself through me. The reciprocal mirroring of Selves in the partners' experience is a constitutive feature of the We-relation in face-to-face situations. Since, however, the We-relation and the partner in it are not grasped reflectively but directly experienced, the multifaceted reflexions of the Self in the mirror of the other Self are not separately brought to consciousness. My experience of the ongoing phases of my own conscious life and my experience of the coordinated phases of your conscious life is unitary: experience in the We-relation is genuinely shared.

This is a significant fact for the structure not only of social relations but also of social interaction in face-to-face situations. I am in a position to witness your projects and to observe their fulfillment or frustration in the course of your actions. Outside an ongoing We-relation I may calculate the objective chances of success for another man's projected goals by drawing upon my stock of knowledge about social reality, and I may interrupt, as it were, an ongoing We-relation in order to do so. But only in the ongoing We-relation may I directly apprehend the outcome of my partner's plans by witnessing the course of his action.

I am inclined, in general, to assign to fellow human beings a world which corresponds to the world as I experience it myself. In the We-relation I do so with infinitely greater confidence because, as we saw, the world within the reach of my fellow-man coincides with mine. I may assume not only that the table in front of me is the same table which is in front of you but also that your experiences of this table correspond to mine. Therefore, I am always able to check the adequacy of the schemata by which I interpret your utterances and expressions by pointing to an object in the world within our common reach. This is an eminently important circumstance in the building up of my stock of knowledge and for my practical adjustment to social reality. Having verified the assumption that you interpret your experience in a way which for all practical purposes is roughly identical with mine, at least with respect to objects in our common environment, I have some justification for generally correlating my interpretive schemes with your expressive schemes.

The community of environment and the sharing of experiences in the We-relation bestows upon the world within the reach of our experience its intersubjective, social character. It is not my environment nor your environment nor even the two added; it is an intersubjective world within reach of our common experience. In this common experience the intersubjective character of the world in general both originates and is continuously confirmed.

The community of the world within reach of our experiences in the We-relation enables me to verify constantly the results of my interpretation of other men's experiences. The fellow-man face to face with me can be always interrogated. Hence I apprehend not only how he interprets his own experiences, that is, what meaning his experiences have for him. We may say that the realization of the correspondence and divergence of the meaning of our experiences originates in the We-relation. We already pointed out that my stock of knowledge, in so far as it refers to that particular fellow-man, and men in general, is constantly verified, corrected, and extended in the We-relation.

My own experiences, too, undergo a certain modification in the We-relation, and the same holds good for my partner. Neither he nor I attend to our respective experiences without awareness of the Other. I realize that my experiences interlock with his and necessarily refer to them. The cross-reference of the partners' experiences in a We-relation has especially important consequences for the structure of social interaction in face-to-face situations. I generally impute a set of genuine "because" and "in-order-to" motives to anybody to whom my actions are directed.[5] In this I rely on my stock of knowledge, which contains typifications of fellow-men in terms of typical sets of invariant "because" and "in-order-to" motives. While a provisional imputation of such motives to others characterizes all social action, interaction in face-to-face situations is privileged in that the motives of a partner in a We-relation are more directly accessible to the actor than the motives of others. It must be noted, however, that the general structure of motivational reciprocity remains the same. In projecting my own action I take account of my fellow-man by fancying – that is to say, rehearsing – likely courses of his future conduct in terms of the invariant motives which I impute to him. My partner's actual conduct then either confirms, approximates, or frustrates my expectations. The project of my action is thus always oriented to my partner by anticipations of his future conduct. But in face-to-face situations, in consequence of the continuous reciprocal modification of experience by the partner in the We-relation, I may "participate" in the constitution of the motives in my partner's conscious life. I am in a position to place your present experiences into an "in-order-to" context by interpreting them as antecedents of your future conduct. At the same time, I may place your present experiences into a "because" context by interpreting them as consequences of your past experiences. My grasp of another man's motives generally orients my action addressed to him; in a We-relation I grasp my fellow-man's motives in the particular fashion just described. I witness the constitution of motivational configurations in my partner's conscious life, then I witness his

[5] See *supra*, p. 109 and "Choosing Among Projects of Action," in *Collected Papers I*, p. 69ff.

reactions to my conduct; and I am present when my "in-order-to" motives become the "because" motives of his actions, and so forth. I always grow older between the rehearsing of the conduct of another man to whom my action is addressed and his actual conduct. But if I have addressed an action to a fellow-man, to a partner in a We-relation, I have not grown older alone; we have grown older together. Since we are jointly engaged in our common experiences, I "participate" in the projection and realization of his plans. Social interaction, characterized in all its forms by an interlocking of the actors' motives, gains an outstanding feature if it occurs in face-to-face situations. The motivational configuration of the actions of my fellow-man, as well as his overt conduct, is integrated into the *common* experience of the We-relation.

3) Direct observations

Our description of social relations in the face-to-face situation revealed the structure of this situation in its fundamental form. We shall now consider a modification of this situation in which I confront a fellow-man, but the fellow-man does not take my presence into account or is not aware of my presence at all. For the social sciences the most important version of this situation is that in which I am the observer of the conduct of a fellow-man. The analysis of observation and of the observer is indispensable for an understanding of the procedures by which the social sciences gather knowledge about social reality.[6]

The social relations in the face-to-face situation are characterized by reciprocity of the Thou-orientations of the two partners. If I am merely observing, my Thou-orientation is, of course, one-sided. My observation is conduct oriented to him, but his conduct need not be oriented to me. The question then arises how I am able to apprehend his conscious life.

In order to answer this question, we may begin by recapitulating those features of the We-relation which also apply to a mere observer. For the observer, too, the body of the Other is a field of direct expression. He, too, may take his observations as expressions that indicate the Other's conscious processes. Words,

[6] Cf. "Common-Sense and Scientific Interpretation of Human Action," *op. cit.*, p. 22f.

signs of any kind, and gestures and movements can be interpreted by the observer as standing in a subjective configuration
of meaning for the individual observed. The observer may
apprehend in a unitary and integrated manner both the manifestations of the Other's conscious processes and the step-by-step
constitution of the processes thus manifested. This is possible
because he witnesses the Other's ongoing experiences in synchrony
with his own interpretations of the Other's overt conduct in an
objective context of meaning. The bodily presence of the Other
offers to the partner in the We-relation as well as to the observer
a maximum of vivid symptoms. The world which is within reach
of the observer is congruent with the world within reach of the
observed person. There is thus a certain chance that the experiences of the world within reach on the part of the observed
person roughly coincide with the corresponding experiences of
the observer. But the observer cannot be certain that this is
really the case. As long as he remains a mere observer, he is not
in a position to verify his interpretation of the Other's experiences
by checking them against the Other's own subjective interpretations. And yet, the facility with which the observer can
transform himself into a partner in a face-to-face social relation
places him in a privileged position relative to the collection of
knowledge about social reality. The observed individual can become a fellow-man who may be questioned, while a mere contemporary is not within my reach Here and Now, and a predecessor is, of course, forever beyond interrogation.

In consequence of the fact that as an observer I am one-sidedly
oriented to the individual observed, the subjective context in
which his experiences are meaningful to me is not co-ordinated
with the subjective context in which my experiences are meaningful to him. Hence there is not the multifaceted reflexion of
mirror-images, characteristic of the We-relation, which enables
me to identify my experiences with his.

The observer is oriented to the Other but does not act upon
him. Therefore, his motives do not interlock with the observed
person's; the observer cannot project his "in-order-to" motives
on the assumption that they will become "because" motives of
the Other. The overt conduct of the observed individual does not
offer adequate clues to the question whether and how his course

of action is fulfilling his subjective projects. Perhaps the observer cannot even say whether the observed fragments of overt conduct constitute an action in the pursuit of a projected goal or whether they are mere behavior.

Since the observer who is interested in the observed individual's motives cannot apprehend these motives as directly as could a partner in a We-relation, he must proceed by one of the following three ways: First, he may remember from his own past experience a course of action similar to the one observed and recall its motive. By matching a given course of action with a given pattern of "because" and "in-order-to" motives, he will ascribe to the individual the motives which he, the observer, might have if only he were performing this action himself. The identification of one's own hypothetical motives with the Other's real motives may be immediate, i.e., it may occur in the course of the Other's ongoing action, or it may take place in a retrospective interpretation of the observed event. Second, if the observer does not find some rule of thumb for the interpretation of the observed course of action in his *own* experience, he may yet find in his general stock of knowledge typifications of the observed individual from which he may derive a typification of the observed individual's typical motives. A complete stranger to our society, let us say, who walked through a lecture hall, a courtroom, and a place of worship would observe in all three places situations that seem roughly alike. Yet, he would be unable to say much, if anything, about the motives of the overt conduct that he observed. If, however, the observer knew from previous experience that here a teacher, there a judge, and there a priest is performing his official duties, he would be able to deduce their typical "because" and "in-order-to" motives from that segment of his stock of knowledge which referred to typical teachers, judges, and priests.

Third, if the observer possesses no knowledge at all about the observed individual, or insufficient knowledge about the type of individual involved, he must fall back upon an inference from "effect to cause." This means that, in observing an accomplished act and its results, he assumes that this particular accomplished act and these results, were, indeed, the "in-order-to" motive of the actor.

These different ways of understanding the motives of individuals under observation do not have the same likelihood of being correct. Aside from the adequacy of one's stock of knowledge concerning typical motivations of typical individuals, the interpretation of other men's "in-order-to" motives will be the more dubious the farther it stands from the vivid context of a We-relation. The information, for example, that the individual one sees speaking to an assembly is a priest does not allow with certainty the conclusion that he is preaching a sermon. To impute to someone an "in-order-to" motive on the basis of an observed accomplished act is even more uncertain. That act may indeed have completely failed to achieve the goal projected by the actor. One's grasp of genuine "because" motives, on the other hand, does not suffer much by the fact that one is merely an observer rather than a partner in a We-relation. Both the observer and the partner in a face-to-face social relation must try to reconstruct, ex post facto, the experiences which motivated the Other before he embarked on a given course of action. With respect to this task which depends on one's "objective" knowledge, the partner's position in a We-relation is not privileged.[7]

The observation of social relations is more complicated, to be sure, than the observation of individual conduct, yet it proceeds according to the same basic principles. The observer must again draw upon his stock of knowledge about social relations in general, this particular social relation, and the partners involved in it. The observer's scheme of interpretation cannot be identical, of course, with the interpretive scheme of either partner in the social relation observed. The modifications of attention which characterize the attitude of the observer cannot coincide with those of a participant in an ongoing social relation. For one thing, what he finds relevant is not identical with what they find relevant in the situation. Furthermore, the observer stands in a privileged position in one respect: he has the ongoing experiences of *both* partners under observation. On the other hand, the observer cannot legitimately interpret the "in-order-to" motives of one participant as the "because" motives of the other, as do the partners themselves, unless the interlocking of motives becomes explicitly manifested in the observable situation.

[7] "Choosing Among Projects of Action," *op. cit.*, pp. 71–72.

III. THE WORLD OF CONTEMPORARIES AS A
STRUCTURE OF TYPIFICATIONS

1) The transition from direct to indirect experience of social reality

In the analysis of the We-relation we found that in face-to-face situations fellow-men are experienced on different levels of intimacy and in different degrees of directness. Within the temporal and spatial immediacy given by the face-to-face situation itself we found differences in the degree of directness which characterize the experience of another Self to be constitutive traits of the concrete We-relation proper. We saw that no matter how indifferent and uninvolved we may be in relation to a particular concrete fellow-man (e.g., a stranger in the subway), the face-to-face experience is essentially direct.

The stratification of attitudes by degrees of intimacy and intensity extends into the world of mere contemporaries, i.e., of Others who are not face-to-face with me, but who co-exist with me in time. The gradations of experiential directness outside the face-to-face situation are characterized by a decrease in the wealth of symptoms by which I apprehend the Other and by the fact that the perspectives in which I experience the Other are progressively narrower. We may illustrate this point by considering the stages by which a fellow-man confronting me becomes a mere contemporary. Now we are still face-to-face, saying good-bye, shaking hands; now he is walking away. Now he calls back to me; now I can still see him waving to me; now he has disappeared around a corner. It is impossible to say at which precise moment the face-to-face situation ended and my partner became a mere contemporary of whom I have knowledge (he has, probably, arrived at home) but no direct experience. The gradations of directness can be also illustrated by the series ranging from a conversation face-to-face, to a conversation by phone, to an exchange of letters, to a message transmitted by a third party. Both examples show a progressive decrease in the wealth of symptoms by which I experience my partner and a progressive narrowing of the perspectives in which my partner appears to me. While we may legitimately distinguish between direct and indirect experiences of social reality, we must realize that these are polar concepts between which exist many concrete transitional forms.

In the routine of everyday life the problem underlying the transition from face-to-face situations to the world of mere contemporaries do not, as a rule become visible. In the routine of everyday life we fit both our own conduct and the conduct of our fellow-man into a matrix of meaning which transcends the Here and Now of present experience. Hence, the attribute of present directness or indirectness of a social relation seems irrelevant to us. The deeper reason for this circumstance lies in the fact that a face-to-face experience of a fellow-man retains its constitutive traits even after I cease to see my fellow-man in person. The ongoing direct experience becomes a past direct experience. As a rule we see no reason why a fellow-man who was a partner in a concrete We-relation, with whom we interacted, whom we have loved or hated, should turn into something "different" merely because he happens to be absent at the moment. We still love him or hate him, as the case may be, and nothing in the routine of everyday life compels us to notice that our experience of him underwent a significant structural modification.

Careful description reveals, however, that such a modification does occur. The recollection of a fellow-man in a face-to-face situation indeed contains the constitutive traits of that situation, and these are structurally different from those which characterize an attitude, or an act of consciousness generally, which is oriented to a mere contemporary. In the face-to-face situation the fellow-man and I were partners in a concrete We-relation. He was present in person, with a maximum of symptoms by which I could apprehend his conscious life. In the community of space and time we were attuned to one another; his Self reflected mine; his experiences and my experiences formed a common stream, *our* experience; we grew older together. As soon as my fellow-man leaves, however, my experience of him undergoes a transformation. I know that he is in some Here and Now of his own, and I know that his Now is contemporaneous with mine, but I do not participate in it, nor do I share his Here. I know that my fellow-man has grown older since he left me, and, upon reflection, I know that, strictly speaking, he has changed with each additional experience, with each new situation. But all this I fail to take into account in the routine of everyday life. I hold on to the familiar image I have of you. I take it for granted that you are as I have known you before. Until further notice I hold invariant that segment of my stock of knowledge which concerns you and which I have built up in face-to-face situations, that is, until I receive information to the contrary. But then this is information about a contemporary to whom I am oriented as a mere contemporary and not as a fellow-man. It is a contemporary, of course, whom I experienced directly before, about whom I have more specific knowledge, gained in the shared experiences of past We-relations, than about others who are and always were mere contemporaries.

In this connection we must discuss the nature of those social relations which, according to Weber [8] are characterized by the "probability of the repeated recurrence of the behavior which corresponds to its subjective meaning, behavior which is an understandable consequence of the meaning and hence expected." Customarily we consider marriage or friendship as predominantly face-to-face relations that contain experiences of a high degree of directness. We are wont to do so, as we pointed out earlier, because of a general tendency to consider an action or a sequence of actions in a framework of larger units irrespective of whether the actors themselves have or have not integrated their actions – i.e., the projects of their actions – into such units. Closer scrutiny resolves the pretended unity of a marriage or a friendship into a manifold sequence of situations. In some of these situations, "marriage" or "friendship" was a face-to-face social relation, in others it was a social relation among mere contemporaries. Taking the terms in their precise sense, these social relations are indeed not continuous – but they are recurrent. Let us investigate then what the participants in a social relation of this type, e.g., two friends, mean when they speak of their friendship:

First, A, speaking of his friendship with B, may be thinking of a series of past face-to-face social relations with B. These past We-relations with B evidently constitute a series rather than an

[8] Max Weber, *The Theory of Social and Economic Organization*, New York, 1947, p. 119.

uninterrupted span. In this recollection A finds both solitary phases of his past experience as well as phases involving We-relations with individuals other than B.

Second, above and beyond concrete We-relations involving B, A may mean that his conduct or some aspect of his conduct is oriented by the fact that there is such a man, B, or, more specifically, that it is oriented by some aspects of B's expected future conduct. Thus, A has an attitude involving B as a (mere) contemporary, and he stands with B in a social relation which is a social relation among (mere) contemporaries. A's actions in this relation are oriented by B as he imagines B's reactions to his conduct. Whereas actions *interlock* in a concrete We-relation, they are just *oriented* reciprocally in a social relation that involves (mere) contemporaries. Thus, we find that social relations between the two friends as (mere) contemporaries are interposed in a discontinuous series of concrete We-relations between them. Third, A may refer to the fact that a face-to-face social relation with B is always restorable – technical hindrances being left out of account – and that he is confident that B will participate as a friend in future We-relations in a manner congruent with the We-relations that A and B experienced in the past.

In the foregoing we concerned ourselves with transitions from face-to-face situations to situations involving mere contemporaries. Thereby we investigated a border province lying between the domain of directly experienced social reality and the indirectly experienced world of contemporaries. The closer we approach the latter, the lower the degree of directness and the higher the degree of anonymity which characterizes my experience of others. Accordingly, the broader world of contemporaries itself contains various strata: My partners in former We-relations who are now mere contemporaries but who are restorable to face-to-face situations; partners in the *former* We-relations of my *present* partner in a We-relation who are potentially accessible to my direct experience (your friend whom I have not met yet); contemporaries of whom I have knowledge and whom I am to meet shortly (Professor X whose books I have read and with whom I have an appointment in the near future); contemporaries of whose existence I am aware, as reference points for typical social functions (post office employees involved in the processing of my letters); collective social realities which are known to me by their function and organization while their personnel remains anonymous – although I could, under certain circumstances, gain direct personal experience of the individuals in question (the House of Lords); collective social realities which are by their very nature anonymous and of which I consequently cannot gain direct personal experience under any circumstances; objective configurations of meaning which are instituted in the world of my contemporaries and which are essentially anonymous in character (the Articles of the Constitution, the rules of French grammar); and, finally, artifacts in the broadest sense, which testify to some subjective meaning-context of some unknown person, i.e., the sense which the artifact "had" for its creator, user, beholder, etc. All these strata of the large domain of indirectly experienced social reality are characterized, in a graduated series, by different degrees of anonymity and by transitions from relative nearness to direct experience to absolute detachment from it.

2) The contemporary as an ideal type and the they-relation

Whereas I experience fellow-men *directly* in the temporal and spatial immediacy of a face-to-face situation, this immediacy is lacking in my experience of mere contemporaries. Contemporaries are not present in person, *but I do know of their co-existence with me in time:* I know that the flux of their experiences is simultaneous with mine. This knowledge, however, is necessarily indirect. Hence, the contemporary is not a Thou in the pregnant sense that this term has in a We-relation. These terms describe the social topography of my Here and Now, whose contents are, of course, continuously changing. The reference point is always my present experiences. A mere contemporary may be a former fellow-man, and I may be counting on meeting him again face-to-face in a recurrent pattern. Yet the structure of the experiences involved differs radically. The Other who is a mere contemporary is not given to me *directly* as a unique particular Self. I do not apprehend his Selfhood in straightforward prepredicative experience. I do not even have an immediate experience of the Other's *existence*. I can only experience the Other in acts of inference by which I judge that the Other is such rather than otherwise, by imputing to him certain typical attributes. *Whereas I experience the individual Thou directly in the concrete We-relation, I apprehend the contemporary only mediately, by means of typifications.* In order to clarify this point we shall investigate various kinds of such mediating typifications by which I apprehend a contemporary.

One way by which my experience of contemporaries can become constituted is by derivation from previous immediate experiences of contemporaries in face-to-face situations. We have already investigated this mode of constitution and found that the knowledge gained directly of a fellow-man in a We-relation is maintained as valid – until further notice – even after the fellow-man moved out of the face-to-face situation. The act by which I apprehend the former fellow-man as a contemporary is thus a typification in the sense that I hold invariant my previously gained knowledge, although my former fellow-man has grown older in the meantime and must have necessarily gained new experiences. Of these experiences I have either no knowledge or only knowledge by inference or knowledge gained through fellow-men or other indirect sources.

Another mode by which experiences of contemporaries are constituted turns out to be merely a variant of the one previously mentioned. Contemporaries whom I apprehend as former fellow-men of my present partner in a We-relation are also experienced mediately, by following the example of my partner in holding invariant *his* former direct experiences of a particular person. Hence, I cannot even fall back upon my own direct experiences of that person but must first interpret the communications of my partner about his former direct experiences and then join him in holding invariant his knowledge about that particular contemporary.

These modes of constitution refer to everything we know of contemporaries through the mediation of our *own* past, direct as well as indirect experiences of Others and to everything we know through the mediation of the past experiences of Others, communicated to us directly as well as anonymously. It is abundantly clear that all such knowledge of contemporaries points back to, and is legitimized by, an originary direct experience of a fellow-man. But I can also gain knowledge about my contemporary social world in other ways than the one just cited. My experiences of things and events in physical reality, of objects manufactured by men, of tools and artifacts, of cultural objects, institutions and action patterns, too, refer to the world of my contemporaries (or point back to the world of my predecessors, a circumstance which we shall discuss later). This is so because I can always interpret them as testimony to the conscious life of human beings who produced and used these tools and artifacts, who adhered to these institutions, performed these actions. Such interpretations are by their very nature derivative. They consist of inferences based on and mediated by my experiences of fellow-men, either of particular fellow-men or of fellow-human beings in general. Face-to-face with a fellow-man I witnessed in simultaneity with my own ongoing conscious life the step-by-step constitution of his conduct, of experiences meaningful to him, that resulted in an accomplished act, artifact, tool, etc. Now I interpret an accomplished act, artifact, tool, etc., as a pointer to such subjective step-by-step processes. Without original experiences of this kind, objects and events in the outer world would be nothing but material things and physical processes without any reference to a human world.

My experiences of contemporaries are thus necessarily derivative and indirect. Nevertheless, it is obvious that I can be oriented to mere contemporaries as I can be oriented to fellow-men. These orientations, too, may range from mere attitudes to social action and social interaction. In analogy to the concept of Thou-orientation we shall subsume all conscious acts oriented to contemporaries under the concept, They-orientation.

In contrast to the way I experience the conscious life of fellow-men in face-to-face situations, the experiences of contemporaries appear to me more or less *anonymous* processes. The object of the They-orientation is my knowledge of social reality in general, of the conscious life of other human beings in general, regardless of whether the latter is imputed to a single individual or not. The object of the They-orientation is *not* the existence of a concrete man, *not* the ongoing conscious life of a fellow-man which is directly experienced in the We-relation, *not* the subjective configuration of meaning which I apprehend if experiences of a fellow-man constitute themselves before my eyes. My knowledge of contemporaries stands by its very nature in an *objective context of meaning*. Only *post hoc* may I append interpretations which refer back to a subjective meaning configuration, a point to which we shall return later when describing the constitution of personal ideal types. My knowledge of the world of contemporaries is typical knowledge of typical processes. Fundamentally, I leave it undecided in whose consciousness such typical processes are occurring. Detached as they are from a subjective configuration of meaning, such processes – typical experiences of "someone" – *exhibit the idealization: "again and again"*, i.e., of typical anonymous repeatability.

The unity of the mere contemporary is originally built up in the unity of *my* experience, more precisely, in a synthesis of *my* interpretations of the Other's experiences. It is not constituted in my direct experience of the unity of *his* ongoing conscious life in the Here and Now of a concrete Thou. Through this synthesis of my interpretations of the typical experiences of a more or less anonymous contemporary I apprehend him as a *personal ideal type*.

It should be clearly recognized that the more complete the substitution of a series of complex, interlocking, and interdependent objective meaning contexts for a subjective configuration of meaning, the more anonymous will be the object of my They-orientation. Our analysis has shown that the synthesis of the interpretations by which I know my contemporaries as ideal types does not apprehend the unique Self of a human being in his vivid present. It is an act of thought that holds invariant some typical attribute of fellow-human beings and disregards the modifications and variations of that attribute "in real life," i.e. when embedded in the ongoing experiences of a concrete and unique individual. Hence, *the personal ideal type merely refers to, but is never identical with, a concrete Other or a plurality of Others*.

This point will be illustrated by a few examples. If I drop a letter into the mailbox, I act in the expectation that certain contemporaries of mine (post office employees) will adequately interpret the wish I signified by writing out an address, attaching a stamp, etc., and will in fact carry it out. The expectation which oriented my action was not directed to specific concrete individuals but to the genus "post office employees." Max Weber pointed out that the acceptance of money as legal tender depends on the subjective chance that other contemporaries will also accept these tiny physical objects as means of payment. This, too, is an example of a They-orientation referring to the typical conduct of typical contemporaries. If I perform or refrain from performing some determinate act in order to avoid the intervention of certain people with badges and uniforms – to adduce another of Weber's examples – that is to say, if I orient my conduct to the law and its enforcement agencies, I stand in a social relation with my contemporaries, personified according to ideal types, i.e., in a They-relation.

In these examples I have acted with the expectation that certain determinate kinds of conduct are likely on the part of others: postal clerks, individuals involved in monetary transactions, policemen. I have a certain attitude toward them: I reckon with them when I plan my actions, in short, I am in a social relation with them. But my partners in these relations do not appear as concrete and specific individuals. They appear as instances of the genus "postal clerk," "user of the currency," "policeman." I ascribe to them specific patterns of conduct, specific functional performances. They are relevant for me as contemporaries only so far as they are typical performers of such functions, that is, as ideal types. In the They-relation I draw upon my stock of knowledge according to which there are "people" who are "typical" clerks, policemen, etc., and who do "typical" things *as* clerks, policemen, etc. I do not care how they "feel" about being clerks and doing police work, how, in other words, they experience their (ongoing) conduct in a subjective context of meaning. For me, their performances stand basically in an objective context of meaning. In the They-relation my partners are not concrete and unique individuals, but *types*.

This essential feature of the experience of contemporaries should not lead one to the false conclusion that one apprehends the conduct of others by typification only in relation to the world of contemporaries. It is true that the experience of contemporaries is *always* in the form of typifications, but the same holds for the apprehension of the world of predecessors. Furthermore, since knowledge of typical patterns of action and of personal ideal types constitutes part of one's stock of knowledge about social reality in general, typifications of this kind are also used in the experience of partners in the concrete We-relation, i.e., of the unique individual face-to-face with me. Consequently, *ideal types serve also as schemes of interpretation for that domain of social reality which is experienced directly*. However, there is an important difference: in the concrete We-relation the typifying schemata are swept along and modified by the unique Thou apprehended in the immediacy of a shared vivid present. The typifying schemata are, so to speak, formal models without content, matched against the concrete fellow-man and thereby deprived of their status as mere typifications. We shall illustrate this point with an example.

I am face-to-face with several fellow-men. Their experiences appear to me as an undivided and unbroken sequence of events in their conscious life. But the "They" with which I am face-to-face can be always resolved into a Thou and Thou and Thou in such manner that I can join with each Thou in a concrete We-relation. If, for example, I am observing three fellow-men playing cards, I can direct my attention to each of the players. In the Thou-orientation I can apprehend the way in which this particular individual is attending to the business at hand, the subjective context of meaning within which he places this business, etc., a context which will vary from player to player. But, as a detached observer, I can also transpose, as it were, the situation from the vivid present into the typified world of contemporaries. I draw upon my stock of knowledge and say: They are playing a game of rummy. Statements of this kind refer to the conscious life of the individual players only in so far as the typical performance "card-playing" is co-ordinated with a sequence of ongoing experiences for each player. These, it may be assumed, stand in a subjective context of meaning for him. But thereby I merely postulate that if, indeed, he is playing rummy, his conduct must be oriented by the rules of the game. This postulate is, of course, generally applicable to people who play rummy, any time, anywhere, and is by no means restricted to the three persons in front of me. No concrete experience of A is identical with any concrete experience of B or C since it belongs to the conscious life of one specific individual at a specific moment of his biography. The concrete experience is unique and cannot be repeated. It is neither identical nor even commensurable with any real experience of B. *The typical – and only the typical – is homogeneous.* Only in so far as I disregard the unique individuals A and B and C and say, "They" are playing cards, do I recognize in them an example of the anonymous genus "card-player." By typifying them I have performed an interpretive act of thought which bestowed anonymity upon A, B, and C.

The objective matrix of meaning which originated in the construction of typical experiences of typical contemporaries, co-ordinated with typical performances, may be retranslated into subjective configurations of meaning. I apply the typifications which are part of my stock of knowledge to concrete fellow-men in face-to-face situations. I apprehend the fellow-men as individuals "like others" of a designated type. At the same time, these fellow-men, as partners in a We-relation, are experienced directly. Therefore, they are "people like others" and yet unique individuals, endowed with a conscious life which goes on before my eyes. This double status of a fellow-man is the basis of a further, more complex transposition: the contemporary who is basically apprehended by me as a type is conceived of as an individual endowed with a "genuine" ongoing conscious life. But I do not grasp his conscious life directly, but only by an act of interpretation. Therefore, the contemporary ultimately remains a type whose consciousness, too, is "typical" and, in that sense, homogeneous.

The concept of the ideal type, so widely used in the social sciences, and the relation of the scientific construct to the common-sense typifications of one's fellow-men and contemporaries needs careful analysis. The complex processes by which "in-order-to" and "because" motives are co-ordinated with typical action patterns and held invariant in relation to the experience and observation of concrete individuals, and the procedures by which typical motives are ascribed to typical individuals, are investigated in more detail elsewhere.[9] In the sequel we shall continue with the discussion of the one aspect of this complex problem that is most important for our present investigation, the anonymity of the ideal type.

[9] Cf. *supra*, "The Social World and the Theory of Social Action"; and *Collected Papers I*, Part I.

3) The strata of anonymity in the world of contemporaries

In the foregoing analysis we considered the constitutive elements of the They-orientation. Within the basic structure of the They-orientation occur, in fact, various concrete experiences of contemporaries. These experiences are, to be sure, necessarily acts of thought by which Others whose existence is assumed or imagined are apprehended with respect to typical attributes. Given this fundamental identity, the experiences are differentiated in various ways. Most important is the fact that – while always indirect – they are not equally anonymous. We may say that the world of contemporaries *is stratified by the relative degree of concreteness or anonymity* that characterizes the ideal type by which Others are apprehended. The more anonymous the personal ideal type that mediates the experience of a contemporary, the more advanced is the substitution of objective matrices of meaning for the subjective meaning configuration ascribed to the Other. The more advanced the substitution, the more dependent is, in turn, the personal ideal type constituting a given experience upon a substratum of more or less anonymous personal ideal types and corresponding matrices of meaning.

The anonymity of an ideal type is a concept that requires further clarification. In a previous step of our investigation we pointed out that the "pure" Thou-orientation consists in the mere – but immediate – awareness of the existence of the Other. The apprehending of a fellow-man according to some characteristic trait presupposes this awareness. Not so in the case of the They-orientation. Even in its "pure" form the They-orientation is based on the positing of a typical attribute in an act of thought. In such an act of thought I posit, of course, the existence or former existence of the typical attribute. But I need not posit the presence of the typical attribute in a given concrete individual at a specific point of the spatio-temporal continuum. The ideal type is anonymous in relation to any existing person. Hence, the contemporary – who can be apprehended only as an ideal type – is anonymous in this sense. The *existence* of the contemporary is not directly experienced, whether it be assumed, considered likely, or even taken for granted. In my present experience the contemporary has the status of an individuated intersection of typical attributes. It should be noted in this context that the character of subjective chance that my contemporary's existence has for me increases the chance-character of my actions addressed to him, in comparison with actions addressed to fellow-men in face-to-face situations. As we shall show in the sequel this has important consequences for the nature of social relations involving mere contemporaries.

The concept, anonymity of the ideal type, may be also understood to refer to the *relative scope* of the typifying scheme. The scope of the typifying scheme is determined by the relative completeness and generality of that segment of the stock of knowledge which guided my selection of the trait to be typified as an invariant attribute within the typifying scheme. If the scheme is derived from previous experiences of a particular fellow-man, the typification is relatively concrete; if it is derived from personal ideal types available in my stock of general knowledge concerning social reality, it is relatively anonymous. We may say that *the degree of concreteness of the typifying scheme is inversely proportionate to the level of generality of those experiences sedimented in the stock of knowledge from which the scheme is derived.*

These remarks make it obvious that each typification involves other typifications. The more substrata of typifying schemes are involved in a given ideal type, the more anonymous it is, and the larger is the region of things simply taken for granted in the application of the ideal type. The substrata, of course, are not explicitly grasped in clear and distinct acts of thought. This becomes evident if one takes social realities such as the state or the economic system or art and begins to explicate all the substrata of typifications upon which they are based.

The relative degree of concreteness or anonymity of an ideal type must, therefore, be connected with the facility with which a They-relation – of which a given type is a constituent – can be transformed into a We-relation. The likelier I am to apprehend directly the ideal-typical traits of "someone" as elements of the ongoing conscious life of a concrete individual, the less anonymous are these traits. We shall illustrate this point by two examples.

I think about the absent friend A in a They-orientation. I know that A is facing a difficult decision. From past direct

experience of A I retain the ideal type "my friend A in general."
I may also form an action-pattern typification, "A's conduct in
face of difficult decisions." This ideal type, too, is They- rather
than Thou- oriented: "People 'like' A are wont to act in such
fashion if facing difficult decisions." Still, the ideal type "my
friend A" is highly concrete, based on past direct experience of
A in face-to-face situations. Furthermore, technical difficulties
aside, my contemporary A can always become my fellow-man A.

Another example: My friend A tells me about X whom he
recently met and whom I do not know. He proceeds to characterize X, that is, he constructs an ideal type of X by keeping invariant his direct experiences of X, thereby transforming them
into typifications. A's typifications depend, of course, upon his
stock of knowledge, his biographical situation, his interests when
meeting X, his interests when telling me about X, etc. I refer the
ideal type, as constructed and communicated to me by A, to my
own stock of knowledge according to my own biographical
situation, my interests, etc. The ideal type of X is therefore not
identical for A and for me. I may even question the validity of
A's characterization of X on the basis of my own characterization
of A: "A is an excitable type ... he is likely to see people in his
own peculiar way."

Both examples are of ideal types that are relatively concrete.
They are derived from first-hand direct experiences of a fellow-
man as an individual. Recollection of that individual's ongoing
conscious life breathes life into the objective matrix of typifications which has replaced, in the present actual experience, the
direct grasp of the unique individual. Ideal types of this kind
may be designated as *characterological personal types*. Another
kind of personal ideal type is the *functional* type, which refers to
contemporaries only with respect to their typical functions. For
illustration we may again refer to the example of the postal
clerk. This ideal type is already more anonymous than the
characterological, since it does not refer to the life of an individual
with whom I stood, now stand, or will ever stand in a We-
relation of any degree of intimacy; even in face-to-face situations
I apprehend him as a "postal clerk." Moreover, when I mail my
letter, I do not address myself even to the personal ideal type,
"postal clerk," for whom his conduct stands in a *specific* sub-

jective meaning context (salary, security, the boss, etc.). For me only the *action pattern*, in this case the standardized typical processing of letters, is relevant. It is only incidental that I append, as it were, to this action pattern "someone" who performs it. The "someone" is, of course, a relatively anonymous personal type.

If the functional ideal type is relatively anonymous in comparison to the characterological ideal type, it is relatively concrete if compared to other ideal-typical schemes, especially those which refer to social collectivities. Typifications of social collectivities, even if they retain personal character, are highly anonymous since the collectivities cannot ever be experienced directly and by their very nature belong to the transcendent social world of mere contemporaries and predecessors. The large class of such typifications also contains different strata of anonymity. The board of directors of a given corporation, for example, or Congress, are typifications of social collectivities which are still *relatively* concrete, since they are based on a limited number of substrata of personal ideal types. But one also uses typifications such as *the* state, *the* people, *the* economy, *the* social classes, etc., as though personal ideal types of contemporaries corresponded to them. This "as though," however, cannot be anything but an anthropomorphism for a completely anonymous context. The implication that this context is, or could be a subjective meaning configuration for a real contemporary is illegitimate. In the words of Max Weber: "But, for the subjective interpretation of action in sociological work, these collectivities must be treated as *solely* the resultants and modes of organization of the particular acts of individual persons, since these alone can be treated as agents in a course of subjectively understandable action." "...... for sociological purposes there is no such thing as a collective personality which 'acts.' When reference is made in a sociological context to a 'state,' a 'nation,' a 'corporation,' a 'family,' or an 'army corps,' or to similar collectivities, what is meant is, on the contrary, *only* a certain kind of development of actual or possible social actions of individual persons." [10] The "activities" of the state can be resolved into actions of state "functionaries," who can be apprehended, indeed, by means of

[10] Max Weber, *op. cit.*, pp. 101–102.

personal ideal types, and to whom one can turn in a They-orientation. In the sociological perspective the state can be considered an abbreviated designation for a highly complex system of interdependent personal ideal types. In the ordinary use of terms such as "the state," however, one naively takes this complex structure of typifications for granted. Furthermore, the objective matrices of meaning which manifest themselves in the anonymous action patterns of functionaries are ascribed, by an unwarranted transposition, to a personal pseudotype of the social collectivity in the same manner in which individual action is coordinated with a typical actor. But no individual consciousness can be construed from which the "activities" of a social collectivity constitute a *subjective* configuration of meaning.

The analysis of the structures of ideal typifications which form the substrata of social collectivities is an important task which sociology still has to accomplish. It will be necessary to describe the stratification of social collectivities in terms of relative anonymity and, according to their origin, in direct or indirect experiences of social reality. It will be also necessary to investigate to what extent it may be possible to speak of a subjective meaning of social collectivities, that is, to what extent "the activities" of a social collectivity, apprehended as typical actions of "functionaries," can be ascribed to subjective *meaning* contexts of the latter and thereby to their "responsibility." This is a problem of particular importance for political and legal theory.

Also deserving of careful analysis is the question under what circumstances and to what extent the concept of social collectivity can serve as a scheme for interpretation of the conduct of contemporaries by virtue of the fact that it subsumes, in an objective matrix, value-judgments which are accepted as valid and "lived by" in a given society or social group.

The observations on social collectivities also apply to systems of signification as, for example, the English language. It is always possible to turn from the objective context of meaning, the structure of the English language, to the highly anonymous personal ideal type, the speaker of English. Yet again, there can be no typical "individual" for whom the objective structure is a subjective meaning configuration. An "objective spirit of language" is an illegitimate fiction.

These remarks apply also to cultural objects of any kind, both ideal and material. Artifacts, for example, can be interpreted with respect to the personal ideal type of their creators and manufacturers, beholders, and users. A tool is the product of past actions, of "someone," and the means for the realization of future action projects of "anyone." The means-end relation constitutes an objective meaning context from which it is always possible to turn to the highly anonymous ideal types of the producer or user.

Here we conclude the description of the levels of anonymity which structure the experience of the world of contemporaries. Beginning with the transitions from direct experience of fellow-men in face-to-face situations to indirect experience of former fellow-men, we described the progressively more anonymous typifications which mediate the experience of transcendent social realities: from the relatively concrete characterological personal ideal type and the relatively more anonymous functional type to the typifying schemes for highly anonymous social collectivities, cultural objects, sign systems, and artifacts.

4) Social relations between contemporaries

As social relations in face-to-face situations are based on the "pure" Thou-orientation, so are social relations between contemporaries based on the "pure" form of the They-orientation. This means that while face-to-face social relations are constituted in the reciprocal mirroring of direct experiences of the Other, the Other is given only as an ideal type in social relations between contemporaries. A person involved in a social relation with a contemporary must be content with reckoning that the Other whom he grasps by a more or less anonymous typification is in his turn oriented to him by means of typification. Social relations involving mere contemporaries have a hypothetical character.

Boarding a train, for example, I orient my conduct by the expectation that certain individuals will perform certain actions which will make it possible and likely that the train will reach its destination. With these individuals, railway employees, I stand in a They-relation by virtue of the fact that, first, my stock of knowledge contains a functional ideal type, railway employee who sees to it that "people like me," i.e., travelers, reach their destinations, and, second, that I orient my conduct in accordance with this ideal type. This example shows also that social relations between contemporaries are characterized not only by the fact that I orient myself in accordance with a personal ideal type but also by my assumption that he, the "railway employee," orients his conduct according to a complementary personal ideal type, "traveler," i.e., anyone who conforms to the action pattern in question. Hence, *in a social relation between* contemporaries, I am in a They-relation. I ascribe, therefore, to my partner a scheme of typifications and expectations relative to *me* as a personal ideal type. *A social relation between contemporaries consists in the subjective chance that the reciprocally ascribed typifying schemes* (and corresponding expectations) *will be used congruently by the partners.* In face-to-face situations there is an immediate reciprocity of my experiences of the Other and of the Other's experiences of me. This reciprocity is replaced in They-relations by acts of reflection on the typifying scheme which presumably orients the conduct of both partners. The validity of my assumption that my partner shares a given typifying scheme with me (railway employee, traveler) cannot be verified, since my partner is not present. Hence, the more highly standardized a given typifying scheme, the better is the subjective chance that the typifying scheme I ascribed to my partner is, indeed, shared by him. This is the case with typifying schemes which are "institutionalized" by law, ordinance, tradition, etc., and with schemes which refer to means-ends relationships, that is, with schemes which are rational in the sense of Weber's analysis. These features of social relations between contemporaries have important consequences. As a result of the fact that They-relations are based on subjective chance, it can be decided only ex post facto whether a given social relation between A and myself really prevailed. Accordingly, the assumption that A and I share a certain typifying scheme, and that A is adequately apprehended by me in terms of the personal ideal type, A can be verified only retrospectively. I can reckon, therefore, with A's in-order-to and because-motives to plan my own conduct only in so far as these are explicitly part of the ideal type as A's invariant and constant motives. Starting with the assumption – which has, of course, merely the character of subjective chance – that my contemporary's typification of me as an ideal type ("client of the postal service") is congruent with my typification of him ("postal clerk"), I fit his "because"-motive into the in-order-to motive of my action project (writing, mailing, processing, etc., of my letter "in order that" X may have a letter from me). In contrast to interaction in face-to-face situations, however, I cannot proceed on the assumption that my "in-order-to" motive will be his "because"-motive. The interlocking of motives characteristic of interaction in the We-relation is replaced in the social relation between contemporaries by the interdependence of the reciprocally ascribed ideal types – which contain invariant motives – of the partners.

Furthermore, whereas my experience of a fellow-man in the We-relation is continuously modified and enriched by the experiences shared by us, this is not the case in the They-relation. Each new experience of contemporaries adds, of course, to my stock of knowledge; and the ideal types by which I am oriented to others in a They-relation do, indeed, undergo modifications as a result of shifts in my situation. But these modifications remain minimal as long as a given situation and my interests in it – which have determined the original application of a given typifying scheme – remain constant.

In the We-relation I can verify my assumption that the way in which I experience my environment can be co-ordinated with the way in which you experience yours. I am wont to extend this assumption to my contemporary and to say that if he were in my situation, his experiences would be roughly identical with mine. This assumption, however, cannot be verified. The question whether my partner's interpretation of the world is congruent with mine cannot be resolved with certainty in a They-relation.

In communicating with my partners in social relations I use sign-systems. The more anonymous my partner, the more "objectively" must I use the signs. Here it becomes obvious again how close is the relation between the degree of anonymity in a social relation and the graduated substitution of objective matrices of meaning for the subjective meaning configurations. I cannot presuppose, for example, that my partner in a They-relation will grasp a nuance of a word or that he will place a statement of mine in the proper context unless I explicitly and "objectively" refer to that context. The direct evidence that I have been understood, which I have if my partner is present in the community of space and time, is lacking in a They-relation.

Finally, it should be noted that They-relations that are from the outset characterized by a relatively low degree of anonymity can be transformed by various transitional phases into a We-relation. Correspondingly, intimate We-relations can be transformed into relatively concrete They-relations. Simmel's discussion of epistolary correspondence provides an excellent analysis of one such transitional phase. In general, we must observe that the transition between the structure of We-relations and the structure of They-relations is fluid. When I attend a performance in a theatre, for example, I am face-to-face with the actor. Yet I am relevant for the actor merely as an anonymous member of the audience.

In this investigation we must forego a discussion of the characteristic features of the observation of contemporaries. The problem is highly relevant for an understanding of the procedures of the empirical social sciences, and was treated in some detail elsewhere.[11]

IV. THE WORLD OF PREDECESSORS
AND THE PROBLEM OF HISTORY

If I have lived through a We-relation or a They-relation, I may recollect my past experiences in them either by reproducing them in my memory step by step or in a unitary grasp of retrospection. In both cases the constitutive characteristics of these experiences remain intact; they are recollected as direct face-to-face experiences of fellow-men or mediated experiences of contemporaries, according to the respective experiential structures. Yet they do not carry a subscript of actuality, but of historicity; they are not ongoing, but past experiences. In addition, another important modification occurred. In the ongoing experience the

---

[11] "Common-Sense and Scientific Interpretation of Human Action," in *Collected Papers I*, esp. pp. 15 f, 39, and "The Social World and the Theory of Social Action." *supra* esp. p. 4 ff.

coming phases of that experience were merely anticipated; the future of the experience was open. Now the anticipations are either fulfilled or frustrated; the experience is completed. Whatever had merely the character of subjective chance in my actual social relation – that is, in particular, the anticipated conduct of my partner – has now become certain one way or another. In planning my action, I projected my partner's anticipated conduct. Now my planned action has run its course, successfully or unsuccessfully, and his anticipated conduct has either occurred or failed to occur. The peculiar temporal structure of action,[12] while remaining intact in the recollection, is now relocated in the new context of temporal closure: e.g., "I wanted this when I started, but I accomplished only that." The *reason* for recollecting formerly experienced social realities, on the other hand, originates in my present situation and is conditioned by the problems and interests of the Here and Now.

The line separating directly experienced social reality and the world of contemporaries from the world of predecessors is fluid. By a shift in interpretation I could take my recollections of past experiences of fellow-men and contemporaries as experiences of past social reality. It should be noted, however, that such recollections are not yet experiences of the world of predecessors in the strict sense. In recollection the genuine contemporaneity in which the experience of the We- or They-relation constituted itself remains preserved. This means that I co-ordinate each past phase of the life of a fellow-man or contemporary with past phases of my own life and that I can turn my attention retrospectively to the step-by-step constitution of subjective meaning contexts in my own consciousness or in the consciousness of my partner in a We- or They-relation.

The world of my predecessors, on the other hand, is obviously characterized by the fact that I cannot co-ordinate my own and my predecessor's conscious lives in genuine contemporaneity. It is a definitively past world; *it has no open future.* In the concrete conduct of my predecessors there is nothing as yet undecided: their actions are accomplished: nothing remains to be anticipated. In contrast to my fellow-men – and in a certain sense also my contemporaries – my predecessors *cannot be experienced*

---

[12] "Choosing Among Projects of Action," in *Collected Papers I.*

as free. The "freedom" of my contemporaries, too, is restricted by the fact that I apprehend them as ideal types whose motives and actions are held constant and invariant. However, while I apprehend my predecessors, too, by ideal-typical constructs, I do not hold invariant anything which is not by its nature invariant. The world of my predecessors is by its very essence constant; everything has already come to pass. Hence, I can be oriented to my predecessors, but I cannot act upon them. But even my orientation to predecessors differs fundamentally from my orientation toward fellow-men and contemporaries. My actions can be said to be oriented by actions of my predecessors only in so far as my experiences of past actions of predecessors become because-motives of my conduct. It may be noted in parentheses that Weber's concept of traditional action affords an example of such conduct. It need not be emphasized that genuine social relations with predecessors are impossible, genuine and regular acts of orientation toward ancestors as, for example, in the ancestor worship of some cultures notwithstanding. Actions of my predecessors which are oriented by anticipations of my future conduct, as in the case of testamentary dispositions, can be reciprocated only by acts of orientation – and, of course, by conduct for which the action of the predecessor is a because-motive.

Experience of the world of predecessors is, of course, indirect. Knowledge of predecessors – just as knowledge of contemporaries – can be derived from communicative acts of fellow-men or contemporaries in which they report their own past experiences (e.g. childhood reminiscences of my father) and their past experiences of fellow-men and contemporaries (e.g. my teacher telling me about a Civil War veteran he knew). These illustrations show clearly how fluid are the transitions from the world of contemporaries to the world of predecessors. My father, for example, stands with me in a We-relation and his childhood experiences, while antedating my birth, are nevertheless experiences of a fellow-man of mine, although they carry a subscript of historicity. Yet they properly belong to the world of my predecessors because I cannot co-ordinate past phases of my own conscious life with these experiences of my fellow-man. Such past direct and indirect experiences of social reality on the part of my fellow-man therefore belong to a genuinely past domain of the social world, but I gain knowledge of it through the mediation of communicative acts in a genuine We- or They-relation. Hence, I can ascribe these communicative acts to a subjective meaning configuration in the conscious life of the communicator.

Second, I gain knowledge of the world of my predecessors through documents and "monuments" in the broadest sense. These are manifestations of the conscious life of my predecessors. It is irrelevant whether they are manifestations of communicative acts of my predecessors intended for posterity, i.e., for us, or whether the communications were intended by my predecessors for their own contemporaries. In so far as my experience of predecessors is mediated by communications of my fellow-men and contemporaries, it is more or less anonymous, more or less concrete, although these characteristics are evidently derived and second-hand, as it were. If I gain knowledge of the world of predecessors through communicative acts on the part of the predecessors, however, the signs used in communication are, first of all, elements in an objective system of meaning and completely anonymous. Yet the signs are also manifestations of the conscious life of the communicator, and I can shift my attention from the objective context of the sign to the subjective configuration of meaning, i.e., the conscious life of the communicator who used the sign in a specific communicative act. By this shift of perspective I achieve a kind of pseudo-contemporaneity of my own conscious life with the conscious life of the communicator. Historical research proper is ordinarily not concerned with the communicating subject. Yet it must not be forgotten that historical sources always refer to direct or indirect experiences of the social reality on the part of the communicator and that this circumstance bestows more or less concreteness or anonymity upon the "objective content" of the sign. In this connection it should be pointed out that the world of predecessors is always a contemporary world of an Other and that it contains, therefore, the same internal stratification of more or less concrete and anonymous experiential structures as my own contemporary social world.

While both the world of contemporaries and the world of predecessors can be experienced only mediately by means of ideal typification, there is an important difference. The predecessor is located in an environment which differs radically from my own but also from that which I ascribe to my contemporaries. In apprehending fellow-men or contemporaries by means of typifying schemes, I can take for granted that the partner in the We- or They-relation shares with me a rather vaguely defined core segment of common knowledge. I can assume, for example, that the highly anonymous personal ideal type, "my contemporary," participates in the equally anonymous – and vaguely defined – "contemporary civilization." The stock of knowledge which was the context for my predecessor's thoughts and actions, on the other hand, is fundamentally different from the stock of knowledge of "our contemporary civilization." Hence, the context of meaning in which a predecessor's experience was located differs radically from the context in which the "same" experience would appear for a contemporary. Consequently, the experience cannot be the "same." I can say, however, that my predecessor's experience was human experience: I can interpret it in the context of my knowledge of the structure of human experience as meaningful experience *in general*.[13]

The schemes which we use in the interpretation of the world of predecessors necessarily differ from the schemes by which the predecessors themselves interpreted their experiences. If I equate the way in which I interpret my experiences with the way in which my predecessor interpreted his, I do so only in a vague and tentative manner. The degree of subjective chance which this equation has is immeasurably greater than that of the same equation applied to contemporaries. This holds even for my interpretation of the objective sign systems by which my predecessors communicated. Sign systems are, of course, invariant, that is, they do not have the open horizon and "freedom" of an ongoing experience. What cannot be decided with certainty, however, is the degree of congruity between the scheme of expression which

---

[13] In the words of Jacob Burckhardt in *Weltgeschichtliche Betrachtungen*, Kröner Ausgabe, p. 5: "*Unser Ausgangspunkt ist der vom einzigen Bleibenden und für uns möglichen Zentrum, von duldenden, strebenden und handelnden Menschen, wie er ist und immer war und sein wird ....*" (We shall start from the one point accessible to us, the one and only center of history - man, suffering, striving, acting, as he is and was and ever will be).

determined my predecessor's communicative acts and my scheme of interpretation. Hence, all interpretation of predecessors' communicative acts has the character of subjective chance. The history of philosophy affords many examples of controversies over what the "correct meaning" of a term is, that is, what meaning was intended by the philosopher in question. Another more specific example is the controversy about the "proper" interpretation of the works of J. S. Bach in terms of the "objectively given" system of musical notation. The interpretation of the communicative acts of contemporaries also has the character of subjective chance, of course, but I can verify my interpretation by questioning my contemporary, if necessary by meeting him face-to-face.

The science of history has the momentous task of deciding which events, actions, and communicative acts to select for the interpretation and reconstruction of "history" from the total social reality of the past. If we look back at the stream of historical events and compare it with the stream of our own past experiences, we find that they are similarly continuous and manifold. Yet the latter occurs in the duration of individual conscious life, the former in objective time.[14] The stream of history contains anonymous events, and homogeneous events repeat themselves. Nevertheless, all historical events *can* be reduced to genuine experiences of other men, experiences which occurred in the duration of individual conscious life and referred to fellow-men and contemporaries. They were experiences which took place in We-relations or They-relations. From one generation to the next the individuals involved in relations of this kind changed. Fellow-men became predecessors: in a manner of speaking, a continuous We-relation exists from the dawn of mankind to this day. The concrete individuals in the relation follow one another, the concrete experiences change, but the relation is maintained. This view of history, while permitting of metaphysical interpretations, is not in itself metaphysical but, rather, the necessary condition for the unity not only of our experience of the world of predecessors but of social reality in general. It is also the condition for the conception of history as a process meaningful

[14] Cf. G. Simmel, *Das Problem der historischen Zeit*, Philosophische Vorträge der Kant-Gesellschaft, 12, Berlin, 1916.

to its subjects. The starting point for historical interpretation may be the objective meaning context of the completed events, of the accomplished actions; but it may be also the subjective meaning context of a We in which every event was located. Hence, there can be a history of "objective facts" as well as a history of conduct, meaningful to the individual historical subject.

In order to conclude the discussion of the several regions of social reality, we shall briefly describe the main features of the world of successors. This domain is totally indeterminate and indeterminable. Hence, our conduct cannot be oriented to the world of successors by any of its characteristics but merely by the knowledge that there will be an – indeterminate – world of successors. We cannot apprehend this domain of social reality by any method, not even by typification. This method, which originates in our experiences of fellow-men, contemporaries and predecessors, cannot be legitimately applied to a reality for which we do not have *any* principles of interpretation based in experience. Only to those fellow-men and contemporaries whom we may assume to predecease, may we apply typifying schemes derived from our experiences of them as fellow-men and contemporaries. Thus, we apprehend, with some degree of likelihood, the character of the transitional region between the world of contemporaries and successors. The farther removed the region from an actual We-relation or They-relation, however, the vaguer the interpretations by which we try to understand it. The world of genuine successors is absolutely free and beyond the grasp of my understanding. Belief in a historical law above history by which not only the past and the present can be explained but also the future predicted evidently has no foundation in the nature of human experience of *social* reality.

V. GLOSSARY

Mitwelt, world of contemporaries
Vorwelt, world of predecessors
Folgewelt, world of successors
Umwelt, fellow-men in direct experience; (*or if the context permits, simply*) fellow-men; the domain of directly experienced social reality. (*Schutz himself used* associates *as well as* consociates, *occasionally, in some contexts, also* fellow-men).

Du-Einstellung, thou-orientation
Du-Beziehung, thou-relation
Ihr-Einstellung, they-orientation
Ihr-Beziehung, they-relation

subjektiver Sinn, subjective meaning

objektiver Sinn, objective meaning

subjektiver Sinnzusammenhang, subjective configuration of meaning

objektiver Sinnzusammenhang, objective matrix of meaning

personaler Idealtypus, personal ideal type

Charakterologischer Idealtypus, characterological ideal type

habitueller Idealtypus, functional ideal type (*the definition by Schutz:" . . . den habituellen Ideal typus. Sein Kennzeichen ist, dass er das mitweltliche alter ego nur in seiner habituellen und deshalb als typisch angesetzten Funktion erfasst."*).

THE PROBLEM OF RATIONALITY IN THE SOCIAL WORLD

I

The problem suggested by the terms "rationality" or "rational action" as used in current literature is most certainly central to the methodology and epistemology of the scientific study of the social world. The terms themselves, however, are not only used with many different meanings – and this sometimes in the writings of the same author as, for instance, Max Weber – but they represent only very inadequately the underlying conceptual scheme. In order to bring out the concealed equivocations and connotations, and to isolate the question of rationality from all the other problems surrounding it, we must go further into the structure of the social world and make more extensive inquiries into the different attitudes toward the social world adopted, on the one hand, by the actor within this world, and, on the other hand, by the scientific observer of it.

What is commonly understood by the term "rational action" is best shown by the definition of "rationality" or "reasonableness" given by Professor Talcott Parsons in his remarkable study on *The Structure of Social Action*: [1]

"Action is rational in so far as it pursues ends possible within the conditions of the situation, and by the means which, among those available to the actor, are intrinsically best adapted to the end for reasons understandable and verifiable by positive empirical science." Indicating in his usual careful manner the methodological point of view from which he contemplates his problem, Professor Parsons comments upon this definition as follows: "Since science is the rational achievement par excellence,

[1] New York, 1937, p. 58.

the mode of approach here outlined is in terms of the analogy between the scientific investigator and the actor in ordinary practical activities. The starting point is that of conceiving the actor as coming to know the facts of the situation in which he acts and thus the condition necessary and means available for the realization of his ends. As applied to the means-end relationship this is essentially a matter of the accurate prediction of the probable effects of various possible ways of altering the situation (employment of alternative means) and the resultant choice among them. Apart from questions relating to the choice of ends and from those relating to 'effort' . . . there is, where the standard is applicable at all, little difficulty in conceiving the actor as thus analogous to the scientist whose knowledge is the principal determinant of his action so far as his actual course conforms with the expectations of an observer who has, as Pareto says, 'a more extended knowledge of the circumstances.' ''

This definition gives an excellent résumé of the widely used concept of rational action in so far as it refers to the level of social theory. It seems important, however, to make more precise the peculiarity of this theoretical level by contrasting it with the other levels of our experience of the social world. We must, therefore, start by examining what we really mean when we speak of different levels in observing the social world. Following this a short description of the social world as it appears to the actor within this world in his everyday life will give us an opportunity of examining whether or not the category of rationality becomes determinative for his actions. Only after these preliminaries shall we examine the social world as it is given to the scientific observer; and together with it we shall have to examine the question of whether the categories of interpretation used by the scientist coincide with those used by the observed actor. Anticipating our results, we may say at once that with the shift from one level to another all the conceptual schemes and all the terms of interpretation must be modified.

II

The fact that the same object has a different appearance to various observers has been illustrated by some philosophers by the example of a city which, though always the same, appears different to different persons according to their individual stand-points. I do not wish to over-work this metaphor, but it helps to make clear the difference between our view of the social world in which we naively live and the social world which is the object of scientific observation. The man brought up in a town will find his way in its streets by following the habits he has acquired in his daily occupations. He may not have a consistent conception of the organization of the city, and, if he uses the underground railway to go to his office, a large part of the city may remain unknown to him. Nevertheless, he will have a proper sense of the distances between different places and of the directions in which the different points are situated relatively to whatever he regards as the center. This center will usually be his home, and it may be sufficient for him to know that he will find nearby an underground line or a bus leading to certain other points to bring them all within his reach. He can, therefore, say that he knows his town, and, though this knowledge is of a very in-coherent kind, it is sufficient for all his practical needs.

When a stranger comes to the town, he has to learn to orientate himself in it and to know it. Nothing is self-explanatory for him and he has to ask an expert, in this case a native, to learn how to get from one point to another. He may, of course, refer to a map of the town, but even to use the map successfully he must know the meaning of the signs on the map, the exact point with-in the town where he stands and its correlative on the map, and at least one more point in order correctly to relate the signs on the map to the real objects in the city.

Entirely different means of orientation must be used by the cartographer who has to draw a map of the city. There are several ways open to him. He can start with a photograph taken from an aeroplane; he can place a theodolite at a known point, measure a certain distance and calculate trigonometrical functions, etc. The science of cartography has developed a standard for such operations, elements the cartographer must know before he begins to draw his map, and rules he must observe if he is to draw his map correctly.

The town is the same for all the three persons we have mention-ed – the native, the foreigner and the cartographer – but for the

native it has a special meaning: "my home town"; for the foreigner it is a place within which he has to live and work for some
time; for the cartographer it is an object of his science, he is
interested in it only for the purposes of drawing a map. We may
say that the same object is considered from different levels.

We should certainly be surprised if we found a cartographer in
mapping a town restricting himself to collecting information from
natives. Nevertheless, social scientists frequently choose this
strange method. They forget that their scientific work is done on
a level of interpretation and understanding different from the
naive attitudes of orientation and interpretation peculiar to
people in daily life. When these social scientists speak of different
levels, they frequently consider the difference between the two
levels as entirely and simply one of the degree of concreteness or
generality. These two terms, however, are no more than chapter
headings for much more complicated problems than those which
they directly suggest.

In our daily life, as in our scientific world, we, as human
beings, all have the tendency to presume, more or less naively,
that what we have once verified as valid will remain valid throughout the future, and that what appeared to us beyond question
yesterday will still be beyond all question to-morrow. This naive
presumption may be made without danger if we deal with propositions of a purely logical character, or with empirical statements of a very high generality, though it can be shown that these
kinds of propositions, too, have only a limited realm of applicability. On the other hand, at a so-called concrete level, we are
forced to admit very many suppositions and implications as
beyond question. We can even consider the level of our actual
research as defined by the total of unquestioned presuppositions
which we make by placing ourselves at the specific standpoint
from which we envisage the interrelation of problems and aspects
under scrutiny. Accordingly, passing from one level to another
would involve that certain presuppositions of our research
formerly regarded as beyond all question would now be called in
question; and what was formerly a *datum* of our problem would
now become problematic itself. But the simple fact that new
problems and aspects of facts emerge with the shift in the point
of view, while others that were formerly in the center of our

question disappear, is sufficient to initiate a thorough modification of the meaning of all the terms correctly used at the former level. Careful control of such modifications of the meaning is, therefore, indispensable if we are to avoid the risk of naively taking over from one level to another terms and propositions whose validity is essentially limited to a certain level, that is, to its implied suppositions.

Philosophical and in particular phenomenological theory has made very important contributions toward the better understanding of this phenomenon. However, we need not concern ourselves here with this very complicated problem from the phenomenological viewpoint. It will be sufficient to refer to an outstanding thinker of the English-speaking world, to William James and his theory of conception. It was he who taught us that each of our concepts has its fringes surrounding a nucleus of its unmodified meaning. "In all our voluntary thinking," he says, "there is some topic or subject about which all the members of the thought revolve. Relation to our topic or interest is constantly felt in the fringe of our concepts. Each word in a sentence is felt, not only as a word, but as having a meaning. The meaning of a word taken thus dynamically in a sentence may be quite different from its meaning if taken statically or without context."

It is not for us to discuss here James's theory of the nature of such fringes and their genesis in the stream of thought. For our purpose it will be sufficient to say that already the connection in which a concept or a term is used and its relation to the topic of interest (and this topic of interest is in our case the *problem)* create specific modifications, of the fringes surrounding the nucleus, or even of the nucleus itself. It was also William James who explained that we do not apperceive isolated phenomena, but rather a field of several interrelated and interwoven things as it emerges in the stream of our thought. This theory explains sufficiently for our purposes the phenomenon of the meaning oı a term being modified as we pass to another level. I think that these superficial references will be sufficient to indicate the nature of the problem we are dealing with.

The term "rationality," or at least the concept it envisages, has, within the framework of social science, the specific role of a "key concept." It is peculiar to key concepts that, once introduced into an apparently uniform system, they constitute the differentiations between the points of view which we call levels. The meaning of such key concepts, therefore, does not depend on the level of the actual research, but, on the contrary, the level on which the research may be done depends upon the meaning attributed to the key concept, the introduction of which has for the first time divided what formerly appeared as a homogeneous field of research into several different levels. Anticipating what we shall have to prove later, we shall say that the level made accessible by the introduction of the term "rational action" as a chief principle of the method of social sciences is nothing else than the level of theoretical observation and interpretation of the social world.

III

As scientific observers of the social world, we are not practically but only cognitively interested in it. That means we are not acting in it with full responsibility for the consequences, but rather contemplating it with the same detached equanimity as physicists contemplate their experiments. But let us remember that notwithstanding our scientific activity we all remain human beings in our daily life – men among fellow-men with whom we are interrelated in very many ways. To be precise, even our scientific activity itself is based on the co-operation between us, the scientists, and our teachers and the teachers of our teachers, a co-operation by mutual influence and mutual criticism; but in so far as scientific activity is socially founded, it is one among other emanations of our human nature and certainly pertains to our daily life, governed by the categories of vocation and avocation, of work and leisure, of planning and accomplishing. Scientific activity as a social phenomenon is one thing, the specific attitude the scientist has to adopt toward his problem is another. Considered purely as a human activity, scientific work is distinguished from other human activities merely by the fact that it constitutes the archetype for rational interpretation and rational action.

In our daily life it is only very rarely that we act in a rational way if we understand this term in the meaning envisaged in Professor Parsons' previously quoted statement. We do not even interpret the social world surrounding us in a rational way, except under special circumstances which compel us to leave our basic attitude of just living our lives. Each of us, so it seems, has naively organized his social world and his daily life in such a way that he finds himself the center of the social cosmos surrounding him. Or, better, he was already born into an organized social cosmos. For him it is a cosmos and it is organized in so far as it contains all the comfortable equipment to render his daily living and that of his fellow-men a routine matter. There are, on the one hand, institutions of various kinds, tools, machines, etc.; on the other hand, habits, traditions, rules and experiences, both actual and vicarious. Furthermore, there is a scale of systematized relations which everyone has with his fellow-men, starting from the relations with members of his immediate family, relations with kinsmen, with personal friends, with people he knows personally, with people he met once in his life, through relations with those anonymous men who work somewhere and in a way he cannot imagine, but with the result that the letter he puts into the pillar box reaches the addressee in time, and that his lamp is lit by the turn of a switch.

Thus the social world with the *"alter egos"* in it is arranged around the self as a center in various degrees of intimacy and anonymity. Here am I and next to me are *"alter egos"* of whom, as Kipling says, I know "their naked souls." Then come those with whom I share time and space and whom I know more or less intimately. Next in order are the manifold relations I have with people in whose personality I am interested, though I have only an indirect knowledge of them such, for instance, as may be obtained from their works or writings or from reports from others. For example, my social relation with the author of the book I am reading is of this kind. On the other hand, I have social relations (in the technical meaning of this term), though superficial and inconsistent ones, with others in whose personalities I am not interested, but who merely happen to perform functions in which I am interested. Perhaps the salesgirl in the store where I buy my shaving cream, or the man who polishes my shoes, are much more interesting personalities than many of my friends. I do not inquire. I am not interested in social contact with those people.

I just want to get my shaving cream and to have my shoes polished by whatever means. In this sense, it makes very little difference to me whether, when I want to make a telephone call, an operator or a dial intervenes. Incidentally – and here we enter the remotest sphere of social relations – the dial, too, has its social function because it derives, as do all products of human activity, from the man who invented, designed and produced it. But if I am not guided by a special motive, I do not ask for the history, genesis, and construction of all the tools and institutions created by other people's activity. Likewise, I do not ask about the personality and destiny of fellow-men whose activity I consider as a purely *typical* function. In any case, and this is important for our problem, I can use the telephone with success without knowing how it functions; I am interested only in the fact that it does function. I do not care whether the result achieved, which alone interests me, is due to the intervention of a human being whose motives remain undisclosed to me or to a mechanism whose operation I do not understand. What counts is the typical character of the occurrence within a typified situation.

Thus, in this organization of the social world by the human being living naively in it, we already find the germ of the system of types and typical relations which we shall recognize later in its fullest ramification as the essential feature of scientific method. This typification is progressive in the same proportion as the personality of the fellow-man disappears beyond the undisclosed anonymity of his function. If we want to do so, we may interpret this process of progressive typification also as one of rationalization. At least it is envisaged by one of the several meanings Max Weber attributes to the term "rationalization" when he speaks of the "disenchantment of the world" (*Entzauberung der Welt*). This term means the transformation of an uncontrollable and unintelligible world into an organization which we can understand and therefore master, and in the framework of which prediction becomes possible.

In my opinion, the fundamental problem of the different aspects under which our fellow-men and their behavior and actions seem given to us has not yet received from sociologists the attention it merits. But if social science, with few exceptions, has failed to consider this kind of rationalization of its conceptual framework, each of us human beings, in "just living along," has already performed this task, and this without planning to do so and without any effort in the performance of his job. In doing so, we are guided neither by methodological considerations nor by any conceptual scheme of means-end relations, nor by any idea of values we have to realize. Our practical interest alone, as it arises in a certain situation of our life, and as it will be modified by the change in the situation which is just on the point of occurring, is the only relevant principle in the building up of the perspective structure in which our social world appears to us in daily life. For, just as all our visual apperceptions are in conformity with the principles of perspective and convey the impressions of depths and distance, so all our apperceptions of the social world necessarily have the basic character of perspective views. Of course the social world of a sixty-year old Chinese Buddhist in the time of the Ming dynasty will be organized in quite a different way from the social world of a twenty-year old American Christian of our own day, but the fact remains that both worlds would be organized, and this within the framework of the categories of familiarity and strangeness, of personality and type, of intimacy and anonymity. Furthermore, each of these worlds would be centered in the self of the person who lives and acts in it.

IV

But let us proceed in our analysis of the knowledge that a man living naively has about the world, the social world as well as the natural. In his daily life the healthy, adult, and wide-awake human being (we are not speaking of others) has this knowledge, so to speak, automatically at hand. From heritage and education, from the manifold influences of tradition, habits and his own previous reflection, his store of experiences is built up. It embraces the most heterogeneous kinds of knowledge in a very incoherent and confused state. Clear and distinct experiences are intermingled with vague conjectures; suppositions and prejudices cross well-proven evidences; motives, means and ends, as well as causes and effects, are strung together without clear understanding of their real connections. There are everywhere gaps, intermissions, discontinuities. Apparently there is a kind of organization by habits, rules, and principles which we regularly apply with success. But the origin of our habits is almost beyond our control; the rules we apply are rules of thumb and their validity has never been verified. The principles we start from are partly taken over uncritically from parents and teachers, partly distilled at random from specific situations in our lives or in the lives of others without our having made any further inquiry into their consistency. Nowhere have we a guarantee of the reliability of all of these assumptions by which we are governed. On the other hand, these experiences and rules are sufficient to us for mastering life. As we normally have to act and not to reflect in order to satisfy the demands of the moment, which it is our task to master, we are not interested in the "quest for certainty." We are satisfied if we have a fair chance of realizing our purposes, and this chance, so we like to think, we have if we set in motion the same mechanism of habits, rules and principles which formerly stood the test and which still stand the test. Our knowledge in daily life is not without hypotheses, inductions, and predictions, but they all have the character of the approximate and the typical. The ideal of everyday knowledge is not certainty, nor even probability in a mathematical sense, but just likelihood. Anticipations of future states of affairs are conjectures about what is to be hoped or feared, or at best, about what can be reasonably expected. When afterwards the anticipated state of affairs takes some form in actuality, we do not say that our prediction has come true or proved false, or that our hypothesis has stood the test, but that our hopes or fears were or were not well founded. The consistency of this system of knowledge is not that of natural *laws*, but that of *typical* sequences and relations.

This kind of knowledge and its organization I should like to call "cook-book knowledge." The cook-book has recipes, lists of ingredients, formulae for mixing them, and directions for finishing off. This is all we need to make an apple pie, and also all we need to deal with the routine matters of daily life. If we enjoy the apple pie so prepared, we do not ask whether the manner of preparing it as indicated by the recipe is the most appropriate from the hygienic or alimentary point of view, or whether it is the shortest, the most economical, or the most efficient. We just eat and enjoy it. Most of our daily activities from rising to going to bed are of this kind. They are performed by following recipes reduced to automatic habits or unquestioned platitudes. This kind of knowledge is concerned only with the regularity as such of events in the external world irrespective of its origin. Because of this regularity it can be reasonably expected that the sun will rise to-morrow morning. It is equally regular, and it can, therefore, with as good reason be anticipated too that the bus will bring me to my office if I choose the right one and pay my fare.

V

The foregoing remarks characterize in a very superficial manner the conceptual scheme of our everyday behavior in so far as the term "conceptual scheme" can be applied at all. Are we to classify a behavior of the type just described as rational or irrational? In order to answer this question we must analyze the various equivocal implications which are hidden in the term "rationality" as it is applied to the level of everyday experience.

1. "Rational" is frequently used as synonymous with "reasonable." Now we certainly act in our daily life in a reasonable way if we use the recipes we find in the store of our experience as already tested in an analogous situation. But acting rationally often means avoiding mechanical applications of precedents, dropping the use of analogies, and searching for a new way to master the situation.

2. Sometimes rational action is put on a par with acting deliberately, but the term "deliberately" itself implies many equivocal elements.

   (a) Routine action of daily life is deliberated in so far as it always relates back to the original act of deliberation which once preceded the building up of the formula now taken by the actor as a standard for his actual behavior.

   (b) Conveniently defined, the term "deliberation" may cover the insight into the applicability to a present situation of a recipe which has proved successful in the past.

   (c) We can give the term "deliberation" a meaning covering

the pure anticipation of the end – and this anticipation is always the motive for the actor to set the action going.

(d) On the other hand, the term "deliberation" as used, for instance, by Professor Dewey in his *Human Nature and Conduct*, means, "a dramatic rehearsal in imagination of various competing possible lines of action." In this sense, which is of the greatest importance for the theory of rationality, we cannot classify as rational the type of everyday actions which we have examined up to now as deliberated actions. On the contrary, it is characteristic of these routine actions that the problem of choice between different possibilities does not enter into the consciousness of the actor. We shall have to come back to the problem of choice immediately.

3. Rational action is frequently defined as "planned" or "projected" action without a precise indication of the meaning of the terms "planned" or "projected." We cannot simply say that the non-rational routine acts of daily life are not consciously planned. On the contrary, they rest within the framework of our plans and projects. They are even instruments for realizing them. All planning presupposes an end to be realized by stages, and each of these stages may be called, from one point of view or another, either means or intermediate ends. Now the function of all routine work is a standardization and mechanization of the means-end relations as such by referring standardized means to standardized classes of ends. The effect of this standardization is that the intermediate ends disappear from the consciously envisaged chain of means which have to be brought about for performing the planned end. But here arises the problem of subjective meaning which we have mentioned before. We cannot speak of the unit-act as if this unit were constituted or demarcated by the observer. We must seriously ask: when does one act start and when is it accomplished? We shall see that only the actor is in a position to answer this question.

Let us take the following example: Assume the professional life of a business man to be organized and planned to the extent that he intends to continue with his business for the next ten years, after which he hopes to retire. To continue his work involves going to his office every morning. For this purpose he has to leave his home at a certain hour, buy a ticket, take the train, etc. He did so yesterday and he will do so to-morrow if nothing extraordinary intervenes. Let us assume that one day he is late and that he thinks: "I shall miss my train – I shall be late at my office. Mr. 'X' will be there already, waiting for me. He will be in a bad humor, and perhaps he will not sign the contract on which so much of my future depends." Let us further assume that an observer watches this man rushing for the train "as usual" (so he thinks). Is his behavior planned, and if so, what is the plan? Only the actor can give the answer because he alone knows the span of his plans and projects. Probably all routine work is a tool for bringing about ends which are beyond routine work and which determine it.

4. "Rational" is frequently identified with "predictable." It is not necessary to return to this question. We have already analyzed the specific form of prediction in everyday knowledge as simply an estimate of likelihood.

5. According to the interpretation of some authors, "rational" refers to "logical." Professor Parsons' definition is one example and Pareto's theory of non-logical action to which he refers is another. In so far as the scientific concept of the rational act is in question, the system of logic may be fully applied. On the level of everyday experience, however, logic in its traditional form cannot render the services we need and expect. Traditional logic is a logic of concepts based on certain idealizations. In enforcing the postulate of clearness and distinctness of the concepts, for instance, traditional logic disregards all the fringes surrounding the nucleus within the stream of thought. On the other hand, thought in daily life has its chief interest precisely in the relation of the fringes which attach the nucleus to the actual situation of the thinker. This is clearly a very important point. It explains why Husserl classifies the greater part of our propositions in daily thought as "occasional propositions," that means, as valid and understandable only relative to the speaker's situation and to their place in his stream of thought. It explains, too, why our everyday thoughts are less interested in the antithesis "true-false" than in the sliding transition "likely-unlikely." We do not make everyday propositions with the purpose of achieving a formal validity within a certain realm which could be recognized

by someone else, as the logician does, but in order to gain knowledge valid only for ourselves and to further our practical aims. To this extent, but only to this extent, the principle of pragmatism is incontestably well founded. It is a description of the style of everyday thought, but not a theory of cognition.

6. A rational act presupposes, according to the interpretation of other authors, a choice between two or more means toward the same end, or even between two different ends, and a selection of the most appropriate. This interpretation will be analyzed in the following section.

VI

As Professor John Dewey has pointed out, in our daily life we are largely preoccupied with the next step. Men stop and think only when the sequence of doing is interrupted, and the disjunction in the form of a problem forces them to stop and rehearse alternative ways – over, around or through – which their past experience in collision with this problem suggest. The image of a dramatic rehearsal of future action used by Professor Dewey is a very fortunate one. Indeed, we cannot find out which of the alternatives will lead to the desired end without imagining this act as already accomplished. So we have to place ourselves mentally in a future state of affairs which we consider as already realized, though to realize it would be the end of our contemplated action. Only by considering the act as accomplished can we judge whether the contemplated means of bringing it about are appropriate or not, or whether the end to be realized accommodates itself to the general plan of our life. I like to call this technique of deliberation "thinking in the future perfect tense." But there is a great difference between action actually performed and action only imagined as performed. The really accomplished act is irrevocable and the consequences must be borne whether it has been successful or not. Imagination is always revocable and can be revised again and again. Therefore, in simply rehearsing several projects. I can ascribe to each a different probability of success, but I can never be disappointed by its failure. Like all other anticipations, the rehearsed future action also has gaps which only the performance of the act will fill in. Therefore the actor will only retrospectively see whether his project has stood the test or proved a failure.

The technique of the choice is this: The mind of the actor runs through one alternative and then through the other till the decision falls from his mind – to use the words of Bergson – as a ripe fruit falls from the tree. But it is a prerequisite of all choice that the actor have clearly in mind that alternative ways of applying different means or even alternative ends do actually exist. It is erroneous to assume that consciousness of such alternatives and therefore choice is necessarily given before every human action and that in consequence all acting involves deliberation and preference. This interpretation uncritically confuses selection in the sense of just singling out without comparison of alternatives, and choice in the sense of electing the preferred. Selection is, as has already been pointed out by James, a cardinal function of human consciousness. Interest is nothing else than selection, but it does not necessarily involve conscious choice between alternatives which presupposes reflection, volition, and preference. When I walk through a garden discussing a problem with a friend and I turn left or right, I do not choose to do so. I have no alternative in mind. It is a question for psychology to determine the motives for such behavior, but I cannot say that I prefer one direction to another.

Undoubtedly there are situations in which each of us sits down and thinks over his problems. In general he will do so at critical points in his life when his chief interest is to master a situation. But even then he will accept his emotions as guides in finding the most suitable solution as well as rational deliberation, and he is right in doing so, because these emotions also have their roots in his practical interest.

He will also appeal to his stock of recipes, to the rules and skills arising out of his vocational life or his practical experiences. He will certainly find many systematized solutions in his standardized knowledge. He may perhaps consult an expert, but again he will get nothing else than recipes and systematized solutions. His choice will be a deliberated one, and having rehearsed all the possibilities of action open to him in the future perfect tense, he will put in action that solution which seems to have the greatest chance of success.

But what are the conditions under which we may classify a deliberated act of choice as a rational one? It seems that we have to distinguish between the rationality of knowledge which is a prerequisite of the rational choice and the rationality of the choice itself. Rationality of knowledge is given only if all the elements from which the actor has to choose are clearly and distinctly conceived by him. The choice itself is rational if the actor selects from among all means within his reach the one most appropriate for realizing the intended end.

We have seen that clearness and distinctness in the strict meaning of formal logic do not belong to the typical style of everyday thought. But it would be erroneous to conclude that, therefore, rational choice does not exist within the sphere of everyday life. Indeed, it would be sufficient to interpret the terms clearness and distinctness in a modified and restricted meaning, namely, as clearness and distinctness adequate to the requirements of the actor's practical interest. It is not our task to examine whether rational acts corresponding with the above-mentioned characteristics do or do not occur frequently in daily life. There is no doubt that "rational acts" together with their antithesis, defined by Max Weber as "traditional" or "habitual" acts, represent rather ideal types which will be found very seldom in their pure form in everyday action. What I wish to emphasize is only that the ideal of rationality is not and cannot be a peculiar feature of everyday thought, nor can it, therefore, be a methodological principle of the interpretation of human acts in daily life. This will become clearer if we discuss the concealed implications of the statement – or better, postulate – that rational choice would be present only if the actor had sufficient knowledge of the end to be realized as well as of the different means apt to succeed. This postulate implies:

  (a) Knowledge of the place of the end to be realized within the framework of the plans of the actor (which must be known by him, too).
  (b) Knowledge of its interrelations with other ends and its compatibility or incompatibility with them.
  (c) Knowledge of the desirable and undesirable consequences which may arise as by-products of the realization of the main end.

(*d*) Knowledge of the different chains of means which technically or even ontologically are suitable for the accomplishment of this end, regardless of whether the actor has control of all or several of their elements.

(*e*) Knowledge of the interference of such means with other ends or other chains of means including all their secondary effects and incidental consequences.

(*f*) Knowledge of the accessibility of those means for the actor, picking out the means which are within his reach and which he can and may set going.

The aforementioned points do not by any means exhaust the complicated analysis which would be necessary in order to break down the concept of rational choice in action. The complications increase greatly when the action in question is a social one, that is, when it is directed towards other people. In this case, the following elements become additional determinants for the deliberation of the actor:

First: The interpretation or misinterpretation of his own act by his fellow-man.

Second: The reaction of the other people and its motivation.

Third: All the outlined elements of knowledge (*a* to *f*) which the actor, rightly or wrongly, attributes to his partners.

Fourth: All the categories of familiarity and strangeness, of intimacy and anonymity, of personality and type, which we have discovered in the course of our inventory of the organization of the social world.

This short analysis shows that we cannot speak of an *isolated* rational act, if we mean by this an act resulting from deliberated choice, but only of *a system* of rational acts.[2]

But where is this *system* of rational action to be found? We have already noted that the concept of rationality has its native place not at the level of the everyday conception of the social world, but at the theoretical level of the scientific observation of it, and it is here that it finds its field of methodological application. Therefore, we have to proceed to the problem of the social sciences and to the scientific methods of its interpretation.

---

[2] See the excellent study which Professor Parsons has devoted to this problem under the heading "Systems of Action and their Units," at the end of his *Structure of Social Action*.

VII

Our analysis of the social world in which we live has shown that each of us considers himself as the center of this world, which he groups around himself according to his own interests. The observer's attitude towards the social world is quite different. This world is not the theatre of his activities, but the object of his contemplation on which he looks with detached equanimity. As a scientist (not as a human being dealing with science) the observer is essentially solitary. He has no companion, and we can say that he has placed himself outside the social world with its manifold relations and its system of interests. Everyone, to become a social scientist, must make up his mind to put somebody else instead of himself as the center of this world, namely, the observed person. But with the shift in the central point, the whole system has been transformed, and, if I may use this metaphor, all the equations proved as valid in the former system now have to be expressed in terms of the new one. If the social system in question had reached an ideal perfection, it would be possible to establish a universal transformation formula such as Einstein has succeeded in establishing for translating propositions in terms of the Newtonian System of Mechanics into those of the theory of Relativity.

The first and fundamental consequence of this shift in the point of view is that the scientist replaces the human beings he observes as actors on the social stage by puppets created by himself and manipulated by himself. What I call "puppets" corresponds to the technical term "ideal types" which Weber has introduced into social science.

Our analysis of our common social world has shown us the origin of typification. We typify, in daily life, human activities which interest us only as appropriate means for bringing about intended effects, but not as emanations of the personality of our fellow-men. The procedure of the scientific observer is on the whole the same. He observes certain events as caused by human activity and he begins to establish a type of such proceedings. Afterwards he co-ordinates with these typical acts typical actors as their performers. He thus ends up by constructing personal ideal types which he imagines as having consciousness. This fictitious consciousness is constructed in such a way that the

fictitious actor, if he were not a dummy but a human being of
flesh and blood, would have the same stream of thought as a
living man acting in the same manner, but with the important
modification that the artificial consciousness is not subjected to
the ontological conditions of human existence. The puppet is not
born, he does not grow up, and he will not die. He has no hopes
and no fears; he does not know anxiety as a chief motive of all
his deeds. He is not free in the sense that his acting could transgress the limits his creator, the social scientist, has fixed. He
cannot, therefore, have other conflicts of interest and motives
than those the social scientist has implanted in him. The personal
ideal type cannot err if to err is not its typical destiny. It cannot
perform an act which is outside the typical motives, the typical
means-ends relations, and outside the typical situation provided
for by the scientist. In short, the ideal type is but a model of a
conscious mind without the faculty of spontaneity and without
a will of its own. In typical situations of our daily life we all, too,
assume certain typical roles. By isolating one of our activities
from its interrelations with all the other manifestations of our
personality, we disguise ourselves as consumers or tax-payers,
citizens, members of a church or of a club, clients, smokers, by-
standers, etc. The traveler, for instance, has to behave in the
specific way he believes the type "railway agent" to expect from
a typical passenger. For us in our daily lives these attitudes are
but roles which we voluntarily assume as expedients and which
we may drop whenever we want to do so. But assuming this role
does not change our general attitude toward the social world or
toward our own life. Our knowledge remains incoherent, our propositions occasional, our future uncertain, our general situation
unstable. The next moment may bring the great cataclysm which
will affect our choice, modify all our plans, perhaps destroy the
value of all our experience. And we keep – even in the role – the
liberty of choice, as far as such liberty exists at all within the
scope of our human and social conditions. This liberty embraces
the possibility of taking off our disguise, of dropping the role,
of recommencing our orientation in the social world. We continue
to be subjects, centers of spontaneous activities, actors.

The puppet called "personal ideal type" is on the contrary,
never a subject or a center of spontaneous activity. He does not

have the task of mastering the world, and, strictly speaking, he has no world at all. His destiny is regulated and determined beforehand by his creator, the social scientist, and with such a perfect pre-established harmony as Leibniz imagined the world created by God. By the grace of its constructor, he is endowed with just that kind of knowledge he needs to perform the job for the sake of which he was brought into the scientific world. The scientist distributes his own store of experience, and that means of scientific experience in clear and distinct terms, among the puppets with which he peoples the social world. But this social world, too, is organized in quite another way; it is not centered in the ideal type; it lacks the categories of intimacy and anonymity, of familiarity and strangeness: in short, it lacks the basic character of perspective appearance. What counts is the point of view from which the *scientist* envisages the social world. This point of view defines the general perspective framework in which the chosen sector of the social world presents itself to the scientific observer as well as to the fictitious consciousness of the puppet type. This central point of view of the scientist is called his "scientific problem under examination."

In a scientific system the problem has exactly the same significance for the scientific activity as the practical interests have for activities in everyday work. The scientific problem as formulated has a two-fold function:

(a)   It determines the limits within which possible propositions become relevant to the inquiry. It thus creates the realm of the scientific subject matter within which all concepts must be compatible.

(b)   The simple fact that a problem is raised creates a scheme of reference for the construction of all ideal types which may be utilized as relevant.

For the better understanding of the last remark we have to consider that the concept "type" is not an independent one but always needs a supplement. We cannot speak simply of an "ideal type" as such; we must indicate the reference scheme within which this ideal type may be utilized, that is, the problem for the sake of which the type has been constructed. To borrow a mathematical term we may say that the ideal type always needs a subscript referring to the problem which determines the formation of all the types to be used. In this sense, the problem under scrutiny is the locus of all possible types which may pertain to the system investigated.

I cannot go further here into the logical foundations of this thesis which I call the *principle of relevance*. But we can interpret it as an application of James's theory concerning the fringes of concepts. The ideal type, too, like all other concepts, has fringes referring to the main topic about which all the members of the thought revolve. It is easy to understand that a shift in the main topic – that is, in the problem – automatically involves a modification in the fringes of each concept revolving about it. And, as a shift in the problem means a modification in the scope of relevance too, we can explain, for the same reason, why new facts emerge with the shift in the point of view, whereas others that were formerly in the center of our question disappear. But this statement is nothing else than the original definition we have given of the passing from one level to another. To be sure, it must be admitted that the term "level" applies strictly only to whole systems of problems; nevertheless, the consequences are, in principle, the same. It seems important to me that the scientist keep in mind that each shift in the problem involves a thorough modification of all the concepts and of all the types with which he is dealing. A great many misunderstandings and controversies in the social sciences have their root in the unmodified application of concepts and types at a level other than that where they have their natural place.

But why form personal ideal types at all? Why not simply collect empirical facts? Or, if the technique of typological interpretation may be applied successfully, why not restrict oneself to forming types of impersonal events, or types of the behavior of groups? Do we not have modern economics as an example of a social science which does not deal with personal ideal types, but with curves, with mathematical functions, with the movement of prices, or with such institutions as bank systems or currency? Statistics has performed the great work of collecting information about the behavior of groups. Why go back to the scheme of social action and to the individual actor?

The answer is this: It is true that a very great part of social science can be performed and has been performed at a level which legitimately abstracts from all that happens in the individual actor. But this operating with generalizations and idealizations on a high level of abstraction is in any case nothing but a kind of intellectual shorthand. Whenever the problem under inquiry makes it necessary, the social scientist must have the possibility of shifting the level of his research to that of individual human activity, and where real scientific work is done this shift will always become possible.

The real reason for this is that we cannot deal with phenomena in the social world as we do with phenomena belonging to the natural sphere. In the latter, we collect facts and regularities which are not understandable to us, but which we can refer only to certain fundamental assumptions about the world. We shall never understand why the mercury in the thermometer rises if the sun shines on it. We can only interpret this phenomenon as compatible with the laws we have deduced from some basic assumption about the physical world. We want, on the contrary, to understand social phenomena, and we cannot understand them apart from their placement within the scheme of human motives, human means and ends, human planning – in short – within the categories of human action.

The social scientist must therefore ask, or he must, at least, always be in a position to ask, what happens in the mind of an individual actor whose act has led to the phenomenon in question. We can formulate this *postulate of the subjective interpretation* more correctly as follows: The scientist has to ask what type of individual mind can be constructed and what typical thoughts must be attributed to it to explain the fact in question as the result of its activity within an understandable relation.

This postulate finds its complement in another which I propose to call, borrowing a term of Max Weber, the *postulate of adequacy*. It may be formulated as follows: Each term used in a scientific system referring to human action must be so constructed that a human act performed within the life-world by an individual actor in the way indicated by the typical construction would be reasonable and understandable for the actor himself, as well as for his fellow-men. This postulate is of extreme importance for the methodology of social science. What makes it possible for a social science to refer at all to events in the life-world is the fact that the interpretation of any human act by the social scientist might be the same as that by the actor or by his partner.

The principle of relevance, the postulate of the subjective interpretation, and that of adequacy, are applicable at each level of social study. For instance, all the historical sciences are governed by them. The next step would be to circumscribe within the social sciences the category of those we call the theoretical ones. The outstanding feature of these theoretical sciences is the interpretation of the social world in terms of a system of determinate logical structure (Parsons, *op. cit.*, p. 7). This system of means-ends relations is also an ideal typical one, but as Professor Parsons had pointed out, it is an analytical one and not a system dealing with concrete actions as he calls it. I once formulated the same idea in the statement that the personal ideal-types of action constructed by the so-called theoretical sciences are of a maximum anonymity, that means, what is typified is the behavior of "people as such" or of "every-man." Whatever formula we may use to describe the peculiarity of the theoretical realm, it is clear that a logically interrelated system presupposes that the means-end relations together with the system of constant motives and the system of life-plans must be constructed in such a way that:

(*a*) it remains in full compatibility with the principles of formal logic;

(*b*) all its elements are conceived in full clearness and distinctness;

(*c*) it contains only scientifically verifiable assumptions, which have to be in full compatibility with the whole of our scientific knowledge.

These three requirements may be condensed into another *postulate* for the building up of the ideal types, that of *rationality*. It may be formulated as follows: The ideal type of social action must be constructed in such a way that the actor in the living world would perform the typified act if he had a clear and distinct scientific knowledge of all the elements relevant to his choice and the constant tendency to choose the most appropriate means for the realization of the most appropriate end. Indeed, as we had anticipated in the beginning, only by the introduction of the key concept of rationality can all the elements be provided for constitution of the level called "pure theory." The postulate of rationality implies, furthermore, that all other behavior has to be interpreted as derivative from the basic scheme of rational acting. The reason for this is that only action within the framework of rational categories can be scientifically discussed. Science does not have at its disposal other methods than rational ones and it cannot, therefore, verify or falsify purely occasional propositions.

As we stated before, each type formed by the scientist has its subscript referring to the main problem. In a theoretical system, therefore, only pure rational types are admitted. But where can the scientist find the guarantee that he is establishing a real unified system? Where are the scientific tools to perform that difficult task? The answer is that in every branch of the social sciences which has arrived at the theoretical stage of its development there is a fundamental hypothesis which both defines the fields of research and gives the regulative principle for building up the system of ideal types. Such a fundamental hypothesis, for instance, is in classical economics the utilitarian principle, and in modern economics the marginal principle. The sense of this postulate is the following: Build your ideal types as if all actors had oriented their life-plan and, therefore, all their activities to the chief end of realizing the greatest utility with the minimum of costs; human activity which is oriented in such a way (and only this kind of human activity) is the subject matter of your science.

But hidden within these statements is a very disturbing question. If the social world as object of our scientific research is but a typical construction, why bother with this intellectual game? Our scientific activity and, particularly, that which deals with the social world, is also performed within a certain means-ends relation, namely, in order to acquire knowledge for mastering the world, the real world, not the one created by the grace of the scientist. We want to find out what happens in the real world and not in the fantasies of a few sophisticated eccentrics.

There are a few arguments for quieting such an interlocutor. First of all, the construction of the scientific world is not an arbitrary act of the scientist which he can perform at his own discretion:

    1. There are the historical boundaries of the realm of his

science which each scientist has inherited from his ancestors as a stock of approved propositions.

2. The postulate of adequacy requires that the typical construction be compatible with the totality of both our daily life and our scientific experience.

But to one who is not satisfied with such guarantees and asks for greater reality, I want to say that I am afraid I do not exactly know what reality is, and my only comfort in this unpleasant situation is that I share my ignorance with the greatest philosophers of all time. Again, I want to quote William James and his profound theory of the different realities in which we live at the same time. It is a misunderstanding of the essential character of science to think that it deals with reality if we consider as the pattern of reality the world of daily life. The world of both the natural and the social scientist is neither more nor less real than the world of thought in general can be. It is not the world within which we act and within which we are born and die. But it is the real home of those important events and achievements which humanity at all times calls culture.

The social scientist, therefore, may continue his work in full confidence. His clarified methods, governed by the postulates mentioned, give him the assurance that he will never lose contact with the world of daily life. And as long as he uses with success methods which have stood this test and still do so, he is quite right in continuing without worrying about methodological problems. Methodology is not the preceptor or the tutor of the scientist. It is always his pupil, and there is no great master in his scientific field who could not teach the methodologists how to proceed. But the really great teacher always has to learn from his pupils. Arnold Schoenberg, the famous composer, starts the preface to his masterly book on the theory of harmony with the sentence: "This book I have learned from my pupils." In this role, the methodologist has to ask intelligent questions about the technique of his teacher. And if those questions help others to think over what they really do, and perhaps to eliminate certain intrinsic difficulties hidden in the foundation of the scientific edifice where the scientists never set foot, methodology has performed its task.

PART II

Applied Theory

THE STRANGER

AN ESSAY IN SOCIAL PSYCHOLOGY

The present paper intends to study in terms of a general
theory of interpretation the typical situation in which a stranger
finds himself in his attempt to interpret the cultural pattern of a
social group which he approaches and to orient himself within it.
For our present purposes the term "stranger" shall mean an adult
individual of our times and civilization who tries to be permanently accepted or at least tolerated by the group which he approaches.
The outstanding example for the social situation under scrutiny
is that of the immigrant, and the following analyses are, as a
matter of convenience, worked out with this instance in view.
But by no means is their validity restricted to this special case.
The applicant for membership in a closed club, the prospective
bridegroom who wants to be admitted to the girl's family, the
farmer's son who enters college, the city-dweller who settles in a
rural environment, the "selectee" who joins the Army, the
family of the war worker who moves into a boom town – all are
strangers according to the definition just given, although in these
cases the typical "crisis" that the immigrant undergoes may
assume milder forms or even be entirely absent. Intentionally
excluded, however, from the present investigation are certain
cases the inclusion of which would require some qualifications
in our statements: (*a*) the visitor or guest who intends to establish
a merely transitory contact with the group; (*b*) children or primi-
tives; and (*c*) relationships between individuals and groups of
different levels of civilization, as in the case of the Huron brought
to Europe – a pattern dear to some moralists of the eighteenth
century. Furthermore, it is not the purpose of this paper to deal

with the processes of social assimilation and social adjustment which are treated in an abundant and, for the most part, excellent literature [1] but rather with the situation of approaching which precedes every possible social adjustment and which includes its prerequisites.

As a convenient starting-point we shall investigate how the cultural pattern of group life presents itself to the common sense of a man who lives his everyday life within the group among his fellow-men. Following the customary terminology, we use the term "cultural pattern of group life" for designating all the peculiar valuations, institutions, and systems of orientation and guidance (such as the folkways, mores, laws, habits, customs, etiquette, fashions) which, in the common opinion of sociologists of our time, characterize – if not constitute – any social group at a given moment in its history. This cultural pattern, like any phenomenon of the social world, has a different aspect for the sociologist and for the man who acts and thinks within it.[2] The sociologist (as sociologist, not as a man among fellow-men which he remains in his private life) is the disinterested scientific on-looker of the social world. He is disinterested in that he intention-ally refrains from participating in the network of plans, means-and-ends relations, motives and chances, hopes and fears, which the actor within the social world uses for interpreting his experiences of it; as a scientist he tries to observe, describe, and classify the social world as clearly as possible in well-ordered terms in accordance with the scientific ideals of coherence, con-sistency, and analytical consequence. The actor within the social world, however, experiences it primarily as a field of his actual and possible acts and only secondarily as an object of his thinking. In so far as he is interested in knowledge of his social world, he organizes this knowledge not in terms of a scientific system but in terms of relevance to his actions. He groups the world around

[1] Instead of mentioning individual outstanding contributions by American writers, such as W. G. Sumner, W. I. Thomas, Florian Znaniecki, R. E. Park, H. A. Miller, E. V. Stonequist, E. S. Bogardus, and Kimball Young, and by German authors, especially Georg Simmel and Robert Michels, we refer to the valuable monograph by Margaret Mary Wood, *The Stranger: A Study in Social Relationship*, New York, 1934, and the bibliography quoted therein.

[2] This insight seems to be the most important contribution of Max Weber's methodological writings to the problems of social science. Cf. the present writer's *Der sinnhafte Aufbau der sozialen Welt*, Vienna, 1932, 2nd ed. 1960.

himself (as the center) as a field of domination and is therefore especially interested in that segment which is within his actual or potential reach. He singles out those of its elements which may serve as means or ends for his "use and enjoyment," [3] for furthering his purposes, and for overcoming obstacles. His interest in these elements is of different degrees, and for this reason he does not aspire to become acquainted with all of them with equal thoroughness. What he wants is *graduated knowledge* of relevant elements, the degree of desired knowledge being correlated with their relevance. Otherwise stated, the world seems to him at any given moment as stratified in different layers of relevance, each of them requiring a different degree of knowledge. To illustrate these strata of relevance we may – borrowing the term from cartography – speak of "isohypses" or "hypsographical contour lines of relevance," trying to suggest by this metaphor that we could show the distribution of the interests of an individual at a given moment with respect both to their intensity and to their scope by connecting elements of equal relevance to his acts, just as the cartographer connects points of equal height by contour lines in order to reproduce adequately the shape of a mountain. The graphical representation of these "contour lines of relevance" would not show them as a single closed field but rather as numerous areas scattered over the map, each of different size and shape. Distinguishing with William James [4] two kinds of knowledge, namely, *"knowledge of acquaintance"* and *"knowledge about,"* we may say that, within the field covered by the contour lines of relevance, there are centers of explicit knowledge *of* what is aimed at; they are surrounded by a halo knowledge *about* what seems to be sufficient; next comes a region in which it will do merely "to put one's trust"; the adjoining foothills are the home of unwarranted hopes and assumptions; between these areas, however, lie zones of complete ignorance.

We do not want to overcharge this image. Its chief purpose has been to illustrate that the knowledge of the man who acts and thinks within the world of his daily life is not homogeneous; it is (1) incoherent, (2) only partially clear, and (3) not at all free from contradictions.

[3] John Dewey, *Logic, the Theory of Inquiry*, New York, 1938, Chap. iv.

[4] For the distinction of these two kinds of knowledge cf. William James, *Principles of Psychology*, New York, 1890, Vol. I, pp. 221–22.

1. It is incoherent because the individual's interests which determine the relevance of the objects selected for further inquiry are themselves not integrated into a coherent system. They are only partially organized under plans of any kind, such as plans of life, plans of work and leisure, plans for every social role assumed. But the hierarchy of these plans changes with the situation and with the growth of the personality; interests are shifted continually and entail an uninterrupted transformation of the shape and density of the relevance lines. Not only the selection of the objects of curiosity but also the degree of knowledge aimed at changes.

2. Man in his daily life is only partially – and we dare say exceptionally – interested in the clarity of his knowledge, i.e., in full insight into the relations between the elements of his world and the general principles ruling those relations. He is satisfied that a well-functioning telephone service is available to him and, normally, does not ask how the apparatus functions in detail and what laws of physics make this functioning possible. He buys merchandise in the store, not knowing how it is produced, and pays with money, although he has only a vague idea of what money really is. He takes it for granted that his fellow-man will understand his thought if expressed in plain language and will answer accordingly, without wondering how this miraculous performance may be explained. Furthermore, he does not search for the truth and does not quest for certainty. All he wants is information on likelihood and insight into the chances or risks which the situation at hand entails for the outcome of his actions. That the subway will run tomorrow as usual is for him almost of the same order of likelihood as that the sun will rise. If by reason of a special interest he needs more explicit knowledge on a topic, a benign modern civilization holds ready for him a chain of information desks and reference libraries.

3. His knowledge, finally, is not consistent. At the same time he may consider statements as equally valid which in fact are incompatible with one another. As a father, a citizen, an employee, and a member of his church he may have the most different and the least congruent opinions on moral, political, or economic matters. This inconsistency does not necessarily originate in a logical fallacy. Men's thinking is distributed over subject

matters located within different and differently relevant levels, and they are not aware of the modifications they would have to make in passing from one level to another. This and similar problems would have to be explored by a logic of everyday thinking, postulated but not attained by all the great logicians from Leibniz to Husserl and Dewey. Up to now the science of logic has primarily dealt with the logic of science.

The system of knowledge thus acquired – incoherent, inconsistent, and only partially clear, as it is – takes on for the members of the in-group the appearance of a *sufficient* coherence, clarity, and consistency to give anybody a reasonable chance of understanding and of being understood. Any member born or reared within the group accepts the ready-made standardized scheme of the cultural pattern handed down to him by ancestors, teachers, and authorities as an unquestioned and unquestionable guide in all the situations which normally occur within the social world. The knowledge correlated to the cultural pattern carries its evidence in itself – or, rather, it is taken for granted in the absence of evidence to the contrary. It is a knowledge of trustworthy *recipes* for interpreting the social world and for handling things and men in order to obtain the best results in every situation with a minimum of effort by avoiding undesirable consequences. The recipe works, on the one hand, as a precept for actions and thus serves as a scheme of expression: whoever wants to obtain a certain result has to proceed as indicated by the recipe provided for this purpose. On the other hand, the recipe serves as a scheme of interpretation: whoever proceeds as indicated by a specific recipe is supposed to intend the correlated result. Thus it is the function of the cultural pattern to eliminate troublesome inquiries by offering ready-made directions for use, to replace truth hard to attain by comfortable truisms, and to substitute the self-explanatory for the questionable.

This "thinking as usual," as we may call it, corresponds to Max Scheler's idea of the "relatively natural conception of the world" (*relativ natürliche Weltanschauung*); [5] it includes the "of-course" assumptions relevant to a particular social group which

[5] Max Scheler, "Probleme einer Soziologie des Wissens," *Die Wissensformen und die Gesellschaft*, Leipzig, 1926, pp. 58ff.; cf. Howard Becker and Hellmuth Otto Dahlke, "Max Scheler's Sociology of Knowledge," *Philosophy and Phenomenological Research*, Vol. II, 1942, pp. 310–22, esp. p. 315.

Robert S. Lynd describes in such a masterly way – together with
their inherent contradictions and ambivalence – as the "Middle-
town-spirit." [6] Thinking-as-usual may be maintained as long as
some basic assumptions hold true, namely: (1) that life and especially social life will continue to be the same as it has been so far;
that is to say, that the same problems requiring the same solutions
will recur and that, therefore, our former experiences will suffice
for mastering future situations; (2) that we may rely on the
knowledge handed down to us by parents, teachers, governments,
traditions, habits, etc., even if we do not understand its origin
and its real meaning; (3) that in the ordinary course of affairs it is
sufficient to know something *about* the general type or style of
events we may encounter in our life-world in order to manage or
control them; and (4) that neither the systems of recipes as schemes
of interpretation and expression nor the underlying basic
assumptions just mentioned are our private affair, but that they
are likewise accepted and applied by our fellow-men.

If only one of these assumptions ceases to stand the test,
thinking-as-usual becomes unworkable. Then a "crisis" arises
which, according to W. I. Thomas' famous definition, "interrupts
the flow of habit and gives rise to changed conditions of consciousness and practice"; or, as we may say, it overthrows precipitously
the actual system of relevances. The cultural pattern no longer
functions as a system of tested recipes at hand; it reveals that
its applicability is restricted to a specific historical situation.

Yet the stranger, by reason of his personal crisis, does not share
the above-mentioned basic assumptions. He becomes essentially
the man who has to place in question nearly everything that
seems to be unquestionable to the members of the approached
group.

To him the cultural pattern of the approached group does not
have the authority of a tested system of recipes, and this, if for
no other reason, because he does not partake in the vivid historical tradition by which it has been formed. To be sure, from the
stranger's point of view, too, the culture of the approached group
has its peculiar history, and this history is even accessible to him.
But it has never become an integral part of his biography, as did

[6] Robert S. Lynd, *Middletown in Transition*, New York, 1937, Chap. xii, and
Knowledge for What?, Princeton, 1939, pp. 58–63.

the history of his home group. Only the ways in which his fathers
and grandfathers lived become for everyone elements of his own
way of life. Graves and reminiscences can neither be transferred
nor conquered. The stranger, therefore, approaches the other
group as a newcomer in the true meaning of the term. At best he
may be willing and able to share the present and the future with
the approached group in vivid and immediate experience; under
all circumstances, however, he remains excluded from such experiences of its past. Seen from the point of view of the approached group, he is a man without a history.

To the stranger the cultural pattern of his home group continues to be the outcome of an unbroken historical development
and an element of his personal biography, which for this very
reason has been and still is the unquestioned scheme of reference
for his "relatively natural conception of the world." As a matter
of course, therefore, the stranger starts to interpret his new social
environment in terms of his thinking as usual. Within the scheme
of reference brought from his home group, however, he finds a
ready-made idea of the pattern supposedly valid within the approached group – an idea which necessarily will soon prove
inadequate.[7]

First, the idea of the cultural pattern of the approached group
which the stranger finds within the interpretive scheme of his
home group has originated in the attitude of a disinterested observer. The approaching stranger, however, is about to transform
himself from an unconcerned onlooker into a would-be member
of the approached group. The cultural pattern of the approached
group, then, is no longer a subject matter of his thought but a
segment of the world which has to be dominated by actions.
Consequently, its position within the stranger's system of relevance changes decisively, and this means, as we have seen, that another type of knowledge is required for its interpretation.
Jumping from the stalls to the stage, so to speak, the former
onlooker becomes a member of the cast, enters as a partner into

---

[7] As one account showing how the American cultural pattern depicts itself as an
"unquestionable" element within the scheme of interpretation of European in-
tellectuals we refer to Martin Gumpert's humorous description in his book, *First
Papers*, New York, 1941, pp. 8–9. Cf. also books like Jules Romains, *Visite chez les
Américains*, Paris, 1930, and Jean Prevost Usonie, *Esquisse de la civilisation améri-
caine*, Paris, 1939, pp. 245–66.

social relations with his co-actors, and participates henceforth in the action in progress.

Second, the new cultural pattern acquires an environmental character. Its remoteness changes into proximity; its vacant frames become occupied by vivid experiences; its anonymous contents turn into definite social situations; its ready-made typologies disintegrate. In other words, the level of environmental experience of social objects is incongruous with the level of mere beliefs about unapproached objects; by passing from the latter to the former, any concept originating in the level of departure becomes necessarily inadequate if applied to the new level without having been restated in its terms.

Third, the ready-made picture of the foreign group subsisting within the stranger's home-group proves its inadequacy for the approaching stranger for the mere reason that it has not been formed with the aim of provoking a response or a reaction from the members of the foreign group. The knowledge which it offers serves merely as a handy scheme for interpreting the foreign group and not as a guide for interaction between the two groups. Its validity is primarily based on the consensus of those members of the home group who do not intend to establish a direct social relationship with members of the foreign group. (Those who intend to do so are in a situation analogous to that of the approaching stranger). Consequently, the scheme of interpretation refers to the members of the foreign group merely as objects of this interpretation, but not beyond it, as addressees of possible acts emanating from the outcome of the interpretive procedure and not as subjects of anticipated reactions toward those acts. Hence, this kind of knowledge is, so to speak, insulated; it can be neither verified nor falsified by responses of the members of the foreign group. The latter, therefore, consider this knowledge – by a kind of "looking-glass" effect [8] – as both irresponsive and irresponsible and complain of its prejudices, bias, and misunderstandings. The approaching stranger, however, becomes aware of the fact that an important element of his "thinking as usual," namely, his ideas of the foreign group, its cultural pattern, and

---

[8] In using this term, we allude to Cooley's well-known theory of the reflected or looking-glass self (Charles H. Cooley, *Human Nature and the Social Order* [rev. ed.; New York, 1922], p. 184).

its way of life, do not stand the test of vivid experience and social interaction.

The discovery that things in his new surroundings look quite different from what he expected them to be at home is frequently the first shock to the stranger's confidence in the validity of his habitual "thinking as usual." Not only the picture which the stranger has brought along of the cultural pattern of the approached group but the whole hitherto unquestioned scheme of interpretation current within the home group becomes invalidated. It cannot be used as a scheme of orientation within the new social surroundings. For the members of the approached group *their* cultural pattern fulfills the functions of such a scheme. But the approaching stranger can neither use it simply as it is nor establish a general formula of transformation between both cultural patterns permitting him, so to speak, to convert all the co-ordinates within one scheme of orientation into those valid within the other – and this for the following reasons.

First, any scheme of orientation presupposes that everyone who uses it looks at the surrounding world as grouped around himself who stands at its center. He who wants to use a map successfully has first of all to know his standpoint in two respects: its location on the ground and its representation on the map. Applied to the social world this means that only members of the in-group, having a definite status in its hierarchy and also being aware of it, can use its cultural pattern as a natural and trustworthy scheme of orientation. The stranger, however, has to face the fact that he lacks any status as a member of the social group he is about to join and is therefore unable to get a starting-point to take his bearings. He finds himself a border case outside the territory covered by the scheme of orientation current within the group. He is, therefore, no longer permitted to consider himself as the center of his social environment, and this fact causes again a dislocation of his contour lines of relevance.

Second, the cultural pattern and its recipes represent only for the members of the in-group a unit of coinciding schemes of interpretation as well as of expression. For the outsider, however, this seeming unity falls to pieces. The approaching stranger has to "translate" its terms into terms of the cultural pattern of his home group, provided that, within the latter, interpretive equivalents exist at all. If they exist, the translated terms may be understood and remembered; they can be recognized by recurrence; they are at hand but not in hand. Yet, even then, it is obvious that the stranger cannot assume that his interpretation of the new cultural pattern coincides with that current with the members of the in-group. On the contrary, he has to reckon with fundamental discrepancies in seeing things and handling situations.

Only after having thus collected a certain knowledge of the interpretive function of the new cultural pattern may the stranger start to adopt it as the scheme of his own expression. The difference between the two stages of knowledge is familiar to any student of a foreign language and has received the full attention of psychologists dealing with the theory of learning. It is the difference between the passive understanding of a language and its active mastering as a means for realizing one's own acts and thoughts. As a matter of convenience we want to keep to this example in order to make clear some of the limits set to the stranger's attempt at conquering the foreign pattern as a scheme of expression, bearing in mind, however, that the following remarks could easily be adapted with appropriate modifications to other categories of the cultural pattern such as mores, laws, folkways, fashions, etc.

Language as a scheme of interpretation and expression does not merely consist of the linguistic symbols catalogued in the dictionary and of the syntactical rules enumerated in an ideal grammar. The former are translatable into other languages; the latter are understandable by referring them to corresponding or deviating rules of the unquestioned mother-tongue.[9] However, several other factors supervene.

1. Every word and every sentence is, to borrow again a term of William James, surrounded by "fringes" connecting them, on the one hand, with past and future elements of the universe of discourse to which they pertain and surrounding them, on the other hand, with a halo of emotional values and irrational implications which themselves remain ineffable. The fringes are the

---

[9] Therefore, the learning of a foreign language reveals to the student frequently for the first time the grammar rules of his mother-tongue which he has followed so far as "the most natural thing in the world," namely, as recipes.

stuff poetry is made of; they are capable of being set to music but they are not translatable.

2. There are in any language terms with several connotations. They, too, are noted in the dictionary. But, besides these standardized connotations, every element of speech acquires its special secondary meaning derived from the context or the social environment within which it is used and, in addition, gets a special tinge from the actual occasion in which it is employed.

3. Idioms, technical terms, jargons, and dialects, whose use remains restricted to specific social groups, exist in every language, and their significance can be learned by an outsider too. But, in addition, every social group, be it ever so small (if not every individual), has its own private code, understandable only by those who have participated in the common past experiences in which it took rise or in the tradition connected with them.

4. As Vossler has shown, the whole history of the linguistic group is mirrored in its way of saying things.[10] All the other elements of group life enter into it – above all, its literature. The erudite stranger, for example, approaching an English-speaking country is heavily handicapped if he has not read the Bible and Shakespeare in the English language, even if he grew up with translations of those books in his mother-tongue.

All the above-mentioned features are accessible only to the members of the in-group. They all pertain to the scheme of expression. They are not teachable and cannot be learned in the same way as, for example, the vocabulary. In order to command a language freely as a scheme of expression, one must have written love letters in it; one has to know how to pray and curse in it and how to say things with every shade appropriate to the addressee and to the situation. Only members of the in-group have the scheme of expression as a genuine one in hand and command it freely within their thinking as usual.

Applying the result to the total of the cultural pattern of group life, we may say that the member of the in-group looks in a single glance through the normal social situations occurring to him and that he catches immediately the ready-made recipe appropriate to its solution. In those situations his acting shows all the marks of habituality, automatism, and half-consciousness. This is

[10] Karl Vossler, *Geist und Kultur in der Sprache*, Heidelberg, 1925, pp. 117ff.

possible because the cultural pattern provides by its recipes typical solutions for typical problems available for typical actors. In other words, the chance of obtaining the desired standardized result by applying a standardized recipe is an objective one; that is open to everyone who conducts himself like the anonymous type required by the recipe. Therefore, the actor who follows a recipe does not have to check whether this objective chance coincides with a subjective chance, that is, a chance open to him, the individual, by reason of his personal circumstances and faculties which subsists independently of the question whether other people in similar situations could or could not act in the same way with the same likelihood. Even more, it can be stated that the objective chances for the efficiency of a recipe are the greater, the fewer deviations from the anonymous typified behavior occur, and this holds especially for recipes designed for social interaction. This kind of recipe, if it is to work, presupposes that any partner expects the other to act or to react typically, provided that the actor himself acts typically. He who wants to travel by railroad has to behave in that typical way which the type "railroad agent" may reasonably expect as the typical conduct of the type "passenger," and vice versa. Neither party examines the subjective chances involved. The scheme, being designed for everyone's use, need not be tested for its fitness for the peculiar individual who employs it.

For those who have grown up within the cultural pattern, not only the recipes and their possible efficiency but also the typical and anonymous attitudes required by them are an unquestioned "matter of course" which gives them both security and assurance. In other words, these attitudes by their very anonymity and typicality are placed not within the actor's stratum of relevance which requires explicit knowledge *of* but in the region of mere acquaintance in which it will do to put one's trust. This interrelation between objective chance, typicality, anonymity, and relevance seems to be rather important.[11]

---

[11] It could be referred to a general principle of the theory of relevance, but this would surpass the frame of the present paper. The only point for which there is space to contend is that all the obstacles which the stranger meets in his attempt at interpreting the approached group arise from the incongruence of the contour lines of the mutual relevance systems and, consequently, from the distortion the stranger's system undergoes within the new surrounding. But any social relationship, and

For the approaching stranger, however, the pattern of the approached group does not guarantee an objective chance for success but rather a pure subjective likelihood which has to be checked step by step, that is, he has to make sure that the solutions suggested by the new scheme will also produce the desired effect for him in his special position as outsider and new-comer who has not brought within his grasp the whole system of the cultural pattern but who is rather puzzled by its inconsistency, incoherence, and lack of clarity. He has, first of all, to use the term of W. I. Thomas, to *define* the situation. Therefore, he cannot stop at an approximate acquaintance with the new pattern, trusting in his vague knowledge *about* its general style and structure but needs an explicit knowledge *of* its elements, inquiring not only into their *that* but into their *why*. Consequently, the shape of his contour lines of relevance by necessity differs radically from those of a member of the in-group as to situations, recipes, means, ends, social partners, etc. Keeping in mind the above-mentioned interrelationship between relevance, on the one hand, and typicality and anonymity, on the other, it follows that he uses another yardstick for anonymity and typicality of social acts than the members of the in-group. For to the stranger the observed actors within the approached group are not – as for their co-actors – of a certain presupposed anonymity, namely, mere performers of typical functions, but individuals. On the other hand, he is inclined to take mere individual traits as typical ones. Thus he constructs a social world of pseudo-anonymity, pseudo-intimacy, and pseudo-typicality. Therefore, he cannot integrate the personal types constructed by him into a coherent picture of the approached group and cannot rely on his expectation of their response. And even less can the stranger himself adopt those typical and anonymous attitudes which a member of the in-group is entitled to expect from a partner in a typical situation. Hence the stranger's lack of feeling for distance, his oscillating between remoteness and intimacy, his hesitation and uncertainty, and his distrust in every matter which seems to be so simple and uncomplicated to those who rely on the efficiency

especially any establishment of new social contacts, even between individuals, in-volves analogous phenomena, although they do not necessarily lead to a crisis.

of unquestioned recipes which have just to be followed but not understood.

In other words, the cultural pattern of the approached group is to the stranger not a shelter but a field of adventure, not a matter of course but a questionable topic of investigation, not an instrument for disentangling problematic situations but a problematic situation itself and one hard to master.

These facts explain two basic traits of the stranger's attitude toward the group to which nearly all sociological writers dealing with this topic have rendered special attention, namely, (1) the stranger's objectivity and (2) his doubtful loyalty.

1. The stranger's objectivity cannot be sufficiently explained by his critical attitude. To be sure, he is not bound to worship the "idols of the tribe" and has a vivid feeling for the incoherence and inconsistency of the approached cultural pattern. But this attitude originates far less in his propensity to judge the newly approached group by the standards brought from home than in his need to acquire full knowledge of the elements of the approached cultural pattern and to examine for this purpose with care and precision what seems self-explanatory to the in-group. The deeper reason for his objectivity, however, lies in his own bitter experience of the limits of the "thinking as usual," which has taught him that a man may loose his status, his rules of guidance, and even his history and that the normal way of life is always far less guaranteed than it seems. Therefore, the stranger discerns, frequently with a grievous clear-sightedness, the rising of a crisis which may menace the whole foundation of the "relatively natural conception of the world," while all those symptoms pass unnoticed by the members of the in-group, who rely on the continuance of their customary way of life.

2. The doubtful loyalty of the stranger is unfortunately very frequently more than a prejudice on the part of the approached group. This is especially true in cases in which the stranger proves unwilling or unable to substitute the new cultural pattern entirely for that of the home group. Then the stranger remains what Park and Stonequist have aptly called a "marginal man," a cultural hybrid on the verge of two different patterns of group life, not knowing to which of them he belongs. But very frequently the reproach of doubtful loyalty originates in the astonishment of

the members of the in-group that the stranger does not accept the total of its cultural pattern as the natural and appropriate way of life and as the best of all possible solutions of any problem. The stranger is called ungrateful, since he refuses to acknowledge that the cultural pattern offered to him grants him shelter and protection. But these people do not understand that the stranger in the state of transition does not consider this pattern as a protecting shelter at all but as a labyrinth in which he has lost all sense of his bearings.

As stated before, we have intentionally restricted our topic to the specific attitude of the approaching stranger which precedes any social adjustment and refrained from investigating the process of social assimilation itself. A single remark concerning the latter may be permitted. Strangeness and familiarity are not limited to the social field but are general categories of our interpretation of the world. If we encounter in our experience something previously unknown and which therefore stands out of the ordinary order of our knowledge, we begin a process of inquiry. We first define the new fact; we try to catch its meaning; we then transform step by step our general scheme of interpretation of the world in such a way that the strange fact and its meaning become compatible and consistent with all the other facts of our experience and their meanings. If we succeed in this endeavor, then that which formerly was a strange fact and a puzzling problem to our mind is transformed into an additional element of our warranted knowledge. We have enlarged and adjusted our stock of experiences.

What is commonly called the process of social adjustment which the newcomer has to undergo is but a special case of this general principle. The adaptation of the newcomer to the in-group which at first seemed to be strange and unfamiliar to him is a continuous process of inquiry into the cultural pattern of the approached group. If this process of inquiry succeeds, then this pattern and its elements will become to the newcomer a matter of course, an unquestionable way of life, a shelter, and a protection. But then the stranger is no stranger any more, and his specific problems have been solved.

THE HOMECOMER

The Phaeacian sailors deposited the sleeping Odysseus on the shore of Ithaca, his homeland, which he had struggled to reach for twenty years of unspeakable suffering. He stirred and woke from sleep in the land of his fathers, but he knew not his whereabouts. Ithaca showed to him an unaccustomed face; he did not recognize the pathways stretching far into the distance, the quiet bays, the crags and precipices. He rose to his feet and stood staring at what was his own land, crying mournfully: "Alas! and now where on earth am I? What do I here myself?" That he had been absent for so long was not the whole reason why he did not recognize his own country; in part it was because the goddess Pallas Athene had thickened the air about him to keep him unknown "while she made him wise to things." Thus Homer tells the story of the most famous home-coming in the literature of the world.[1]

To the homecomer home shows – at least in the beginning – an unaccustomed face. He believes himself to be in a strange country, a stranger among strangers, until the goddess dissipates the veiling mist. But the homecomer's attitude differs from that of the stranger. The latter is about to join a group which is not and never has been his own. He knows that he will find himself in an unfamiliar world, differently organized than that from which he comes, full of pitfalls and hard to master.[2] The homecomer, however, expects to return to an environment of which he always had and – so he thinks – still has intimate knowledge and which he has just to take for granted in order to find his

---

[1] The presentation follows the translation of Homer's *Odyssey* by T. E. Shaw ("Lawrence of Arabia"), New York, 1932.
[2] Cf. *supra*, "The Stranger."

bearings within it. The approaching stranger has to anticipate in a more or less empty way what he will find; the homecomer has just to recur to the memories of his past. So he feels; and because he feels so, he will suffer the typical shock described by Homer.

These typical experiences of the homecomer will be analyzed in the following *in general terms* of social psychology. The returning veteran is, of course, an outstanding example of the situation under scrutiny. His special problems, however, have recently been widely discussed in many books and articles,[3] and it is not my aim to refer to them otherwise than as examples. We could refer also to the traveler who comes back from foreign countries, the emigrant who returns to his native land, the boy who "made good" abroad and now settles in his home town.[4] They all are instances of the "homecomer," defined as one who comes back for good to his home, – not as one returning for a temporary stay, such as the soldier on a thirty-day leave or the college boy spending the Christmas vacation with his family.

What, however, has to be understood by "home"? "Home is where one starts from," says the poet.[5] "The home is the place to which a man intends to return when he is away from it," says the jurist.[6] The home is starting-point as well as terminus. It is the null-point of the system of co-ordinates which we ascribe to the world in order to find our bearings in it. Geographically "home" means a certain spot on the surface of the earth. Where I happen to be is my "abode"; where I intend to stay is my "residence"; where I come from and whither I want to return is my "home." Yet home is not merely the homestead – my house, my room, my garden, my town – but everything it stands for. The symbolic

---

[3] We mention, in the first place, Professor Willard Waller's *Veteran Comes Back*, New York, 1944, an excellent sociological analysis of the civilian made into a professional soldier and of the soldier-turned-veteran who comes back to an alien homeland; also – Professor Dixon Wecter, *When Johnny Comes Marching Home*, Cambridge 1944, with valuable documents relating to the American soldier returning from four wars and very helpful bibliographical references; finally, the discussion of the veteran problem in the *New York Herald Tribune*, "Annual Forum on Current Problems," October 22, 1944 (Sec. VIII), especially the contributions of Mrs. Anna Rosenberg, Lieutenant Charles G. Bolte, and Sergeant William J. Caldwell. See also the very interesting collection of servicemen's *Letters Home*, arranged and edited by Mina Curtiss, Boston, 1944.

[4] Cf. the fine analysis of this situation in Thomas Wolfe's short story, "The Return of the Prodigal," in *The Hills Beyond*, New York, 1941.

[5] T. S. Eliot, *Four Quartets*, New York, 1943, p. 17.

[6] Joseph H. Beale, *A Treatise on the Conflict of Laws*, New York, 1935, I, p. 126.

character of the notion "home" is emotionally evocative and hard to describe. Home means different things to different people. It means, of course, father-house and mother-tongue, the family, the sweetheart, the friends; it means a beloved landscape, "songs my mother taught me," food prepared in a particular way, familiar things for daily use, folkways, and personal habits – briefly, a peculiar way of life composed of small and important elements. likewise cherished. *Chevron*, a Marine Corps newspaper, inquired what United States soldiers in the South Pacific miss most, outside of families and sweethearts. Here are some of the answers: " 'A fresh lettuce and tomato sandwich with icecold fresh milk to wash it down.' 'Fresh milk and the morning paper at the frontdoor.' 'The smell of a drugstore.' 'A train and the engine whistle.' " [7] All these things, badly missed if not available were probably not particularly appreciated so long as they were accessible at any time. They had just their humble place among the collective value "homely things." Thus, home means one thing to the man who never has left it, another thing to the man who dwells far from it, and still another to him who returns.

"To feel at home" is an expression of the highest degree of familiarity and intimacy. Life at home follows an organized pattern of routine; it has its well-determined goals and well-proved means to bring them about, consisting of a set of traditions, habits, institutions, timetables for activities of all kinds, etc. Most of the problems of daily life can be mastered by following this pattern. There is no need to define or redefine situations which have occurred so many times or to look for new solutions of old problems hitherto handled satisfactorily. The way of life at home governs as a scheme of expression and interpretation not only my own acts but also those of the other members of the in-group. I may trust that, using this scheme, I shall understand what the Other means and make myself understandable to him. The system of relevances [8] adopted by the members of the in-group shows a high degree of conformity. I have always a fair chance – subjectively and objectively – to predict the Other's action toward me as well as the Other's reaction to my own social

---

[7] Quoted from *Time*, June 5, 1944; other examples can be found in Wecter, *op. cit.*, pp. 495ff.

[8] Concerning this term, cf. "The Stranger," *supra*, pp. 92, 102.

acts. We not only may forecast what will happen tomorrow, but we also have a fair chance to plan correctly the more distant future. Things will in substance continue to be what they have been so far. Of course, there are new situations, unexpected events. But at home, even deviations from the daily routine life are mastered in a way defined by the general style in which people at home deal with extraordinary situations. There is a way – a proved way – for meeting a crisis in business life, for settling family problems, for determining the attitude to adopt toward illness and even death. Paradoxically formulated, there is even a routine way for handling the novel.

In terms of social relationships, it could be said that life at home is, for the most part, actually or at least potentially life in so-called primary groups. This term was coined by Cooley [9] to designate intimate face-to-face relationship and has become a current, although contested,[10] feature of sociological textbooks. It will be helpful for our purpose to analyze some of the implications hidden in this highly equivocal term.

First of all, we have to distinguish between face-to-face relationships and intimate relationships. A face-to-face relationship presupposes that those who participate in it have space and time in common as long as the relation lasts. Community of space means, on the one hand, that for each partner the Other's body, his facial expressions, his gestures, etc., are immediately observable as symptoms of his thought. The field of the Other's expressions is wide open for possible interpretation, and the actor may control immediately and directly the effect of his own social acts by the reaction of his fellow. On the other hand, community of space means that a certain sector of the outer world is equally accessible to all the partners in the face-to-face relationship. The same things are within reach, within sight, within hearing, and so on. Within this common horizon there are objects of common interest and common relevance; things to work with or upon, actually or potentially. Community of time does not refer so

---

[9] Charles H. Cooley. *Social Organization*, New York, 1909, Chaps. iii–v.

[10] Cf. R. M. MacIver, *Society*, New York, 1937, chapter on the "Primary Group and Large Scale Association" (esp. p. 236 n.); Edward C. Jandy, *Charles H. Cooley, His Life and Social Theory*, New York, 1942, pp. 171–81; Ellsworth Faris, "Primary Group, Essence and Accident," *American Journal of Sociology*, XXX, July, 1932, p. 41–45; Frederick R. Clow, "Cooley's Doctrine of Primary Groups," *American Journal of Sociology*, XXV, November, 1919, pp. 326–47.

much to the extent of outer (objective) time shared by the partners but to the fact that each of them participates in the onrolling inner life of the Other. In the face-to-face relation I can grasp the Other's thoughts in a vivid present as they develop and build themselves up, and so can he with reference to my stream of thought; and both of us know and take into account this possibility. The Other is to me, and I am to the Other, not an abstraction, not a mere instance of typical behavior, but, by the very reason of our sharing a common vivid present, this unique individual personality in this unique particular situation. These are, very roughly outlined, some of the features of the face-to-face relation which we prefer to call the "pure we-relation." It is, indeed, of outstanding importance in its own right because it can be shown that all other social relationships can, and for certain purposes have to be, interpreted as derived from the pure we-relation.

Yet it is important to understand that the pure we-relation refers merely to the formal structure of social relationships based upon community of space and time. It may be filled with a great variety of contents showing manifold degrees of intimacy and anonymity. To share the vivid present of a woman we love or of the neighbor in the subway are certainly different kinds of face-to-face relations. Cooley's concept of primary groups, however, presupposes a particular content of such a relationship – namely, intimacy.[11] We have to forego here the analysis of this ill-defined term which could be made explicit only by embarking upon an investigation of the layers of personality involved, the schemes of expression and interpretation presupposed, and the common system of relevance referred to by the partners. It suffices that the category of intimacy is independent of that of the face-to-face relation.

However, the term "primary group," as generally used, implies a third notion, which itself is independent of either of the two mentioned above, namely, the recurrent character of certain social relationships. It is by no means restricted to pure we-relations and to intimate relations, although we are going to choose our examples from them. A marriage, a friendship, a

---

[11] We disregard here entirely Cooley's untenable theory of "primary ideals," such as loyalty, truth, service, kindness, etc.

family group, a kindergarten, does not consist of a permanent, a strictly continuous, primary face-to-face relationship but rather of a series of merely intermittent face-to-face relationships. More precisely, the so-called "primary groups" are institutionalized situations which make it possible to re-establish the interrupted we-relation and to continue where it was broken off last time. There is, of course, no certainty, but just a mere chance, that such a re-establishment and continuation will succeed. But it is characteristic in the primary group as conceived by Cooley that the existence of such a chance is taken for granted by all its members.

After these parenthetical and all too casual explications, we may, for the present purpose, stick to our previous statement that life at home means, for the most part, life in actual or potential primary groups. The meaning of this statement has now become clear. It means to have in common with others a section of space and time, and therewith surrounding objects as possible ends and means, and interests based upon as underlying more or less homogeneous system of relevances; it means, furthermore, that the partners in a primary relationship experience one another as unique personalities in a vivid present, by following their unfolding thought as an ongoing occurrence and by sharing, therefore, their anticipations of the future as plans, as hopes or as anxieties; it means, finally, that each of them has the chance to re-establish the we-relation, if interrupted, and to continue it as if no intermittence had occurred. To each of the partners the Other's life becomes, thus, a part of his own autobiography, an element of his personal history. What he is, what he grew to be, what he will become is codetermined by his taking part in the manifold actual or potential primary relationships which prevail within the home-group.

This is the aspect of the social structure of the home world for the man who lives in it. The aspect changes entirely for the man who has left home. To him life at home is no longer accessible in immediacy. He has stepped, so to speak, into another social dimension not covered by the system of co-ordinates used as the scheme of reference for life at home. No longer does he experience as a participant in a vivid present the many we-relations which form the texture of the home group. His leaving home has replaced these vivid experiences with memories, and these memories preserve merely what home life meant up to the moment he left it behind. The ongoing development has come to a standstill. What has been so far a series of *unique* constellations, formed by individual persons, relations, and groups, receives the character of mere *types*; and this typification entails, by necessity, a deformation of the underlying structure of relevances. To a certain degree the same holds good for those left behind. By cutting off the community of space and time, for example, the field within which the Other's expressions manifest themselves and are open to interpretation has been narrowed. The Other's personality is no longer accessible as a unit; it has been broken down into pieces. There is no longer the total experience of the beloved person, his gestures, his way of walking and of speaking, of listening and of doing things; what remains are recollections, a photograph, some handwritten lines. This situation of the separated persons is, to a certain degree, that of those in bereavement; "partir, c'est mourir un peu."

To be sure, there still are means of communication, such as the letter. But the letter-writer addresses himself to the typification of addressee as he knew him when they separated, and the addressee reads the letter as written by the person typically the same as the one he left behind.[12] Presupposing such a typicality (and any typicality) means assuming that what has been proved to be typical in the past will have a good chance to be typical in the future, or, in other words, that life will continue to be what it has been so far: the same things will remain relevant, the same degree of intimacy in personal relationships will prevail, etc. Yet by the mere change of surroundings, other things have become important for both, old experiences are re-evaluated; novel ones, inaccessible to the Other, have emerged in each partner's life. Many a soldier in the combat line is astonished to find letters from home lacking any understanding of his situation, because they underscore the relevance of things which are of no importance to him in his actual situation, although they would be the subject of many deliberations if he were at home and had to handle them. This change of the system of relevance has its corollary in the

[12] Cf. Georg Simmel's excellent analysis of the sociology of the letter in his *Soziologie, Untersuchungen über die Formen der Vergesellschaftung*, Leipzig, 1922, pp. 379–82.

changing degree of intimacy. The term "intimacy" designates *here* merely the degree of reliable knowledge we have of another person or of a social relationship, a group, a cultural pattern, or a thing. As far as a person is concerned, intimate knowledge enables us to interpret what he means and to forecast his actions and reactions. In the highest form of intimacy, we know, to quote Kipling, the Other's "naked soul." But separation conceals the Other behind a strange disguise hard to remove. From the point of view of the absent one the longing for re-establishing the old intimacy – not only with persons but also with things – is the main feature of what is called "home-sickness." Yet, the change in the system of relevance and in the degree of intimacy just described is differently experienced by the absent one and by the home group. The latter continues its daily life within the customary pattern. Certainly, this pattern, too, will have changed and even in a more or less abrupt way. But those at home, although aware of this change, lived together through this changing world, experienced it as changing in immediacy, adapted their interpretative system, and adjusted themselves to the change. In other words, the system may have changed entirely, but it changed as a system; it was never disrupted and broken down; even in its modification it is still an appropriate device for mastering life. The in-group has now other goals and other means for attaining them, but still it remains an in-group.

The absent one has the advantage of knowing the general style of this pattern. He may from previous experiences conclude what attitude mother will take to the task of running the household under the rationing system, how sister will feel in the war plant, what a Sunday means without pleasure driving.[13] Those left at home have no immediate experience of how the soldier lives at the front. There are reports in the newspapers and over the radio, recitals from homecomers, movies in technicolor, official and unofficial propaganda, all of which build up a stereotype of the soldier's life "somewhere in France" or "somewhere in the Pacific." For the most part, these stereotypes are not spontaneous-

---

[13] This, of course, does not hold in case of a violent destruction of the home by catastrophies or enemy action. Then, however, not only may the general style of the pattern of home life have changed entirely but even the home itself may have ceased to exist. The absent one is then "homeless" in the true sense and has no place to return to.

ly formed but are directed, censored for military or political
reasons, and designed to build up morale at the home front or to
increase the efficiency of war production or the subscription to
war bonds. There is no warrant whatsoever that what is described as typical by all these sources of information is also relevant to the absent member of the in-group. Any soldier knows
that his style of living depends upon the military group to which
he belongs, the job allotted to him within this group, the attitude
of his officers and comrades. That is what counts, and not the
bulletin "All quiet on the western front." But whatever occurs
to him under these particular circumstances is his individual,
personal, unique experience which he never will allow to be typified. When the soldier returns and starts to speak – if he starts
to speak at all – he is bewildered to see that his listeners, even
the sympathetic ones, do not understand the uniqueness of these
individual experiences which have rendered him another man.
They try to find familiar traits in what he reports by subsuming
it under *their* preformed types of the soldier's life at the front.
To them there are only small details in which his recital deviates
from what every homecomer has told and what they have read
in magazines and seen in the movies. So it may happen that many
acts which seem to the people at home the highest expression of
courage are to the soldier in battle merely the struggle for survival
or the fulfilment of a duty, whereas many instances of real endur-
ance, sacrifice, and heroism remain unnoticed or unappreciated
by people at home.[14]

This discrepancy between the uniqueness and decisive importance that the absent one attributes to his experiences and
their pseudo-typification by the people at home, who impute to
them a pseudo-relevance, is one of the biggest obstacles to mutual
re-establishment of the disrupted we-relations. Yet the success or
failure of the homecoming will depend upon the chance of transforming these social relations into recurrent ones. But, even if
such a discrepancy did not prevail, the complete solution of this
problem would remain an unrealizable ideal.

What is here in question is nothing less than the irreversibility

---

[14] "Without exception G.I.'s most dislike tinhorn war and home-front heroics" is
the summary of a poll by *Time* correspondents: "What kind of movies do G.I.'s like?"
Time, August 14, 1944.

of inner time. It is the same problem which Heraclitus visualized with his statement that we cannot bathe twice in the same river; which Bergson analyzed in his philosophy of the *durée;* which Kierkegaard described as the problem of "repetition"; which Péguy had in mind in saying that the road which leads from Paris to Chartres has a different aspect from the road which leads from Chartres to Paris; and it is the same problem which, in a somewhat distorted fashion, occupies G. H. Mead's *Philosophy of the Present.* The mere fact that we grow older, that novel experiences emerge continuously within our stream of thought, that previous experiences are permanently receiving additional interpretative meanings in the light of these supervenient experiences, which have, more or less, changed our state of mind – all these basic features of our mental life bar a recurrence of the same. Being recurrent, the recurrent is not the same any more. Repetition might be aimed at and longed for: what belongs to the past can never be reinstated in another present exactly as it was. When it emerged, it carried along empty anticipations, horizons of future developments, references to chances and possibilities; now, in hindsight, these anticipations prove to have been or not to have been fulfilled; the perspectives have changed; what was merely in the horizon has shifted toward the center of attention or disappeared entirely; former chances have turned into realities or proved to be impossibilities – briefly, the former experience has now another meaning.

This is certainly not the place to embark upon an analysis of the highly complicated philosophical problems of time, memory, and meaning here involved. They are just mentioned for two reasons: first, in the present state of the social sciences it always seems to be useful to show that the analysis of a concrete sociological problem, if only driven far enough, necessarily leads to certain basic philosophical questions which social scientists cannot dodge by using unclarified terms such as "environment," "adjustment," "adaptation," "cultural pattern," and so on. Second, this set of problems determines decisively the form, if not the content, of the attitude of the homecomer even if he does not find that substantial changes have occurred in the life of the home group or in its relations to him. Even then, the home to which he returns is by no means the home he left or the home which he recalled and longed for during his absence. And, for the same reason, the homecomer is not the same man who left. He is neither the same for himself nor for those who await his return.

This statement holds good for any kind of home-coming. Even if we return home after a short vacation, we find that the old accustomed surroundings have received an added meaning derived from and based upon our experiences during our absence. Whatever the accompanying evaluation may be, things and men will, at least in the beginning, have another face. It will need a certain effort to transform our activities again into routine work and to reactivate our recurrent relations with men and things. No wonder, since we intended our vacation to be an interruption of our daily routine.

Homer tells of the landing of Odysseus' comrades at the island of the lotus-eaters. The lotus-eaters devised not death for the intruders but gave them a dish of their lotus flowers; and as each tasted this honeysweet plant, the wish to return grew faint in him: he preferred to dwell forever with the lotus-eating men, feeding upon lotus and letting fade from his mind all longing for home.

To a certain extent, each homecomer has tasted the magic fruit of strangeness, be it sweet or bitter. Even amid the overwhelming longing for home there remains the wish to transplant into the old pattern something of the novel goals, of the newly discovered means to realize them, of the skills and experiences acquired abroad. We cannot be astonished, therefore, that a United States War Department survey of June, 1944,[15] showed that 40 per cent of the discharged veterans being sent back to civilian life through eastern "separation centers" did not want their old jobs back and did not want even to return to their old communities. On the Pacific Coast the percentage of those men was even greater.

A small-town newspaper celebrated the home-coming of the local hero, giving a full account of his feats of extraordinary boldness, efficient leadership, steadfastness, and willingness to assume responsibility. The recital ends with the enumeration of the decorations justly awarded to him and with the statement that Lieutenant X. had always enjoyed the good will of his community

[15] According to *Time*, June 12, 1944.

where he had served for years as cigar clerk in a prominent local store. This case seems to be a rather typical one. A young man lives for years in a small town, a regular fellow, liked by everybody, but in an occupation which, honorable as it is, does not give him any chance to prove his worth. Quite possibly, he himself was not aware of what he could perform. The war gives him such an opportunity; he makes good and receives the reward he deserves. Can we expect, can we wish, that such a man should come home not only to family and sweetheart but also to his place behind the cigar counter? Have we not to hope that Lieutenant X. will avail himself of the facilities provided by Congress in the "G.I. Bill of Rights" to obtain a position in civil life more appropriate to his gifts?

But – and here we touch upon a chief problem of the homecomer – it is unfortunately an unwarranted assumption that social functions which stood the test within one system of social life will continue to do so if transplanted into another system. This general proposition is especially applicable to the problem of the returning veteran. From the sociological point of view, army life shows a strange ambivalence. Considered as an in-group, the army is characterized by an exceptionally high degree of constraint, of discipline imposed authoritatively upon the behavior of the individual by a controlling normative structure. The sense of duty, comradeship, the feeling of solidarity, and subordination are the outstanding features developed in the individual – all this, however, within a frame of means and ends imposed by the group and not open to his own choice. These features prevail in times of peace as well as in times of war. However, in times of war they do not regulate the behavior of the members of the in-group in relation to members of the out-group – that is, the enemy. The combatant's attitude toward the enemy in battle is, and is supposed to be, rather the opposite of disciplined constraint. War is the archetype of that social structure which Durkheim calls the state of "*anomie*." The specific valor of the fighting warrior consists in his will and adroitness in overcoming the Other in a desperate struggle of power, and it cannot be easily used within that pattern of civilian life which has prevailed in Western democracies. Moreover, the homecoming soldier returns to an in-group, the homeworld in the postwar period, which itself is marked by a certain degree of *anomie*, of lack of control and discipline. He finds, then, that *anomie* is no longer to be the basic structure of his relations with the out-group but is a feature of the in-group itself, toward the members of which he cannot apply the techniques permitted and required within the *anomie* situation of battle. In this civil world he will have to choose his own goals and the means to attain them and can no longer depend upon authority and guidance. He will feel, as Professor Waller puts it, like a "motherless child."

Another factor supervenes. In times of war the members of the armed forces have a privileged status within the community as a whole. "The best for our boys in the service" is more than a mere slogan. It is the expression of prestige deservedly accorded to those who might have to give their life for their country or at least to those who left family, studies, occupation, and the amenities of civil life for a highly valued interest of the community. The civilian looks at the man in uniform as an actual or future fighter; and so, indeed, the man in uniform looks at himself, even if he performs merely desk work in an army office somewhere in the United States. This humbler occupation does not matter; to him, too, the induction marked a turning-point in his life. But the discharged homecomer is deprived of his uniform and with it of his privileged status within the community. This does not mean that he will lose, by necessity, the prestige acquired as an actual or potential defender of the homeland, although history does not show that exaggerated longevity is accorded to the memory of glory. This is partly because of the disappointment at home that the returning veteran does not correspond to the pseudo-type of the man whom they have been expecting.

This leads to a practical conclusion. Much has been done and still more will be done to prepare the homecoming veteran for the necessary process of adjustment. However, it seems to be equally indispensable to prepare the home group accordingly. They have to learn through the press, the radio, the movies, that the man whom they await will be another and not the one they imagined him to be. It will be a hard task to use the propaganda machine in the opposite direction, namely, to destroy the pseudotype of the combatant's life and the soldier's life in general and to replace it by the truth. But it is indispensable to undo the glorification of a questionable Hollywood-made heroism by bringing out the real picture of what these men endure, how they live, and what they think and feel – a picture no less meritorious and no less evocative.

In the beginning it is not only the homeland that shows to the homecomer an unaccustomed face. The homecomer appears equally strange to those who expect him, and the thick air about him will keep him unknown. Both the homecomer and the welcomer will need the help of a Mentor to "make them wise to things."

THE WELL-INFORMED CITIZEN

AN ESSAY ON THE SOCIAL DISTRIBUTION OF KNOWLEDGE

I

The outstanding feature of a man's life in the modern world is his conviction that his life-world as a whole is neither fully understood by himself nor fully understandable to any of his fellow-men. There is a stock of knowledge theoretically available to everyone, built up by practical experience, science, and technology as warranted insights. But this stock of knowledge is not integrated. It consists of a mere juxtaposition of more or less coherent systems of knowledge which themselves are neither coherent nor even compatible with one another. On the contrary, the abysses between the various attitudes involved in the approach to the specialized systems are themselves a condition of the success of the specialized inquiry.

If this is true for the various fields of scientific inquiry it is for even better reasons valid for the various fields of practical activity. Where our practical interests predominate we are satisfied with our knowledge that certain means and procedures achieve certain desired or undesired results. The fact that we do not understand the Why and the How of their working and that we do not know anything of their origin does not hinder us from dealing undisturbed with situations, things, and persons. We use the most complicated gadgets prepared by a very advanced technology without knowing how the contrivances work. No car driver is supposed to be familiar with the laws of mechanics, no radio listener with those of electronics. One may even be a successful businessman without an insight into the functioning of the market, or a banker without a smattering of monetary theory. The same holds good for the social world we live in. We rely upon the fact that our fellow-men will react as we antici- pate if we act toward them in a specific way, that institutions such as governments, schools, courts, or public utilities will function, that an order of laws and mores, of religious and politi- cal beliefs, will govern the behavior of our fellow-men as it governs our own. In terms of the social group we may say with Scheler that any in-group has a relatively natural concept of the world which its members take for granted.

Useful as this concept is in many respects, it is clear that all the members of an in-group do not accept the same sector of the world as granted beyond question and that each of them selects different elements of it as an object of further inquiry. Knowledge is socially distributed and the mechanism of this distribution can be made the subject matter of a sociological discipline. True, we have a so-called sociology of knowledge. Yet, with very few exceptions, the discipline thus misnamed has approached the problem of the social distribution of knowledge merely from the angle of the ideological foundation of truth in its dependence upon social and, especially, economic conditions, or from that of the social implications of education, or that of the social role of the man of knowledge. Not sociologists but economists and philosophers have studied some of the many other theoretical aspects of the problem. The economists discovered that certain concepts of economics, such as perfect competition and monopoly and all their intermediate forms, presuppose that the various actors in the world of economics are conceived as possessed of a varying stock of knowledge of the economic means, ends, procedures, chances, and risks involved in the same situ- ation. Philosophers, in their turn, have dealt with the inter- subjective character of knowledge, intersubjective not only because it refers to the one real world common to all of us and because it is subject to confirmation and refutation by others, but also because the personal knowledge of each of us refers to the knowledge acquired by others – our teachers and predecessors – and handed down to us as a preorganized stock of problems, with the means for their solution, procedural rules, and the like. All these manifold problems belong to a theoretical science dealing with the social distribution of knowledge. The present inquiry is just one modest step in this direction. Its purpose is to investigate what motives prompt grown-up men living their everyday life in our modern civilization to accept unquestioningly *some* parts of the relatively natural concept of the world handed down to them and to subject *other* parts to question.

II

For the purpose of our study let us construct three ideal types which shall be called the expert, the man on the street, and the well-informed citizen.

The expert's knowledge is restricted to a limited field but therein it is clear and distinct. His opinions are based upon warranted assertions; his judgments are not mere guesswork or loose suppositions.

The man on the street has a working knowledge of many fields which are not necessarily coherent with one another. His is a knowledge of recipes indicating how to bring forth in typical situations typical results by typical means. The recipes indicate procedures which can be trusted even though they are not clearly understood. By following the prescription as if it were a ritual, the desired result can be attained without questioning why the single procedural steps have to be taken and taken exactly in the sequence prescribed. This knowledge in all its vagueness is still *sufficiently* precise for the practical purpose at hand. In all matters not connected with such practical purposes of immediate concern the man on the street accepts his sentiments and passions as guides. Under their influence, he establishes a set of convictions and unclarified views which he simply relies upon as long as they do not interfere with his pursuit of happiness.

The ideal type that we propose to call the well-informed citizen (thus shortening the more correct expression: the citizen who aims at being well informed) stands between the ideal type of the expert and that of the man on the street. On the one hand, he neither is, nor aims at being, possessed of expert knowledge; on the other, he does not acquiesce in the fundamental vagueness of a mere recipe knowledge or in the irrationality of his unclarified passions and sentiments. To be well informed means to him to arrive at *reasonably founded* opinions in fields which as he knows are at least mediately of concern to him although not bearing upon his purpose at hand.

All three types thus roughly outlined are, of course, mere constructs devised for the purpose of the present investigation. As a matter of fact, each of us in daily life is at any moment simultaneously expert, well-informed citizen, and man on the street, but in each case with respect to different provinces of knowledge. Moreover, each of us knows that the same holds good for each of his fellow-men, and this very fact codetermines the specific type of knowledge employed. For example, for the man on the street it is sufficient to know that there are experts available for consultation should he need their advice in achieving his practical purpose in hand. His recipes tell him when to see a doctor or a lawyer, where to get needed information and the like. The expert, on the other hand, knows very well that only a fellow expert will understand all the technicalities and implications of a problem in his field, and he will never accept a layman or dilettante as a competent judge of his performances. But it is the well-informed citizen who considers himself perfectly qualified to decide who *is* a competent expert and even to make up his mind after having listened to opposing expert opinions.

Many phenomena of social life can be fully understood only if they are referred to the underlying general structure of the social distribution of knowledge thus outlined. This resource alone makes possible a sociological theory of professions, of prestige and competence, of charisma and authority, and leads to the understanding of such complicated social relationships as those existing among the performing artist, his public, and his critics, or among manufacturer, retailer, advertising agent, and consumer, or among the government executive, his technical adviser, and public opinion.

III

The three types of knowledge discussed above differ in their readiness to take things for granted. The zone of things taken for granted may be defined as that sector of the world which, in connection with the theoretical or the practical problem we are concerned with at a given time, does not seem to need further inquiry, although we do not have clear and distinct insight into, and understandings of, its structure. What is taken for granted is, until invalidation, believed to be simply "given" and "given-as-it-appears-to-me" – that is, as I or others whom I trust have experienced and interpreted it. It is this zone of things taken for granted within which we have to find our bearings. All our possible questioning for the unknown arises only within such a world of supposedly preknown things, and presupposes its existence. Or, to use Dewey's terms, it is the indeterminate situation from which all possible inquiry starts with the goal of transforming it into a determinate one. Of course, what is taken for granted today may become questionable tomorrow, if we are induced by our own choice or otherwise to shift our interest and to make the accepted state of affairs a field of further inquiry.

In referring to a shift of our own interest we have touched upon the core of our problem. Before we can proceed in our analysis of the three types of knowledge under consideration, it is necessary to clarify the relationship between interest and the distribution of knowledge.

It is our interest at hand that motivates all our thinking, projecting, acting, and therewith establishes the problems to be solved by our thought and the goals to be attained by our actions. In other words, it is our interest that breaks asunder the unproblematic field of the preknown into various zones of various relevance with respect to such interest, each of them requiring a different degree of precision of knowledge.

For our purposes we may roughly distinguish four regions of decreasing relevance. First, there is that part of the world within our reach which can be immediately observed by us and also at least partially dominated by us – that is, changed and rearranged by our actions. It is that sector of the world within which our projects can be materialized and brought forth. This zone of primary relevance requires an optimum of clear and distinct understanding of its structure. In order to master a situation we have to possess the know-how – the technique and the skill – and also the precise understanding of why, when, and where to use them. Second, there are other fields not open to our domination but mediately connected with the zone of primary relevance because, for instance, they furnish ready-made tools to be used for attaining the projected goal or they establish the conditions upon which our planning itself or its execution depends. It is sufficient to be merely familiar with these zones of minor relevance, to be acquainted with the possibilities, the chances, and risks they may contain with reference to our chief interest. Third, there are other zones which, *for the time being*, have no such connection with the interests at hand. We shall call them relatively irrelevant, indicating thereby that we may continue to take them for granted as long as no changes occur within them which might influence the relevant sectors by novel and unexpected chances or risks. And, finally, there are the zones which we suggest calling absolutely irrelevant because no possible change occurring within them would – or so we believe – influence our objective at hand. For all practical purposes a mere blind belief in the That and the How of things within this zone of absolute irrelevancy is sufficient.

But this description is much too rough and requires several qualifications. First, we have spoken of an "interest at hand" which determines our system of relevances. There is, however, no such thing as an isolated interest at hand. The single interest at hand is just an element within a hierarchical system, or even a plurality of systems, of interests which in everyday life we call our plans – plans for work and thought, for the hour and for our life. To be sure, this system of interests is neither constant nor homogeneous. It is not constant because in changing from any Now to the succeeding Now the single interests obtain a different weight, a different predominance within the system. It is not homogeneous because even in the simultaneity of any Now we may have most disparate interests. The various social roles we assume simultaneously offer a good illustration. The interests I have in the same situation as a father, a citizen, a member of my church or of my profession, may not only be different but even incompatible with one another. I have, then, to decide which of these disparate interests I must choose in order to define the situation from which to start further inquiry. This choice will state the problem or set the goal in respect to which the world we are living in and our knowledge of it are distributed in zones of various relevance.

Second, the terms "zones" or "regions" of various relevance

might suggest that there are closed realms of various relevance in our life-world and, correspondingly, of various provinces of our knowledge of it, each separated from the other by clean-cut border lines. The opposite is true. These various realms of relevances and precision are intermingled, showing the most manifold interpenetrations and enclaves, sending their fringes into neighbor provinces and thus creating twilight zones of sliding transitions. If we had to draw a map depicting such a distribution figuratively it would not resemble a political map showing the various countries with their well-established frontiers but rather a topographical map representing the shape of a mountain range in the customary way by contour lines connecting points of equal altitude. Peaks and valleys, foothills and slopes, are spread over the map in infinitely diversified configurations. The system of relevances is much more similar to such a system of isohypses than to a system of coordinates originating in a center O and permitting measurement by an equidistant network.

Third, we have to define two types of systems of relevances which we propose to call the system of intrinsic, and the system of imposed, relevances. Again, these are merely constructive types which in daily life are nearly always intermingled with one another and are very rarely found in a pure state. Yet it is important to study them separately in their interaction. The intrinsic relevances are the outcome of our chosen interests, established by our spontaneous decision to solve a problem by our thinking, to attain a goal by our action, to bring forth a projected state of affairs. Surely we are free to choose what we are interested in, but this interest, once established, determines the system of relevances intrinsic to the chosen interest. We have to put up with the relevances thus set, to accept the situation determined by their internal structure, to comply with their requirements. And yet they remain, at least to a certain extent, within our control. Since the interest upon which the intrinsic relevances depend and in which they originate has been established by our spontaneous choice, we may at any time shift the focus of this interest and thereby modify the relevances intrinsic to it, obtaining thus an optimum of clarity by continued inquiry. This whole process will still show all the features of a spontaneous performance. The character of all these relevances as intrinsic relevances – that is, intrinsic to a chosen interest – will be preserved.

We are, however, not only centers of spontaneity, gearing into the world and creating changes within it, but also the mere passive recipients of events beyond our control which occur without our interference. Imposed upon us as relevant are situations and events which are not connected with interests chosen by us, which do not originate in acts of our discretion, and which we have to take just as they are, without any power to modify them by our spontaneous activities except by transforming the relevances thus imposed into intrinsic relevances. While that remains unachieved, we do not consider the imposed relevances as being connected with our spontaneously chosen goals. Because they are imposed upon us they remain unclarified and rather incomprehensible.

It is not our business to handle here in detail the import of relevances imposed upon the individual by events in his personal life, such as disease, bereavement, acts of God, or the metaphysical problems of fate, destiny, providence, or the feeling of being "thrown into the world" which Heidegger considers a fundamental condition of human existence. But the imposed relevances have an important function within the social sphere, the study of which will lead us back to our main problem.

IV

Our outline of the various zones of relevance revealed the world within my reach as the core of primary relevance. This world within my own reach is first of all that sector of the world within my actual reach; then, that sector which formerly was in my actual reach and is now within my potential reach because it can be brought back again within my actual reach; and finally, there is within my attainable reach what is within the actual reach of you, my fellow-man, and would be within my actual reach if I were not here where I am but there where you are – briefly, if I were in your place. Thus, actually or potentially, one sector of the world is within my and my fellow-man's common reach; it is within *our* reach, provided – and this restriction is highly important – that my fellow-man has a definite place within the world of my reach as I have in his. We have, then, a common surrounding to be defined by our common interests, his and mine. To be sure, he and I will have a different system of relevances and a different knowledge of the common surrounding if for no other reason than that he sees from "there" everything that I see from "here." Nevertheless, I may within this common surrounding and within the zone of common interests establish social relationships with the individualized Other; each may act upon the Other and react to the Other's action. In short, the Other is partially within my control as I am within his, and he and I not only know of this fact but even know of our mutual knowledge which itself is a means for exercising control. Spontaneously turning to each other, spontaneously "tuning in" ourselves to each other, we have at least *some* intrinsic relevances in common.

But only *some*. In any social interaction there remains a portion of each partner's system of intrinsic relevances not shared by the Other. This has two important consequences. In the first place, let Peter and Paul be partners in a social interaction of any kind whatever. In so far as Peter is the object of Paul's action and has to take into account Paul's specific goals which he, Peter, does not share, Paul's intrinsic relevances are to Peter imposed relevances and vice versa. (The concept of imposed relevances applied to social relationships does not contain any reference to the problem of whether or not the imposition involved is accepted by the partner. It seems that the degree of readiness to accept or not to accept, to give place to, or to resist, the imposition of the Other's intrinsic relevances could be used advantageously for a classification of the various social relationships). In the second place, Peter has full knowledge only of his own system of intrinsic relevances. Paul's system of intrinsic relevances, as a whole, is not fully accessible to Peter. In so far as Peter has a partial knowledge of it – at least he will know what Paul imposes upon him – this knowledge will never have that degree of precision that would be sufficient if what is merely relevant to Peter by imposition were an element of his, Peter's, system of intrinsic relevances. Imposed relevances remain empty, unfulfilled anticipations.

Such is the distribution of knowledge in the social relationship between individuals if each has his definite place in the world

of the Other, if each is under the Other's control. To a certain
extent the same holds good for the relationship between in-
groups and out-groups if each of them is known to the Other in its
specificity. But the more the Other becomes anonymous and the
less his place in the social cosmos is ascertainable to the partner,
the more the zone of common intrinsic relevances decreases and
that of imposed ones increases.

Extending reciprocal anonymity of partners is, however, characteristic of our modern civilization. We are less and less determined in our social situation by relationships with individual
partners within our immediate or mediate reach, and more and
more by highly anonymous types which have no fixed place in
the social cosmos. We are less and less able to choose our partners
in the social world and to share our social life with them. We
are, so to speak, potentially subject to everybody's remote control. No spot of this globe is more distant from the place where we
live than sixty airplane hours; electric waves carry messages in
a fraction of a second from one end of the earth to the other;
and very soon every place in this world will be the potential
target of destructive weapons released at any other place. Our
own social surrounding is within the reach of everyone, everywhere; an anonymous Other, whose goals are unknown to us
because of his anonymity, may bring us together with our system
of interests and relevances within his control. We are less and
less masters in our own right to define what is, and what is not,
relevant to us. Politically, economically, and socially imposed
relevances beyond our control have to be taken into account by
us as they are. Therefore, we have to know them. But to what
extent?

V

This question leads us back to the three ideal types of knowledge described in the beginning as the expert, the well-informed
citizen, and the man on the street. The last-named lives, in a
manner of speaking, naively in his own and his in-group's intrinsic relevances. Imposed relevances he takes into account
merely as elements of the situation to be defined or as data or
conditions for his course of action. They are simply given and

it does not pay to try to understand their origin and structure. Why some things are more relevant than others, why zones of seemingly intrinsic irrelevancy may conceal elements which might be imposed upon him tomorrow as matters of highest relevance is not his concern; these questions do not influence his acting and thinking. He will not cross the bridge before he reaches it, and he takes it for granted that he will find a bridge when he needs it and that it will be strong enough to carry him. That is one of the reasons why in forming his opinions he is much more governed by sentiment than by information, why he prefers, as statistics have amply shown, the comic pages of the newspapers to the foreign news, the radio quizzes to news commentators.

The expert, as we understand this term, is at home only in a system of imposed relevances – imposed, that is, by the problems pre-established within his field. Or to be more precise, by his decision to become an expert he has accepted the relevances imposed within his field as the intrinsic, and the only intrinsic, relevances of his acting and thinking. But this field is rigidly limited. To be sure, there are marginal problems and even problems outside his specific field, but the expert is inclined to assign them to another expert whose concern they are supposed to be. The expert starts from the assumption not only that the system of problems established within his field is relevant but that it is the only relevant system. All his knowledge is referred to this frame of reference which has been established once and for all. He who does not accept it as the monopolized system of his intrinsic relevances does not share with the expert a universe of discourse. He can expect from the expert's advice merely the indication of suitable means for attaining pregiven ends, but not the determination of the ends themselves. Clemenceau's famous statement that war is too important a business to be left exclusively to generals illustrates the way in which a man oriented toward more comprehensive ends reacts to expert advice.

The well-informed citizen finds himself placed in a domain which belongs to an infinite number of possible frames of reference. There are no pregiven ready-made ends, no fixed border lines within which he can look for shelter. He has to choose the frame of reference by choosing his interest; he has to investigate the zones of relevances adhering to it; and he has to gather as much knowledge as possible of the origin and sources of the relevances actually or potentially imposed upon him. In terms of the classification previously used, the well-informed citizen will restrict, in so far as is possible, the zone of the irrelevant, mindful that what is today relatively irrelevant may be imposed tomorrow as a primary relevance and that the province of the so-called absolutely irrelevant may reveal itself as the home of the anonymous powers which may overtake him. Thus, his is an attitude as different from that of the expert whose knowledge is delimited by a single system of relevances as from that of the man on the street which is indifferent to the structure of relevance itself. For this very reason he has to form a reasonable opinion and to look for information. What, however, are the sources of this information, and for what reason may the citizen consider them sufficient to enable him to form an opinion of his own?

VI

Again we are referred to a main problem of the theory of the social distribution of knowledge. It seems to be a mere truism to state that only an exceedingly small part of our actual and potential knowledge originates in our own experience. The bulk of our knowledge consists in experiences which not we but our fellow-men, contemporaries or predecessors, have had, and which they have communicated or handed down to us. We shall call this kind of knowledge socially derived knowledge. But why do we believe in it? All socially derived knowledge is based upon an implicit idealization which can be roughly formulated as follows: "I believe in the experience of my fellow-man because if I were (or had been) in his place I would have (or would have had) the same experiences as he has (or had), could do just as he does (or did), would have the same chances or risks in the same situation. Thus, what to him is (or was) a really existing object of his actual experience is to me a speciously existing object of a possible experience." This is the basic idealization and we cannot enter here into the various modifications of the typical style in which socially derived knowledge is experienced. Within the frame of this paper we have to restrict ourselves to a few examples which are by no means exhaustive.

Socially derived knowledge may originate in four different ways. First, it may come from the immediate experience of another individual who communicates this experience to me. For present purposes such an individual shall be called the eyewitness. My belief in his report is based on the fact that the reported event occurred in the world within his reach. From "there," from his position in space and time, things could be observed and events experienced which were not observable from "here," from my position; but if I were "there" and not "here," I would have experienced the same. This belief presupposes, furthermore, a certain conformity of my system of relevances with that of the eyewitness. Otherwise I am inclined to assume that I would have observed certain aspects of the reported event which remained unnoticed by the reporter or vice versa.

The second source of socially derived knowledge may be the immediate experience of another individual – not necessarily an eyewitness and not necessarily reporting directly to me – to whom the observed event has its place in a system of intrinsic relevances of a configuration substantially different from my own. We will call such an individual an insider. My belief in his report is based on the assumption that the insider, because he experiences the reported event in a unique or typical context of relevance, "knows it better" than I would if I observed the same event but was unaware of its intrinsic significance.

Third, there is the opinion of another individual, based by him on facts collected from some source or other of immediate or socially derived knowledge but arranged and grouped according to a system of relevances similar to my own. Such an individual shall be called an analyst. His opinion carries the more weight with me the more I can control the facts upon which it is based and the more I am convinced of the congruity of his system of relevances with my own.

And finally, there is the opinion of another individual based on the same sources as those of the analyst but grouped according to a system of relevances considerably different from my own. He shall be called the commentator. His opinion is trusted if it enables me to form a sufficiently clear and precise knowledge of the underlying deviating system of relevances.

It is clear that the eyewitness, the insider, the analyst, and the commentator represent merely four of many ideal types of transmission of socially derived knowledge. None of these types is likely to be found in its purity. Any historiographer, teacher, editorialist, or propagandist will represent a mixture of several of the ideal types outlined. For the classification of a communicator according to these types it is immaterial whether he is or is not an expert, whether he uses this or that system of signs, symbols or artifacts for communicating, whether the communication occurs in face-to-face or any other social relationship, whether the informant is intimately known to us or whether he remains more or less anonymous. But all these factors are extremely important, even decisive, for the weight which we, the information-seeking citizens, accord the source of our socially derived knowledge.

It is impossible to enter here into all the implications of the problem. Yet even the rudimentary picture outlined would be incomplete without mentioning briefly another aspect of the social distribution of knowledge which, to a certain extent, is the opposite of socially derived knowledge. We shall call it socially approved knowledge. Any knowledge, our own originary experiences as well as any kind of socially derived knowledge, receives additional weight if it is accepted not only by ourselves but by other members of our in-group. I believe my own experiences to be correct beyond doubt if others whom I consider competent corroborate what I found, either out of their own experiences or merely because they trust me. If I consider my father, my priest, my government to be authoritative, then their opinions have special weight and this weight itself has the character of an imposed relevance. The power of socially approved knowledge is so extended that what the whole in-group approves – ways of thinking and acting, such as mores, folkways, habits – is simply taken for granted; it becomes an element of the relatively natural concept of the world, although the source of such knowledge remains entirely hidden in its anonymity.

Thus, the zone of things taken for granted, the relatively natural concept of the world from which all inquiry starts and which all inquiry presupposes, reveals itself as the sediment of previous acts of experiencing – my own as well as of others – which are socially approved.

Let me close with a few remarks on the nature and function of the interplay between socially derived and socially approved knowledge and draw just one practical conclusion for the diagnosis of our present situation.

Socially approved knowledge is the source of prestige and authority; it is also the home of public opinion. Only he is deemed to be an expert or a well-informed citizen who is socially approved as such. Having obtained this degree of prestige the expert's or the well-informed citizen's opinions receive additional weight in the realm of socially derived knowledge. In our time, socially approved knowledge tends to supersede the underlying system of intrinsic and imposed relevances. Polls, interviews, and questionnaires try to gauge the opinion of the man on the street, who does not even look for any kind of information that goes beyond his habitual system of intrinsic relevances. His opinion, which is public opinion as it is understood nowadays, becomes more and more socially approved at the expense of informed opinion and therefore imposes itself as relevant upon the better-informed members of the community. A certain tendency to misinterpret democracy as a political institution in which the opinion of the uninformed man on the street must predominate increases the danger. It is the duty and the privilege, therefore, of the well-informed citizen in a democratic society to make his private opinion prevail over the public opinion of the man on the street.

DON QUIXOTE AND THE PROBLEM OF REALITY

"Under what circumstances do we think things real?" William
James asks this question in one of the most remarkable chapters
of his *Principles of Psychology* [1] and starts from there to develop
his theory of various orders of reality. Any object, so he finds,
which remains uncontradicted is *ipso facto* believed and posited
as absolute reality. And a thing thought of cannot be contradicted
by another, unless it begins the quarrel by saying something inadmissible about that other. If this is the case, then the mind must
take its choice of which to hold by. All propositions, whether
attributive or existential, are believed through the very fact of
being conceived, unless they clash with other propositions believed at the same time, by affirming that their terms are the
same with the terms of these other propositions. The whole distinction between real and unreal, the whole psychology of belief,
disbelief, and doubt, is, always according to William James,
grounded on two mental facts: first that we are liable to think
differently of the same object; and secondly, that when we have
done so, we can choose which way of thinking to adhere to and
which to disregard. The origin and fountainhead of all reality,
whether from the absolute or the practical point of view is thus,
subjective, is ourselves. Consequently, there exist several,
probably an infinite number of various orders of reality, each with
its own special and separate style of existence, called by James
"sub-universes." Among them is the world of the senses or
physical "things" as experienced by common sense, which is the
paramount reality; the world of science; the world of ideal relations; of "idols of the tribe"; the supernatural worlds, such as
the Christian heaven and hell; the numerous worlds of individual

[1] Vol. II, pp. 287ff.

opinion; and, finally, the worlds of sheer madness and vagary, also infinitely numerous. Every object we think of gets referred to at least one world or another of this or some similar list. Each world, whilst it is attended to, is real after its own fashion, and any relation to our mind at all in the absence of a stronger relation with which it clashes, suffices to make an object real.

So far we have considered William James. This is not the place to investigate by what means mind bestows an accent of reality on one of these sub-universes and withdraws it from others; nor how the transition from one realm of reality to the other occurs; nor, finally, what features of consciousness characterize the various provinces or sub-universes of reality.[2] The few sentences quoted from William James delimit our purpose, which is to analyze the problem of reality in Cervantes' Don Quixote. The thesis we want to submit is that Cervantes' novel deals systematically with the very problem of multiple realities stated by William James and that the various phases of Don Quixote's adventures are carefully elaborated variations of the main theme, viz. how we experience reality. This problem has many aspects, dialectically intertwined. There is the world of Don Quixote's madness, the world of chivalry, a sub-universe of reality incompatible with the paramount reality of daily life, in which the barber, the priest, the housekeeper and the niece simply live along, taking it for granted beyond question. How does it come that Don Quixote can continue to bestow the accent of reality on his sub-universe of phantasy if it clashes with the paramount reality in which there are no castles and armies and giants but merely inns and flocks of sheep and windmills? How is it possible that the private world of Don Quixote is not a solipsistic one, that there are other minds within this reality, not merely as objects of Don Quixote's experience, but sharing with him, at least to a certain extent, the belief in its actual or potential reality? And, finally, neither Don Quixote's sub-universe of madness nor the paramount reality of the senses, as William James calls it, in which we Sancho Panzas live our daily lives, turns out to be as monolithic as it seems. Both contain, as it were, enclaves of experience

---

[2] A first attempt to analyze these problems has been made in the writer's paper "On Multiple Realities," in Collected Papers I, The Problem of Social Reality, Phaenomenologica, The Hague, 1962, pp. 229–234.

transcending the sub-universes taken for granted by either Don
Quixote or Sancho Panza and referring to other realms of reality
not compatible with either of them. There are enigmatic and
frightful nocturnal noises, there is death and dream, vision and
art, prophecy and science. How does Don Quixote, how do we
Sancho Panzas succeed in maintaining the belief in the reality
of the closed sub-universe once chosen as the home base in spite
of the various irruptions of experiences which transcend it?

Let us look first at Don Quixote's world of chivalry. Doubtless it is a closed sub-universe, and doubtless he bestows upon it
the accent of reality. Again and again the ingenious knight refutes
any doubt on the part of outsiders that the heroes of whom the
books of chivalry give an account have ever lived and that their
adventures occurred as described in the books. He has good
arguments to proffer. The institution of knights errant, he explains to the canon of Toledo,[3] is universally acknowledged and
authenticated. The story of Fierrabras took place in the time of
Charlemagne, the deeds of King Arthur are recorded in the
histories and annals of England, in the King's Armory in Madrid
Roland's horn can be seen even to this day. Furthermore, the
books which deal with the life and history of the knights describe
in all details the family, time, place, action of this or that knight
day by day. Based on these reports, Don Quixote can describe
Amadis of Gaul with all his features, characteristics and actions
so that he may say he has seen him with his own eyes. He calls
this an "evidence infallible" for their existence.[4] In addition,
is it thinkable that books printed by royal license lie? And how
can one possibly doubt that giants existed in reality? In the island
of Sicily shinbones and shoulder blades have been discovered of a
size which show their owners were giants as tall as towers. Also
the Holy Scriptures, which cannot depart from the truth by so
much as an inch, know giants such as Goliath.[5] If we examine
why, within the reality of our natural attitude, we believe in
historical events we can only refer to arguments similar to those
of Don Quixote: to documents, monuments, authenticated ac-
counts by witnesses and uninterrupted tradition. And there may

---

[3] pp. 436–440. All quotations refer to the translation by J. M. Cohen, published by
Penguin Books, Middlesex, 1950.

[4] *Ibid.*, p. 478.

[5] *Ibid.*, p. 479.

be well-founded disputes among the historians of the world of Don Quixote, such as his controversy with the crazy Cardenio over the question whether Master Elisabat was or was not Queen Madasima's lover.[6]

Knight errantry is first of all a way of life. It fulfills a heavenly mission. Knights errant are "God's ministers on earth, and the arms by which His justice is executed here."[7] In this iron age it is their profession to roam the world, righting wrongs and relieving injuries.[8] But chivalry is not only a way of life, it is a science, more, the queen of all sciences, which comprises all or most sciences in the world. He who professes knight errantry must be a jurist and know the laws of person and property; he must be a theologian so that he may give the reasons for the Christian rules he professes; a physician and especially a herbalist in order to prepare a flask of the balsam of Fierrabras, of which a few drops heal a knight cut through the middle, provided the parts are fitted together before the blood congeals;[9] an astronomer to know by the stars how many hours of the night have passed and in what part of the world he is; he must know how to shoe a horse, how to mend a saddle, how to swim. And above all, he has to be a maintainer of truth, although its defense may cost him his life.[10]

This world of chivalry has its own legal and economic system. Knights errant are exempt from all jurisdiction, their law is their sword, their charter their courage, their statutes their own will.[11] Where have you ever heard of a knight errant being brought before a judge, however many homicides he may have committed?[12] What knight errant ever paid taxes, customs or toll? What tailor was ever paid by him for a suit of clothes? What warden who received him in his castle ever made him pay his score?[13] And most certainly they did not pay wages to their squires. They made them governors of some islands or rulers of one or the other conquered kingdom.[14]

[6] *Op. cit.*, p. 198.
[7] *Ibid.*, p. 98.
[8] *Ibid.*, p. 158.
[9] *Ibid.*, p. 80.
[10] *Ibid.*, p. 582f.
[11] *Ibid.*, p. 410.
[12] *Ibid.*, p. 80.
[13] *Ibid.*, p. 410.
[14] *Ibid.*, p. 511.

This sub-universe is characterized by peculiar modifications of the basic categories of thought, namely space, time, and causality. The kingdom of Micomicona in Ethiopia,[15] the Empire of Trapezunt [16] are well determined geographic concepts; the second region of air, where hail and snow is born, and the third of fire, where lightning and thunderbolts are made [17] are established by celestial physics. And all these places can easily be brought within reach: the sage, necromancer or magician who looks after the knight's affairs – and certainly every knight, to be a true one, has such a friend [18] – picks him up in his bed and next day he will be a thousand miles away from his place; or he sends him a chariot of fire or a hippogryph or Clavileño, the wooden horse, or an enchanting boat. Otherwise it would be impossible for a knight fighting in the Armenian mountains with a dragon to be saved at the last minute by his friend who was just a moment ago in England.[19] Don Quixote spends four nights in the cave of Montesinos, although those who wait for him at the entrance of the cave state that he was away a little more than an hour [20] – a problem similar to that which in our day Bergson has analyzed in discussing the time concept of Einstein's theory of relativity.[21] All this is due to the work of the enchanters, the friendly and the hostile ones, who fulfill in Don Quixote's sub-universe the role of causality and motivation. Their activity is the basic category of Don Quixote's interpretation of the world. It is their function to translate the order of the realm of phantasy into the realms of common-sense experience, to transform the real giants attacked by Don Quixote, for instance, into phantoms of windmills. Enchanters, so we learn, can transform all things and change their natural shapes. But, strictly speaking, what they change is the scheme of interpretation prevailing in one sub-universe into the scheme of interpretation valid in another. Both refer to the same matter of fact which is, in terms of Don Quixote's private sub-universe, Mambrino's miraculous helmet, and, in terms of Sancho

---

[15] *Ibid.*, p. 252.
[16] *Ibid.*, p. 33.
[17] *Ibid.*, p. 731.
[18] *Ibid.*, p. 270.
[19] *Ibid.*, p. 271.
[20] *Ibid.*, p. 620.
[21] Cf. the dialogue between Pierre in the flying missile and Paul waiting at the gun in *Durée et Simultanéité*, Paris, 1922.

Panza's paramount reality of everyday life, an ordinary barber's basin. Thus, it is the function of the enchanters' activities to guarantee the coexistence and compatibility of several sub-universes of meaning referring to the same matters of fact and to assure the maintenance of the accent of reality bestowed upon any of such sub-universes. Nothing remains unexplained, para-doxical or contradictory, as soon as the enchanter's activities are recognized as a constitutive element of the world. But to Don Quixote the existence of enchanters is much more than a mere hypothesis. It is a historical fact proved by all the sacred source books reporting on matters of chivalry. Of course, this fact is not verifiable by ordinary means of sense perception. For magicians never allow themselves to be seen,[22] and it is clear that the axiom of enchantment, which makes the reconciliation between the sub-universe of phantasy and the paramount reality possible, cannot itself be subjected to a test originating within one of these sub-universes.

Our enlightened age is certainly not prepared to accept the agency of invisible enchanters as a principle of explanation of the occurrences and facts in the causal structure of the world. To be sure, we acknowledge the existence of invisible viruses, or of neutrinos or of an "Id" in the sense of psychoanalysis as the causal source of observed phenomena. But who would dare to compare these findings of our scientists with the activities of the en-chanters of the madman Don Quixote? Yet, in the latter's theory, the activity of invisible enchanters has a great advantage over the explanatory principles of modern science just mentioned: the enchanters themselves have their motives for acting as they do and these motives are understandable to us human beings. Some of them bear the knight malice because they know through their art and spells that in the fullness of time Don Quixote will conquer one of their favorite knights in combat and that they will not be able to gainsay or avert what Heaven has decreed.[23] But friendly enchanters also interfere: the sage who is on Don Quixote's side shows a rare foresight in making Mambrino's helmet, that object of immense value, appear to every one a barber's basin, thus protecting its owner from persecution by all

² *Don Quixote*, p. 126.
³ *Op. cit.*, p. 65.

those who would understand its true meaning.[24] And it also happens, for instance in the miraculous adventure with the enchanted boat, that two powerful enchanters meet in opposition, one frustrating the other's design.[25] Here we have all the elements of Greek theology at the time of Homer: the envy of the gods, their intervention in favor of their protégés, their struggle for power, their subjection under inevitable fate. To be sure, if we introduce the enchanters into the causal chain, we cannot solve the Cartesian doubt about whether the world is governed by an evil genius or by God. But we are sure that whatever happens, happens reasonably, that is, within the motivation of the enchanters. We might be tempted to speak of a non-Hegelian dialectic in a similar way in which we speak of a non-Euclidian geometry.

These are the main features of Don Quixote's closed sub-universe upon which he has bestowed the accent of reality, his home-base from which he interprets all the other provinces of reality. But this his private world comes into contact with the world of his fellow-men, and both, Don Quixote and the others, have to come to terms with the conflicts arising between the disparate schemes of interpretation prevailing in each of them. In the description of the various adventures Don Quixote meets on his three expeditions Cervantes shows in a highly systematic way the typical solutions for this problem and it would be a rather tempting task to analyze them step by step. This purpose cannot be achieved within the frame of the present paper. We have to restrict ourselves to a general survey and to the analysis of a few adventures.

The social world which Don Quixote meets on each of his three expeditions takes a radically different attitude to his private world of phantasy, which is to him a highly meaningful one, but a world of madness to his fellow-men. On the first short expedition Don Quixote is alone. He is merely involved in an inner dialogue with the unknown sage, whoever he may be, who will commit the chronicle of his deeds to future generations. But otherwise Don Quixote remains undisturbed master in his sub-universe; he is not refuted by the behavior of his fellow-men who, as Cervantes

[24] *Ibid.*, p. 204.
[25] *Ibid.*, p. 661.

states, "fall in with his humor." [26] To Don Quixote there is
really a fortress with towers in shining silver, a dwarf's trumpet
announcing the approaching knight, beauteous maidens taking
the air at the castle's gate, and a castellan. Only to the observer
there is an inn, a swineherd blowing his horn, two women of easy
virtue and an innkeeper. Nothing and nobody, however – to
revert to the quotation from William James at the beginning –
starts a quarrel by saying something inadmissible which would
contradict the experience held by Don Quixote to be true. The
innkeeper receives him in a way appropriate for a knight, permits
him the watch of arms, performs the ceremony of knighting him;
nor do the silk-merchants on horseback, who are reluctant to
acknowledge without proof that Dulcinea is the most beauteous
maiden, or their muleteer behave in a way incompatible with the
pattern of interpretation taken for granted in the world of chivalry. Thus, Don Quixote's actions remain performable within the
paramount reality of daily life in spite of his phantastic motives,
and no enchanters are needed to reconcile the disparate schemes
of interpretation.

The activity of the enchanters appears for the first time during
the interlude between the first and second expedition when the
priest and the barber try to cure Don Quixote by burning his
books and walling up his library. This event is explained as the
work of Don Quixote's archenemy, the magician Freston, and
the knight understands this perfectly well, taking it as a real
occurrence. From now on he uses the fact of enchantment in
order to maintain the accent of reality on his private sub-universe
of chivalry if this world clashes with the paramount reality of
those of his fellow-men who come in contact or conflict with
him. For on this second expedition Don Quixote is no longer
alone. He has to establish a "sub-universe of discourse" with the
fellow-men with whom he shares a face-to-face relationship within the world of common sense. This refers first of all to Sancho
Panza, his squire, the representative of everyday thinking who
has always a treasure of proverbs at his command, in order to
explain everything in terms of knowledge just taken for granted.
But if the things and occurrences experienced by both of them
are interpreted in accordance with different schemes of inter-

[26] *Op. cit.*, p. 25.

pretation, are they still *common* experiences of the *same* objects?
Our relationship with the social world is based upon the assumption that in spite of all individual variations the same objects are
experienced by our fellow-men in substantially the same way as by
ourselves and vice versa, and also that our and their schemes
of interpretation show the same typical structure of relevances.
If this belief in the substantial identity of the intersubjective
experience of the world breaks down, then the very possibility
of establishing communication with our fellow-men is destroyed.
In such a crisis situation we become convinced that each of us
lives in the impenetrable shell of his solipsistic prison, the Others
becoming mere mirages to us, we to the Others, we to ourselves.
There are two possibilities: either experiences of the objective
world turn out to be mere illusions (and in Don Quixote's terminology this means that the enchanter has transformed the objective world); or I myself have changed my identity (and this
means I am enchanted myself). On the other hand, it is precisely
the assumed activity of the enchanters, who change and alter all
our deeds and transform them according to their pleasure, which
leads to the effect that what seems to Don Quixote Mambrino's
helmet appears to Sancho as a barber's basin and to another as
something else .[27] This is not to Sancho's liking. To him, the neo-
positivistic empiricist, the pains in his shoulders caused by the
blanket-tossing in the inn vouch for the reality of his tormentors,
the innkeepers and the muleteer, and he refuses to accept Don
Quixote's explanation that they were phantoms in an enchanted
castle. Where you start recognizing people who have names, there
is no enchantment involved, says he. But slowly Sancho accepts
the knight's scheme of interpretation. Enchantment is to Sancho
at least plausible, and at the end of the second part, after Don
Quixote's defeat by the Knight of the Moon, it becomes a fact.
"For all this episode seemed to him to be happening in a dream
and the whole business to be a matter of enchantment." [28] With
great skill Cervantes shows this transition and the devices by
which a common sub-universe of discourse is established between
knight and squire. Both have good arguments for explaining away
discrepancies. Don Quixote admits that Sancho is not a knight

[27] *Op. cit.*, p. 204.
[28] *Ibid.*, p. 890.

and, therefore, subject to other laws; [29] perhaps his fear prevents
him from seeing and hearing right [30] ; if Sancho stealthily followed
the two flocks of sheep for a short while he would discover
that they were re-transformed into two armies as described by Don
Quixote.[31] On the other hand, Sancho is inclined to believe that
the Knight's misfortunes are due to the fact that he has broken
a solemn oath; [32] or perhaps that he has power over real giants,
but no power at all over phantoms.[33] And having discovered that
he has to accept enchantment as a scheme of interpretation in
order to establish a universe of discourse with Don Quixote. Sancho learns to express himself like a follower of the Greek skeptic
philosophers. He corrects several times his original statement
that what Don Quixote declares to be Mambrino's helmet is just
a barber's basin, and worth a *real* if it's worth a farthing. "It's
like nothing so much as a barber's basin. Just like it, it is."[34] And
later on,[35] he speaks even of a "basin-helmet." Toward the end
of the first part,[36] the story of this adventure is used to develop,
like in a stretto of a complicated fugue, the main theme of intersubjective reality in new elaborations. In the inn – to Don Quixote an enchanted castle – all the main actors of the story have
assembled. The barber, the former owner of the basin-helmet,
which Don Quixote had acquired in due combat, appears and
claims his property and also the pack-saddle which Sancho on
this occasion has taken away from his mule. The company in the
inn decides to carry the joke further and confirms to the despair
of the robbed owner that the object in question is, as Don Quixote
maintains, a helmet and not a barber's basin. An expert opinion,
furnished by master Nicholas, Don Quixote's barber friend,
corroborates this finding. The former owner cannot understand
how so many honorable gentlemen can possibly say that this is
not a basin but a helmet. But if this is right, he argues, then the
pack-saddle of his mule must be a horse's harness since Don
Quixote maintains that he had met him riding a silver colored

[29] *Ibid.*, p. 128.
[30] *Ibid.*, p. 137.
[31] *Ibid.*, p. 138.
[32] *Ibid.*, p. 142.
[33] *Op. cit.*, p. 252.
[34] *Ibid.*, p. 162.
[35] *Ibid.*, p. 395.
[36] *Ibid.*, pp. 404ff.

steed. In terms of formal logic this argument is perfectly correct. Don Quixote refuses to interfere in the matter of the pack-saddle because this does not refer to a question of chivalry, and he, being a knight, might be subject to the spells in this enchanted castle. He admits that the thing looks to him rather like a pack-saddle, but he leaves the decision to the others because their understanding will be free and they will be able to judge the affairs of this castle as they really are and not as they appear to him, Don Quixote. Those who are in the plot affirm by secret vote that the object is not the pack-saddle of a mule but the harness of a horse. The former owner, under whose eyes the objects have turned into a helmet and a horse-harness, is more than perplexed, but, as a good democrat, he submits to the majority vote, stating: "Might is right." A bystander, taking the role of a scientific observer, is, however, not satisfied. If this is not a concerted joke, he cannot understand how intelligent men can insist that these things are not a basin and a pack-saddle. Such a statement goes against obvious truth and good sense, and the whole world won't convince him to the contrary. As a sound method to decide such an argument, a general battle starts between the parties. "At last," comments Cervantes, "the uproar was quelled for a time, the pack-saddle remained a harness till Judgement Day, and in Don Quixote's imagination the basin remained a helmet and the inn a castle." [37] The abyss between the two sub-universes can neither be overcome by formal logic, nor by consent of the majority, nor by military victory.

The second part of the novel, written ten years later, transposes the dialectic of intersubjectivity into a new dimension. If during the first two expeditions Don Quixote met fellow-men, he encountered them in a face-to-face relationship, and none of the partners had previous knowledge of the other. But before Don Quixote starts for his third expedition the history of his earlier adventures was described in a book read by the greater part of the persons he was to meet. This anonymous audience of readers has formed an ideal type of Don Quixote's personality and his ways of acting and reacting; they expect from him a certain type of behavior, which includes his expectations of their reactions, and they are prepared to orient their own behavior toward the

[37] *Op. cit.*, p. 408.

knight in such a way that it might be interpreted by him as an adequate response to his own actions. In order to humor him and to establish with him a universe of discourse, they build up within the reality of their daily-life-world a world of play, of joke, of make-believe and "let's pretend," which, so they hope, will be taken by Don Quixote as reality in terms of his private sub-universe. But since they never bestow upon their make-believe world the accent of reality, they cannot succeed in establishing a universe of discourse with Don Quixote and, consequently, they cannot enter into a true social relationship with him. This leads, as we shall see, to the personal tragedy and the downfall of the knight.

His personal tragedy is first of all due to the weakening of his faith in Dulcinea's reality. When Sancho learns that the knight's lady Dulcinea of Toboso is nobody else than the farmer's daughter Aldonza Lorenzo, he doubts everything the enamoured knight has stated of her. "Do you think," Sancho, the knight answers, "that the Amarylisses, Phylisses, Sylvias ... and all the rest the books ... are full of, were real flesh-and-blood ladies, and the mistresses of the writers who wrote about them? Not a bit of it. Most of them were invented to serve as subjects for verses ... I am quite satisfied, therefore, to imagine and believe that the good Aldonza Lorenza is lovely and virtuous and, for my part, I think of her as the greatest princess of the world." [38] And here Don Quixote makes a statement which is at the core of our problem and surpasses in its logical boldness all the paradoxes of Russell's theory of classes which can also be found in Cervantes' novel,[39] as Hermann Weyl has already pointed out. *"To make an end of the matter, I imagine all I say to be true, neither more nor less."* This is the basic axiom which identifies truth with existence in the particular sub-universe upon which the accent of reality has been bestowed.

In the second part of the novel the Duchess receives Don Quixote in the "let's pretend" world she has carefully built up for him. She refers to the aforequoted statement of the knight which she read in the published first part, as well as to the fact that Don Quixote never met Dulcinea, and expresses doubt of Dulcinea's

[38] *Op. cit.*, p. 210.
[39] *Ibid.*, p. 798f.

real existence. "God alone knows," answers Don Quixote, "whether Dulcinea exists on earth or not or whether she is phantastic or not phantastic. *These are not matters whose verification can be carried out to the full.* I neither engendered nor bore my lady, though I contemplate her in her ideal form, as a lady with all the qualities needed to win her fame in all quarters of the world".[40] Only merchants of Toledo going to buy silk in Marcia want the knight to show them Dulcinea, or at least a portrait of her, before they are willing to admit that she is the most beauteous maiden.[41] Only a Sancho dares to admit to Don Quixote during the third expedition, when they look in vain for Dulcinea's palace in Toboso, that he too has never seen the peerless lady and that his seeing her and the reply he brought to the knight were of his invention. But that is not enough. Three country girls on their donkeys come along the road, and Sancho describes them to Don Quixote as the princess Dulcinea in all her glory, accompanied by her damsels, riding hackneys as white as snow. But Don Quixote, to his despair, can only see village-girls on their donkeys, – at least they look so to him [42] – and he is inclined to doubt his own immediate experience. Most certainly the enchanters have put clouds and cataracts into his eyes and *for them alone and no others* have changed Dulcinea to a poor peasant girl. Yet there is still a more horrible possibility. Perhaps, the enchanter has at the same time turned him, Don Quixote, into the appearance of some spectre to make it abominable for Dulcinea's sight .[43] This is the same problem handled by Kafka in his novel, *Metamorphosis*, in which a man finds himself one morning transformed into a gigantic bug. Don Quixote starts to doubt his own identity. The situation becomes more complicated by the fact that later on Don Quixote, in the vision he has in the cave of Montesinos, sees Dulcinea transformed into the peasant girl and comes to the conclusion that she must be enchanted, transformed, not only for him but also to Sancho and everyone else.[44] However, he is in doubt and remains in doubt whether what he saw in the cave of Montesinos was reality, dream, or pure fiction

[40] *Ibid.*, p. 680, italics added.
[41] *Op. cit.*, p. 50.
[42] *Ibid.*, p. 529.
[43] *Ibid.*, p. 530.
[44] *Ibid.*, p. 522.

of his own making. He asks the prophesying ape of Master Pedro[45] and later on the enchanted head [46] whether the account he gave of his experiences in the cave was truth or dream, imagined or real and twice receives the answer that it was a mixture of both. For even within the sub-universe of Don Quixote's private world there is the possibility of dream and imagination, a world of phantasy within the world of phantasy; even in this sub-universe the frontiers of reality are gliding, even here there are enclaves mirrored into it from other sub-universes.

To Sancho who knows that the whole story of his first and second encounter with Dulcinea is just his own invention the situation seems perfectly clear, and Don Quixote's recital of his vision in the cave of Montesinos convinces him finally beyond doubt that his master was out of his mind and mad on all counts.[47] But his righteous conviction is shaken when he confesses later on [48] to the Duchess that he just made Don Quixote believe his encounters with Dulcinea and that her enchantment is no more true than that the moon is a green cheese. The Duchess answers that in her opinion Sancho's tricking scheme was the invention of the enchanters, that the peasant girl is really and truly Dulcinea, and that it was good Sancho who was deceived though he may think he was the deceiver. The Duchess takes, therewith, the Hegelian point of view of the "cunning of Reason," which makes man unwillingly and unknowingly a tool of its higher purpose. This possibility Sancho has to admit and also that if the Duchess is right he has to believe what Don Quixote contends he had seen in the cave. But, says Sancho, it must have been contrariwise as the Duchess says. It can't be presumed that he, Sancho, could invent such a shrewd trick on the spur of the moment with his poor wits, and his master can't be so mad as to accept something so far beyond all probability on his weak persuasion. The truth may be that it was a peasant girl he saw, he took her for a peasant girl and a peasant girl he judged her to be. But if it was Dulcinea it can't be laid to his account, only to that of the very active and exceedingly meddlesome enchanter at work.[49] Sancho's admission

---

[45] *Op. cit.*, p. 637.
[46] *Ibid.*, p. 874.
[47] *Ibid.*, p. 621.
[48] *Ibid.*, p. 689.
[49] *Op. cit.*, p. 690.

of the possibility that his empirical peasant girl, whom he has transformed into a fictitious Dulcinea, was perhaps indeed the noumenal Dulcinea, completes the dialectic of the intersubjective experience of reality.

We mentioned before that the world of phantasy is not a unified realm, that there are phantasies within phantasies, subuniverses within sub-universes, which may conflict with one another and both with the reality of daily life. An example of such a situation can be found in one of the most profound chapters of Cervantes' work in which Don Quixote attends Master Pedro's puppet show "The Releasing of Melisandra." From his books of chivalry Don Quixote knows all the details of the story of how Don Gaiferos liberates the lady Melisandra from Moorish slavery, which is to him a historical fact. At the beginning of the puppet show he criticizes certain details of the presentation as contrary to fact, for instance, that the Moorish King gives alarm signals for the persecution of the fugitives by ringing bells from all the towers of the mosques, whereas in reality, the Moors used for such purposes trumpets and kettledrums. But soon the play takes hold of Don Quixote and creates in him fear and compassion in the good Aristotelian manner. What he knew from his books as historical facts occur now, as represented by Master Pedro's puppets, under his eyes in the vivid present. While it lasts, the course of events is still uncertain and can be influenced by his interference. And seeing the pack of Moors persecuting the fugitives, he thinks that it is his duty to help so famous a king and so lovely a lady. He unsheathes his sword and rains blows with fury upon the puppet-heathenry, not heeding the exhortation of the desperate Master Pedro to reflect that these are not real Moors but only little pasteboard figures. Afterwards, when Master Pedro requires payment for the damage done to his puppetry, Don Quixote assures him [50] that all that had passed had seem to him a real occurrence. Melisandra *was* Melisandra, Gaiferos Gaiferos, Charlemagne Charlemagne. Therefore he was stirred to anger and conscious of his mission that as a knight errant he had to give aid and protection to the persecuted people.

Don Quixote touches here on the profound and unsolved problem of the reality of the work of art, especially of the theater.

[50] *Op. cit.*, p. 643.

Also we, Sancho Panzas of the common-sense world, by taking our seat in the audience, are willing to shift the accent of reality from the surrounding world of our daily life to the world on the stage as soon as the curtain rises. We, too, live in a different realm of reality while the play goes on than during the intermission. Also to us Lear is Lear, Regan Regan, Kent Kent. But this reality of the events on the stage is of an entirely different kind than that of our daily life. The latter is the only sub-universe into which we can gear with our actions, which we can transform and change by them and within which we can establish communication with our fellow-men. This fundamental characteristic of the reality of our daily life – or is it merely an axiom of our bestowing the accent of reality upon it? – is precisely the reason why this sub-universe is experienced by us as the paramount reality of circumstances and environment with which we have to come to terms. We, the audience, the beholders, are powerless with respect to the reality of the work of art or the theater; as beholders we have to suffer or to enjoy it, but we are not in the position to interfere with it, to change it by our actions. Here is perhaps one of the roots of the particular phenomenological structure of the aesthetic experience. But to follow this idea up would lead too far afield. At any rate, Don Quixote, who takes another sub-universe than the paramount reality of daily life as his home-base, cannot "realize" that the world of the theater is separated from that of his private sub-universe of phantasy. Melisandra and her liberation are environmental circumstances also in his world of chivalry. Strictly speaking, we find in his adventure with the puppet show the clash between three realms of reality: that of the phantastic world of chivalry, within which a knight has to interfere in order to help a beautiful lady; that of the theater, in which all this is merely represented in the way of make-believe by living actors or puppets without admitting any interference by the audience; and third, the sad reality of everyday life, in which pasteboard figures can be smashed and in which the master of the show presents a bill for the damage that the intrusion of our dreams into the world of reality has caused.

Another adventure, that of the enchanted boat, shows the clash between three other realms of reality: the world of chivalry, of common sense, and of science. Don Quixote and Sancho, riding along the Ebro river, find a little boat without oars, made fast on the trunk of a tree. Don Quixote thinks that this boat "without the possibility of error" [51] summons him to embark and to travel in the twinkling of an eye six or seven thousand miles in order to succor some noble person in distress. They tie up Rosinante and Dappel, Sancho's donkey, to a tree, embark and weigh anchor. While Sancho is in fear and despair because he hears Dappel braying anxiously, Don Quixote thinks that they have already traveled two thousand miles or more and either have passed or will shortly pass the equinoctial line which, according to Ptolemy, the best cosmographer known, divides and cuts the opposing poles at equal distances. In order to verify this belief, Don Quixote turns to the exact methods of the natural sciences. The first method would be exact measurement with the help of an astrolabe, but such an instrument is not at his disposal. The second method is that of an experiment based upon an empirical law which so far seems to have stood the test and has therefore, as we would say in our modern language, been accepted in the corpus of geographical science. The law, discovered and tested by "the Spaniards and those who embark at Cadiz to go to the East Indies" states "that as soon as the equinoctial line has been passed, the lice die on everybody aboard ship." Sancho just has to make this scientific experiment. If he passes his hand over his thigh and catches anything living, they shall have no doubt on the score, and if not then they have passed. Yet Sancho, thinking in common-sense terms, protests vigorously. There is no need to make this experiment, for he can see with his own eyes that they have not drawn two yards off where Dappel and Rosinante are. To this highly unscientific objection Don Quixote takes the position of the rigorous empirical scientist, who, entrenched in his sub-universe of scientific reality, requires verification of any empirical statement: "Make the investigation I ask of you, Sancho, and do not worry about any others, for you know nothing about the colures, lines, parallels, zodiacs, ecliptics, poles, solstices, equinoxes, planets ... which are the measures of which the celestial and terrestrial spheres are composed. But if you had that knowledge, or part of it, you would clearly see how many parallels we have cut, how many signs seen, and what constel-

[51] *Op. cit.*, p. 656.

lations we have left behind and are now leaving. Once more I ask you, feel and fish!'' Sancho obeys, raises his head, looks at his master and says: ''Either the test is false or we haven't got where your Worship says.'' [52]

Clearly, the sub-universe of scientific interpretation of the world clashes here with that of common sense. But we do need the activity of enchanters to reconcile them. There remains still the possibility outlined by the great methodologist Sancho: the test might be false. If the theory that all lice die when the ship crosses the equinoctial line is an empirical law, and if it turns out that the line has been crossed indeed, although lice are found, then the law has been invalidated by this single contradictory fact and has to be eliminated from the corpus of science and to be replaced by a better founded one. This is so because the closed sub-universe of scientific reality, although necessarily different from that of common sense, of everyday life is, also necessarily, tied to the process of empirical verification within the common-sense world in which we live and which we take for granted as our paramount reality. On the other hand, our seeing with our own eyes Rosinante and Dappel is no objection to the scientific requirement of ascertaining our location within the universe in terms of the scientific realities of colures, lines, ecliptics, etc. And if it turns out that our seeing Rosinante was just a delusion, a mere appearance or phantom, then the scientific explanation, in order to be valid and real in terms of the sub-universe of science, has to keep open, if not to explain, the *possibility* of such delusion within the paramount reality of common sense. But still more interesting is the insight that also the fictional sub-universe of Don Quixote knows ''matters of fact'' and beliefs, permitting controlled analysis and empirical verification and that it is compatible or incompatible with the sub-universe of science to the same extent as our world of common sense. To be sure, in terms of the latter the ''matters of fact'' in the world of Don Quixote's fictitious space, in which we can travel several thousand miles in the twinkling of an eye, is still a location within the whole universe, the same universe which can be described in terms of the scientific system of colures, lines, ecliptics, etc.

The most penetrating analysis of the problem of delusion and

[52] *Op. cit.*, p. 659.

perception and of intersubjectivity as a constitutive element of reality can be found in the chapter which describes the voyage of Don Quixote and Sancho Panza on Clavileño, the wooden horse. Unfortunately, space does not permit a detailed description of the events at the Court of the Duke and the Duchess, who, by establishing a "let's pretend" world, carefully prepare this extraordinary adventure, which, in my opinion, constitutes the acme of the saga of Don Quixote. Don Quixote is advised that a wooden horse, Clavileño, has been sent by a magician in order to carry the knight and his squire through the air to a distant kingdom where an afflicted lady has to be re-instated in her rights. Don Quixote and Sancho are installed on the back of the wooden horse and blindfolded. As instructed, the knight turns the wooden peg which supposedly sets the horse in motion, and the voyage begins. In the most refined way, devices are prepared to make the delusion of flying plausible to our travelers, who, of course, do not leave the ground. People shout: "Now you are beginning to mount and soar to the astonishment of all of us below!" "Now you are in the air already, cleaving it more swiftly than an arrow!" [53] Sancho, still thinking in terms of common sense, wonders: "How can they say we're flying so high when their voices reach us here, and they seem to be speaking just beside us?" "Pay no attention to that," answers Don Quixote, "for as these matters of flights are out of the ordinary course of things, you will see and hear what you please a thousand miles away." Rightly Don Quixote points out that the scheme of interpretation in terms of common-sense reality is no longer applicable to situations, which by transcending this reality, void the axiomatic foundations of all possible explanations valid within the sub-universe just left. Blinded or blindfolded as we are when plunging into the realm of the transcendental, we cannot check the testimony of our fellow - men by our own sense perceptions. It is the same problem which, nearly at the same time as Cervantes, Shakespeare has dealt with in the grandiose scene in *King Lear* when the blinded Gloucester is induced by Edgar to believe that he has jumped from the cliff of Dover to end his life but survived.[54]

Don Quixote, on his immovable horse, feels a breeze striking

[53] *Op. cit.*, p. 730.
[54] IV, 6.

him, caused by bellows operated by the duke's servants; he feels warmth, thanks to pieces of tow easily lit by them. Applying this scientific knowledge to explain his sense impressions in terms of the realm of phantasy, Don Quixote tells Sancho his conclusion that they must have reached the third region of the air, the region of fire where lightnings and thunderbolts are prepared. Sancho decides to take off the bandage covering his eyes, when an explosion occurs, after which the travelers find themselves again at their starting point. The Duke and the Duchess have with delight followed the dialogue of the travelers during their voyage and are, after its end, eager to learn from them what they experienced while riding Clavileño. They are exactly in the position of a modern psychologist in the laboratory who experiments with his subjects, using the so-called auto-kinetic phenomenon. The well-known psychologist Muzafer Sherif, for instance, instructs his subjects that in the darkened laboratory a light (which is physically stationary, of course) will move to the right or left as the case may be; thereafter he checks the answer given by the individual and finally repeats the same experiment in group-situations, in which each subject reports his judgement aloud, thus influencing the others' statements and being influenced by them. First Sancho has to report, and his story resembles very much a wild science-fiction tale of our times. He maintains among other things that they have reached the celestial constellation Capricorn and that he played for an hour with the "seven she-goats" of which it is composed, while Clavileño waited for him, etc. But Don Quixote was with him. As in Professor Sherif's experiment, he heard Sancho's tale. Can he confirm it? "As all these matters and all such happenings are out of the order of nature," he says, "it is no wonder that Sancho says what he does. I can only answer for myself".[55] In order to reach a celestial constellation they would have had to pass beyond the region of fire. They may have touched it, but it is unbelievable that they have passed it. This cannot be without being scorched. "So seeing that we are not burned," Don Quixote concludes, "either Sancho is lying or Sancho is dreaming." It is highly interesting that Don Quixote, who is fully aware that the whole adventure is out of the order of nature, refers to this very order of nature to establish

[55] Op. cit., p. 733.

the premises of his perfectly logical conclusion. Would it not be possible that the wizards who constructed Clavileño permitted the crossing of the fiery region without being burned? This is a very important point: in order to explain the inconsistencies between two sub-universes, we have to resort to the interpretational rules constitutive of a third one, although we know very well that either realm is separated from the other and irreducible to the third. But Don Quixote still keeps open the possibility of Sancho's having been dreaming. He knows from his own vision in the cave of Montesinos how difficult it is to establish the border line between fiction and reality. He approaches Sancho and whispers in his ear: "Sancho, if you want me to believe what you saw in the sky, I wish you to accept my account of what I saw in the Cave of Montesinos. I say no more." [56]

Miguel Unamuno, in his wonderful commentary on Don Quixote, interprets this statement of the knight as the expression of the highest magnanimity of his candid soul, since Don Quixote is well convinced that what he experienced in the cave of Montesinos was true and what Sancho tells cannot be true. But another interpretation is possible. Don Quixote is convinced that only the experiencing self can judge upon which sub-universe it has bestowed the accent of reality. Intersubjective experience, communication, sharing of something in common presupposes, thus, in the last analysis faith in the Other's truthfulness, animal faith in the sense of Santayana; it presupposes that I take for granted the Other's possibility of bestowing upon one of the innumerable sub-universes the accent of reality, and on the other hand, that he, the Other, takes for granted that I, too, have open possibilities for defining what is my dream, my phantasy, my real life. This is the last insight into the intersubjective dialectic of reality, it seems to me, and therefore the climax in the analysis of this problem in Cervantes' work.

This is also the turning point in the personal tragedy of Don Quixote. With the explosion of Clavileño – or better with the impossibility of establishing intercommunication in the sub-universe of phantasy – he loses his magic power of self-enchantment. Faced with Sancho's lies he feels the hybris he committed

---

[56] *Op. cit.*, p. 735.

in intermingling reality and phantasy in his recital of his adventures in the cave – the terms "reality" and "phantasy," here used from the point of view of the reality of Don Quixote's private world. He feels that he has transgressed the self-established frontiers of reality of his private province and that he has indulged within its limits in dreams, intermingling thus two realms of reality and sinning against the spirit of truth, the defense of which is the first task of the knight errant. When he returned from the Cave of Montesinos, Don Quixote spoke like his younger brother Segismundo in Calderon's "La Vida es Sueño": "God pardon you my friends," says Don Quixote, "for you have robbed me of the sweetest existence and most delightful vision any human being ever enjoyed or beheld. Now, indeed, I positively know that the pleasures of this life pass like a shadow and a dream." [57] Yet the transcendental experience that life might be a dream does not only put in question the common-sense reality of everyday life but of any sub-universe taken for granted so far. The true tragedy for Don Quixote is his discovery that even his private sub-universe, the realm of chivalry, might be just a dream and that its pleasures pass like shadows. This creates not only a conflict of consciousness which thus becomes, in Hegel's words, an "unhappy" one, but also of conscience, especially so when the Clavileño adventure proves that even Sanchos are capable of intermingling elements of dreams with their reality of everyday life. Don Quixote's insight that only mutual faith in the Other's terms of reality guarantees intercommunication, his appeal to Sancho to believe his visions if he wants his own to be believed, is a kind of declaration of bankruptcy; and the knight's final words on this occasion. "I say no more," heighten the tragedy of this unhappy consciousness and conscience. It is his bad faith which in the remaining chapters leads to his downfall and the destruction of his sub-universe. He becomes aware of the reality of everyday life, and no enchanter helps him to transform it. His capacity to interpret the common-sense reality in terms of his private universe is broken. Whereas the disenchantment of Dulcinea fails, his own succeeds completely. The great process of disillusionment consists in a piecemeal withdrawal of the

[57] Op. cit., p. 614.

accent of reality from his private sub-universe, the world of chivalry. This world – to revert to William James' statement with which this study opened – clashed finally with the realities of everyday life to such an extent that this mind had to make the choice of which to stand by. After having maintained vigorously his original choice through all his adventures, after having developed a scientific system – or even perhaps a kind of theology – of the magic activities of the enchanters, whose mission is to reconcile the contradictory schemes of interpretations, he loses faith in this fundamental principle of his metaphysics and cosmogony. He finds himself at the end a homecomer to a world to which he does not belong, enclosed in everyday reality as in a prison, and tortured by the most cruel jailer: the common-sense reason which is conscious of its own limits. The intrusion of the transcendental into this world of everyday life is either denied or dissimulated by common reason. But it shows its invincible force in the experience of all of us that the world of everyday life with its things and occurrences, its causal connections of natural laws, its social facts and institutions is just imposed upon us, that we can understand and master it only to a very limited extent, that the future remains open, undisclosed and unascertainable, and that our only hope and guidance is the belief that we will come to terms with this world for all good and practical purposes if we behave as others behave, if we take for granted what others believe beyond question. All this presupposes our faith that things will continue to be what they have been so far and that what our experience of them has taught us will also stand the test in the future. Having lost with his knight errantry his heavenly mission, Don Quixote has to prepare himself after his spiritual death for his physical end. And so he dies, no longer Don Quixote de la Mancha, but Alonso Quixano the Good, a man who considers himself of clear judgment, free from the misty shadows of ignorance with which his dwelling in the province of phantasy has obscured it.[58] Samson Carrasco, in his epitaph, says of him that he lived as a fool and yet died wise. But does not the meaning of wisdom and foolishness depend upon the sub-universe within which alone these yardsticks are valid? What is foolishness, what

[58] *Op. cit.*, p. 936.

wisdom in the whole universe which is the sum total of all of our sub-universes? "We have only to commend ourselves to God and let fortune take what course it will," says Sancho,[59] who, in spite of all temptations of the transcendental, remains deeply rooted in the heritage of common sense.

[59] *Ibid.*, p. 169.

MAKING MUSIC TOGETHER

A STUDY IN SOCIAL RELATIONSHIP

I

Music is a meaningful context which is not bound to a conceptual scheme. Yet this meaningful context can be communicated. The process of communication between composer and listener normally requires an intermediary: an individual performer or a group of coperformers. Among all these participants there prevail social relations of a highly complicated structure.

To analyze certain elements of this structure is the purpose of this paper. The discussion is not aimed at problems commonly relegated to the realm of the so-called sociology of music, although it is believed that an investigation of the social relationships among the participants in the musical process is a prerequisite for any research in this field; nor is it concerned with a phenomenology of musical experience, although some elementary observations regarding the structure of music will have to be made. The chief interest of our analysis consists in the particular character of all social interactions connected with the musical process: they are doubtless meaningful to the actor as well as to the addressee, but this meaning structure is not capable of being expressed in conceptual terms; they are founded upon communication, but not *primarily* upon a semantic system used by the communicator as a scheme of expression and by his partner as a scheme of interpretation.[1] For this very reason it can be hoped that a study of the social relationships connected with the musical process may lead to some insights valid for many other forms of social intercourse, perhaps even to illumination of a certain aspect

[1] The system of musical notation, as will be shown, has quite another function and a merely secondary one.

of the structure of social interaction as such that has not so far attracted from social scientists the attention it deserves. This introductory statement requires some clarification.

When sociologists speak of social interaction they usually have in mind a set of interdependent actions of several human beings, mutually related by the meaning which the actor bestows upon his action and which he supposes to be understood by his partner. To use Max Weber's terminology, these actions have to be oriented in their course with reference to one another. In studying the process of communication as such, most sociologists have taken as a model either the interplay of significative gestures or language in the broadest sense of this term. G. H. Mead, for example, finds that two wrestlers communicate with each other by a "conversation of gestures" which enables either of the participants to anticipate the other's behavior and to orient his own behavior by means of such anticipation.[2] We may also say that two chess players who both know the functional significance of each chessman in general, as well as within the unique concrete constellation at any given moment of a particular game, communicate their thoughts to each other in terms of the "vocabulary" and "syntax" of the scheme of expression and interpretation common to both of them, which is determined by the body of the "rules of the game." In the case of ordinary speech or the use of written symbols, it is assumed that each partner interprets his own behavior as well as that of the other in conceptual terms which can be translated and conveyed to the other partner by way of a common semantic system.

In any of these cases the existence of a semantic system – be it the "conversation of significant gestures," the "rules of the game," or "language proper" – is simply presupposed as something given from the outset and the problem of "significance" remains unquestioned. The reason for this is quite clear: in the social world into which we are born, language (in the broadest sense) is admittedly the paramount vehicle of communication; its conceptual structure and its power of typification make it the outstanding tool for the conveying of meaning. There is even a strong tendency in contemporary thought to identify meaning with

[2] G. H. Mead, *Mind, Self, and Society*, Chicago, 1937, pp. 14, 63, 253ff.

its semantic expression and to consider language, speech, symbols, significant gestures, as the fundamental condition of social intercourse as such. Even Mead's highly original endeavor to explain the origin of language by an interplay of significant gestures – his famous example of the dogfight – starts from the supposition that a prelinguistic "conversation" of "attitudes" is possible. It is not necessary to accept Mead's basic position of "social behaviorism" in order to admit that, as has so often happened, he has seen a crucial problem more clearly than others. Nevertheless, the solution he offers only appears to remove the difficulties connected with the basic issue, namely, whether the communicative process is really the foundation of all possible social relationships, or whether, on the contrary, all communication presupposes the existence of some kind of social interaction which, though it is an indispensable condition of all possible communication, does not enter the communicative process and is not capable of being grasped by it. It is currently rather fashionable to dismiss problems of this kind with a haughty reference to the question of the priority of the chicken or the egg. Such an attitude not only reflects an unfamiliarity with the philosophical issue discussed by the Schoolmen under the heading of priority, but also constitutes a self-made obstacle to a serious analysis of the various problems of foundation important especially for the social sciences.

As far as the question under scrutiny is concerned, the concrete researches of many sociologists and philosophers have aimed at certain forms of social intercourse which necessarily precede all communication. Wiese's "contact-situations," Scheler's perceptual theory of the alter ego, to a certain extent Cooley's concept of the face-to-face relationship, Malinowski's interpretation of speech as originating within the situation determined by social interaction, Sartre's basic concept of "looking at the Other and being looked at by the Other" (le regard), all these are just a few examples of the endeavor to investigate what might be called the "mutual tuning-in relationship" upon which alone all communication is founded. It is precisely this mutual tuning-in relationship by which the "I" and the "Thou" are experienced by both participants as a "We" in vivid presence.

Instead of entering here into the complicated philosophical

analysis of this problem,[3] it may be permissible to refer to a series of well-known phenomena in the social world in which this pre-communicative social relationship comes to the foreground. Mead's example of wrestlers has already been mentioned. It is typical for a set of similar interrelated activities such as the relationship between pitcher and catcher, tennis players, fencers, and so on; we find the same features in marching together, dancing together, making love together, or making music together, and this last-named activity will serve as an example for analysis in the following pages. It is hoped that this analysis will in some measure contribute to clarification of the structure of the mutual tuning-in relationship, which originates in the possibility of living together simultaneously in specific dimensions of time. It is also hoped that the study of the particular communicative situation within the musical process will shed some light on the non-conceptual aspect involved in any kind of communication.

II

Certain elements of the social structure of the musical process were analyzed in one of the later writings of the famous French sociologist, Maurice Halbwachs.[4] The paper in question deserves special attention because it was written as a kind of introduction to a major study on the nature of time, which was unfortunately never completed owing to the author's tragic death in the concentration camp of Buchenwald in July 1944.[5]

Halbwachs' basic position is well known. He assumed that all kinds of memory are determined by a social framework and that individual memory cannot be conceived of without the assumption of a collective memory from which all individual recollection derives. This basic principle – which it is not our concern to criticize here – was applied to the problem of musical communication because the author felt that the very structure of music – its development within the flux of time, its detachment

[3] Mead's *Philosophy of the Present*, Chicago, 1932, is just one example of how investigations of this kind have to be carried out and where they lead.

[4] Maurice Halbwachs, "La mémoire collective chez les musiciens," in *Revue philosophique*, March-April 1939, pp. 136–65.

[5] Four chapters from the manuscript were published posthumously under the title, "Mémoire et société," in *L' Année sociologique*, 3rd Series, Vol. I, Paris, 1949, pp. 11–197.

from anything that lasts, its realization by re-creation – offers an excellent opportunity for demonstrating that there is no other possibility of preserving a set of recollections with all their shades and details except by recourse to the collective memory. In other words, Halbwachs was primarily concerned with analyzing the social structure of music. Curiously enough, he divided the realm of music into two distinct parts: music as experienced by the educated musician and music as experienced by the layman. With regard to the former, Halbwachs came to the conclusion that it is first of all the possibility of translating music into visual symbols – that is, the system of musical notation – which makes transmission of music possible. To be sure, the signs of musical notation are not images of the sounds. They are, however, means of expressing in a conventional language all the commands which the musician must obey if he wants to reproduce a piece of music properly. The conventional character of the signs of musical notation and their combination consists in the fact that they have meaning merely by continuous reference to the group which invented and adopted them. This group, the "society" of educated musicians, lives in a world exclusively filled with sounds and is interested in nothing else but creating or listening to a combination of sounds. Even the invention of new combinations of sounds is possible only within the framework of the socially conditioned musical language (which, for Halbwachs, was identical with the system of musical notation). The creative act of the composer is merely a discovery in the same world of sounds that is accessible exclusively to the society of musicians. It is precisely because the composer accepts the conventions of this society and because he penetrates more deeply into them than others that he can make his discoveries. The musical language is not an instrument invented afterward in order to put down and to transmit to other musicians what one of them has spontaneously invented. On the contrary, it is this very language which creates music.

This is roughly Halbwachs' main argument for the social character of the musician's music. Yet the child or the musically uneducated person learns nursery rhymes, anthems, popular songs, dance or march melodies by rote without any knowledge of musical notation. How is this possible and how can this kind of memory for sound combinations be referred to the collective memory? Halbwachs' answer is that the layman's memory of musical events is also founded upon the collective memory but always attached to metamusical experiences.[6] The melody of a song is remembered because the words – a social product – are remembered. As for dances or marches or other pieces of music dissociated from words, it is the rhythm of marching, dancing, speaking, that serves as the carrier of the musical recollection. Yet rhythm does not exist in nature; it, too, is a result of our living in society. The insulated individual could not discover rhythm. No evidence is offered for this statement (which I believe to be wrong) except reference to the rhythmical character of work songs and of our speech. Both words and rhythms are of social origin and so, consequently, are the layman's musical experiences. But they refer to a world in which other than exclusively sonorous events exist and to a society not exclusively interested in musical texture. So much for Halbwachs.

Interesting as Halbwachs' analysis is, it suffers from various shortcomings. In the first place, it seems to me that the distinction between a musician's music and music accessible to the layman is without any foundation in fact. But postponing the discussion of this question and restricting ourselves for the time being to the province of music allegedly accessible only to the educated musician, the following objections to Halbwachs' theory must be raised: (1) He identifies the musical thought with its communication. (2) He identifies musical communication with musical language which to him is the system of musical notation. (3) He identifies musical notation with the social background of the musical process.

In regard to the first objection, it is clear that from the point of view of the composer a musical thought may be conceived without any intention of communication. This thought may be a perfect piece of music, having its specific meaning structure; it may be remembered at will without being translated into actual sounds or into the visible form of notation. This is, of course, not a particularity of the musical process. It has been said that Raphael would have been one of the greatest painters even if he had been born without arms. In general, all kinds of mental ac-

---

[6] This term is not used by Halbwachs, but probably renders what he meant.

tivities performed in phantasy may be perfectly meaningful and capable of being mentally reproduced within the solitude of the individual consciousness. All our unexpressed thoughts, our day dreams as well as projects for future action never carried out, show these features. But any kind of communication between man and his fellow-man and therefore the communication of musical thoughts presupposes an event or a series of events in the outer world which functions, on the one hand, as a scheme of expression of the communicator's thought and, on the other hand, as a scheme of interpretation of such thought by the addressee. Musical thoughts can be transmitted to others either by the mechanics of audible sound or by the symbols of musical notation.

It is hard to understand why Halbwachs regarded only the latter as the appropriate form of musical communication. Obviously he took as a model of his analysis the situation in which the composer has to communicate his musical idea to the performer by way of a system of visible signs before the performer can translate these ideas into sounds to be grasped by the listener. But this procedure has nothing to do with the particularities of musical communication as such; it is a more or less technical question. We may perfectly well understand an improvisation executed by one or several instrumentalists. Or we may, with Tovey, foresee a revolution in the process of musical communication by means of the microscopic study of phonographic records. "There is nothing to prevent the individual production of music directly in terms of the phonographic needle. That is to say, the composer, untrammeled by the technique of instruments, will prescribe all producible timbre in whatever pitches and rhythms he pleases, and will have no more direct cooperation with the craftsman who models the phonographic wave-lines, than the violinist may with Stradivarius." [7]

Musical notation is, therefore, just one among several vehicles of communicating musical thought. But musical notation is by no means identical with musical language. Its semantic system is of quite another kind than that of ideograms, letters, or mathematical or chemical symbols. The ideogram refers immediately to the represented concept and so does the mathematical or chemical

[7] Donald Francis Tovey, "Music," in *Encyclopaedia Britannica*, 14th ed.

symbol. The written word in our alphabetic languages refers to the sound of the spoken word and through it as an intermediary to the concept it conveys. As stated above, the meaning of a musical process cannot be related to a conceptual scheme, and the particular function of musical notation today as well as in its historical development reflects this situation. The musical sign is nothing but instruction to the performer to produce by means of his voice or his instrument a sound of a particular pitch and duration, giving in addition, at certain historical periods, suggestions as to tempo, dynamics, and expression, or directions as to the connection with other sounds (by such devices as ties, slurs, and the like). All these elements of the tonal material can only be approximately prescribed and the way to obtain the indicated effect is left to the performer. "The composer's specific indications are themselves not always a part of his original creation but rather one musician's message to another about it, a hint about how to secure in performance a convincing transmission of the work's feeling content without destroying its emotional and intellectual community," says a well-known composer and critic.[8] And the conductor, Furtwängler, is certainly right in stating that the composer's text "cannot give any indication as to the really intended volume of a *forte*, the really intended speed of a *tempo*, since every *forte* and every *tempo* has to be modified in practice in accordance with the place of the performance and the setting and the strength of the performing group" and that "the expression marks have intentionally a merely symbolic value with respect to the whole work and are not intended to be valid for the single instrument, wherefore an '*ff*' for the bassoon has quite another meaning than for the trombone." [9]

Thus, all musical notation remains of necessity vague and open to manifold interpretations, and it is up to the reader or performer to decipher the hints in the score and to define the approximations. These limits vary widely in the course of the historical development of musical culture. The more closely we approach the present in the study of the history of music, the lower the level of the general musical culture of performers and

[8] Virgil Thompson, *The Art of Judging Music*, New York, 1948, p. 296.
[9] Wilhelm Furtwängler, "Interpretation – eine musikalische Schicksalfrage," in *Das Atlantisbuch der Musik*, Zurich, 1934, pp. 609ff.

of listeners, and the stronger the tendency of the composer to make his system of notation as exact and precise as possible, that is, to limit more and more the performer's freedom of interpretation. To be sure, all signs of musical notation are conventional; but, as has been shown, the system of musical notation is more or less accidental to the process of musical communication. A social theory of music therefore does not have to be founded on the conventional character of the visual signs but rather on the sum total of what we have just called musical culture against the background of which the reader's or performer's interpretation of these signs takes place.

III

To make this web of social relationships called musical culture clearer, let us imagine a lonely performer of a piece of music sitting at his piano before the score of a sonata by a minor master of the nineteenth century which, we assume, is entirely unknown to him. Furthermore, we assume that our piano player is equally proficient as a technician and sight reader and that consequently no mechanical or other external obstacle will hinder the flux of his performance.

Yet, having hardly made these two assumptions, we hesitate. Are they indeed compatible with each other? Can we really maintain that the sonata in question is *entirely* unknown to our performer? He could not be an accomplished technician and sight reader without having attained a certain level of musical culture enabling him to read offhand a piece of music of the *type* of that before him. Consequently, although this particular sonata and perhaps all the other works of this particular composer might be unknown to him, he will nevertheless have a well-founded knowledge of the type of musical form called "sonata within the meaning of nineteenth century piano music," of the type of themes and harmonies used in such compositions of that period, of the expressional contents he may expect to find in them – in sum, of the typical "style" in which music of this kind is written and in which it has to be executed. Even before starting to play or to read the first chord our musician is referred to a more or less clearly organized, more or less coherent, more or less distinct set

of his previous experiences, which constitute in their totality a
kind of preknowledge of the piece of music at hand. To be sure,
this preknowledge refers merely to the *type* to which this individual piece of music belongs and not to its particular and unique
individuality. But the player's general preknowledge of its
typicality becomes the scheme of reference for his interpretation
of its particularity. This scheme of reference determines, in a
general way, the player's anticipations of what he may or may not
find in the composition before him. Such anticipations are more
or less empty; they may be fulfilled and justified by the musical
events he will experience when he starts to play the sonata or
they may "explode" and be annihilated.

In more general terms, the player approaching a so-called
unknown piece of music does so from a historically – in one's own
case, autobiographically – determined situation, determined by
his stock of musical experiences at hand in so far as they are
typically relevant to the anticipated novel experience before
him.[10] This stock of experiences refers indirectly to all his past
and present fellow-men whose acts or thoughts have contributed
to the building up of his knowledge. This includes what he has
learned from his teachers, and his teachers from their teachers;
what he has taken in from other players' execution; and what he
has appropriated from the manifestations of the musical thought
of the composer. Thus, the bulk of musical knowledge – as of
knowledge in general – is socially derived. And within this
socially derived knowledge there stands out the knowledge transmitted from those upon whom the prestige of authenticity and
authority has been bestowed, that is, from the great masters
among the composers and the acknowledged interpreters of their
work. Musical knowledge transmitted by them is not only socially
derived; it is also socially approved [11] being regarded as authentic

[10] All this is by no means limited to the situation under scrutiny. Indeed, our
analysis has so far been merely an application of Husserl's masterful investigations
into the structure of our experience. According to him the factual world is always
experienced as a world of preconstituted types. To embark upon the importance of
this discovery by Husserl, especially for the concept of type, so fundamental for all
social sciences, is not within the scope of the present paper. This theory has been
touched upon in Husserl's *Ideas: General Introduction to Pure Phenomenology*,
translated by W. R. Boyce Gibson, London-New York, 1931 § 47, p. 149. and has been
fully developed in his *Erfahrung und Urteil*, Prague, 1939, pp. 35ff., 139–43, 394–403.

[11] With regard to the concepts of socially derived and socially approved knowledge,
see *supra*, "The Well-Informed Citizen," especially pp. 131 ff.

and therefore more qualified to become a pattern for others than knowledge originating elsewhere.

IV

In the situation we have chosen to investigate – the actual performance of a piece of music – the genesis of the stock of knowledge at hand with all its hidden social references is, so to speak, prehistoric. The web of socially derived and socially approved knowledge constitutes merely the setting for the main social relationship into which our piano player (and also any listener or mere reader of music) will enter: that with the composer of the sonata before him. It is the grasping of the composer's musical thought and its interpretation by re-creation which stand in the center of the player's field of consciousness or, to use a phenomenological term, which become "thematic" for his ongoing activity. This thematic kernel stands out against the horizon of preacquired knowledge, which knowledge functions as a scheme of reference and interpretation for the grasping of the composer's thought. It is now necessary to describe the structure of this social relationship between composer and beholder,[12] but before entering into its analysis it might be well to forestall a possible misunderstanding. It is by no means our thesis that a work of music (or of art in general) cannot be understood except by reference to its individual author or to the circumstances – biographical or other – in which he created this particular work. It is certainly not a prerequisite for the understanding of the musical content of the so-called Moonlight Sonata to take cognizance of the silly anecdotes which popular belief attaches to the creation of this work; it is not even indispensable to know that the sonata was composed by a man called Beethoven who lived then and there and went through such and such personal experiences. Any work of art, once accomplished, exists as a meaningful entity independent of the personal life of its creator.[13] The social relationship between composer and beholder as it is understood here is established exclusively by the fact that a be-

[12] The term "beholder" shall include the player, listener, and reader of music.
[13] This problem has been discussed for the realm of poetry by E. M. W. Tillyard and C. S. Lewis in their witty and profound book, *The Personal Heresy, a Controversy*, London-New York, 1939.

holder of a piece of music participates in and to a certain extent re-creates the experiences of the – let us suppose, anonymous – fellow-man who created this work not only as an expression of his musical thoughts but with communicative intent.

For our purposes a piece of music may be defined [14] – very roughly and tentatively, indeed – as a meaningful arrangement of tones in inner time. It is the occurrence in inner time, Bergson's *durée*, which is the very form of existence of music. The flux of tones unrolling in inner time is an arrangement meaningful to both the composer and the beholder, because and in so far as it evokes in the stream of consciousness participating in it an interplay of recollections, retentions, protentions, and anticipations which interrelate the successive elements. To be sure, the sequence of tones occurs in the irreversible direction of inner time, in the direction, as it were, from the first bar to the last. But this irreversible flux is not irretrievable. The composer, by the specific means of his art,[15] has arranged it in such a way that the consciousness of the beholder is led to refer what he actually hears to what he anticipates will follow and also to what he has just been hearing and what he has heard ever since this piece of music began. The hearer, therefore, listens to the ongoing flux of music, so to speak, not only in the direction from the first to the last bar but simultaneously in a reverse direction back to the first one.[16]

It is essential for our problem to gain a clearer understanding of the time dimension in which music occurs. It was stated above

[14] An excellent survey of philosophical theories of music can be found in Susanne K. Langer, *Philosophy in a New Key*, Cambridge, 1942, Ch. 8, "On Significance in Music," and Ch. 9, "The Genesis of Artistic Import," although the author's own position seems unsatisfactory. It may be summed up in the following quotation: "Music has all the earmarks of a true symbolism, except one: the existence of an *assigned connotation* . . . It is a limited idiom like an artificial language, *only even less successful; for music at its highest, though clearly a symbolic form, is an unconsummated symbol.* Articulation is its life but not assertion; expressiveness, not expression."

[15] Some of these specific means are essential to any kind of music, others belong merely to a particular musical culture. Rhythm, melody, tonal harmony, technique of diminution, and the so-called forms based on what Tovey calls the larger harmony, such as Sonata, Rondo, Variations, and so on, are certainly characteristic of the musical culture of the nineteenth century. It may be hoped that intensified research in the phenomenology of musical experience will shed some light upon the difficult problem as to which of these means of meaningful arrangement of tones is essential to music in general, regardless of what its particular historical setting may be.

[16] This insight has been formulated in an unsurpassable way by St. Augustine in Book XI, Ch. 38, of his *Confessions*.

that the inner time, the *durée*, is the very form of existence of music. Of course, playing an instrument, listening to a record, reading a page of music all these are events occurring in outer time, the time that can be measured by metronomes and clocks, that is, the time that the musician "counts" in order to assure the correct "tempo." But to make clear why we consider inner time the very medium within which the musical flow occurs, let us imagine that the slow and the fast movement of a symphony each fill a twelve-inch record. Our watches show that the playing of either record takes about three and a half minutes. This is a fact which might possibly interest the program maker of a broadcasting station. To the beholder it means nothing. To him it is not true that the time he lived through while listening to the slow movement was of "equal length" with that which he dedicated to the fast one. While listening he lives in a dimension of time incomparable with that which can be subdivided into homogeneous parts. The outer time is measurable; there are pieces of equal length; there are minutes and hours and the length of the groove to be traversed by the needle of the record player. There is no such yardstick for the dimension of inner time the listener lives in; there is no equality between its pieces, if pieces there were at all.[17] It may come as a complete surprise to him that the main theme of the second movement of Beethoven's Pianoforte Sonata in d-minor, Op. 31, No. 2, takes as much time in the mere clock sense – namely, one minute – as the last movement of the same sonata up to the end of the exposition.[18]

The preceding remarks serve to clarify the particular social relationship between composer and beholder. Although separated by hundreds of years, the latter participates with quasi simultaneity in the former's stream of consciousness by performing with him step by step the ongoing articulation of his musical thought. The beholder, thus, is united with the composer by a time dimension common to both, which is nothing other than a derived form of the vivid present shared by the partners in a

[17] We do not need the reference to the specific experience of listening to music in order to understand the incommensurability of inner and outer time. The hand of our watch may run equally over half the dial, whether we wait before the door of a surgeon operating on a person dear to us or whether we are having a good time in congenial company. All these are well-known facts.

[18] Donald Francis Tovey, *Beethoven*, London-New York, 1945, p. 57.

genuine face-to-face relation [19] such as prevails between speaker and listener.

But is this reconstruction of a vivid present, this establishment of a quasi simultaneity, specific to the relationship between the stream of consciousness of the composer and that of the beholder? Can it not also be found in the relationship between the reader of a letter with its writer, the student of a scientific book with its author, the high school boy who learns the demonstration of the rule of the hypotenuse with Pythagoras? Certainly, in all these cases the single phases of the author's articulated thought are polythetically – that is, step by step – coperformed or reperformed by the recipient, and thus a quasi simultaneity of both streams of thought takes place. The reader of a scientific book, for instance, builds up word by word the meaning of a sentence, sentence by sentence that of a paragraph, paragraph by paragraph that of a chapter. But once having coperformed these polythetic steps of constituting the conceptual meaning of this sentence (paragraph, chapter), the reader may grasp the outcome of this constitutive process, the resulting conceptual meaning, in a single glance – monothetically, as Husserl puts it [20] – that is, independently of the polythetic steps in which and by which this meaning has been constituted. In the same way I may grasp monothetically the meaning of the Pythagorean theorem $a^2 + b^2 = c^2$, without restarting to perform the single mental operations of deriving it step by step from certain assured premises, and I may do so even if I have forgotten how to demonstrate the theorem.

The meaning of a musical work,[21] however, is essentially of a polythetical structure. It cannot be grasped monothetically. It consists in the articulated step-by-step occurrence in inner time, in the very polythetic constitutional process itself. I may give a name to a specific piece of music, calling it "Moonlight Sonata" or "Ninth Symphony"; I may even say, "These were variations with a finale in the form of a passacaglia," or characterize, as

---

[19] This term, here and in the following paragraphs, is not used in the sense that Charles Horton Cooley used it in *Social Organization*, New York, 1937, Chs. 3–5; it signifies merely that the participants in such a relation share time and space while it lasts. An analysis of Cooley's concept can be found *supra*, "The Homecomer," pp. 109 ff.

[20] Husserl, *Ideas* (cited above) § 118, 119, pp. 334ff.

[21] Also of other time-objects such as dance or poetry (see footnote 22).

certain program notes are prone to do, the particular mood or emotion this piece of music is supposed to have evoked in me. But the musical content itself, its very meaning, can be grasped merely by reimmersing oneself in the ongoing flux, by reproducing thus the articulated musical occurrence as it unfolds in polythetic steps in inner time, a process itself belonging to the dimension of inner time. And it will "take as much time" to reconstitute the work in recollection as to experience it for the first time. In both cases I have to re-establish the quasi simultaneity of my stream of consciousness with that of the composer described herein before.[22]

We have therefore the following situation: two series of events in inner time, one belonging to the stream of consciousness of the composer, the other to the stream of consciousness of the beholder, are lived through in simultaneity, which simultaneity is created by the ongoing flux of the musical process. It is the thesis of the present paper that this sharing of the other's flux of experiences in inner time, this living through a vivid present in common, constitutes what we called in our introductory paragraphs the mutual tuning-in relationship, the experience of the "We," which is at the foundation of all possible communication. The peculiarity of the musical process of communication consists in the essentially polythetic character of the communicated content, that is to say, in the fact that both the flux of the musical events and the activities by which they are communicated, belong to the dimension of inner time. This statement seems to hold good for any kind of music. There is, however, one kind of music – the polyphonic music of the western world – which has the magic power of realizing by its specific musical means the possibility of living simultaneously in two or more fluxes of events. In polyphonic writing each voice has its particular meaning; each represents a series of, so to speak, autarchic musical events; but this flux is designed to roll on in simultaneity with other series of musical events, not less autarchic in themselves, but coexisting

---

[22] This thesis is simply a corollary to the other – that the meaning context of music is not related to a conceptual scheme. A poem, for instance, may *also* have a conceptual content, and this, of course, may be grasped monothetically. I can tell in one or two sentences the story of the ancient mariner, and in fact this is done in the author's gloss. But in so far as the poetical meaning of Coleridge's poem surpasses the conceptual meaning – that is, in so far as it *is* poetry – I can only bring it before my mind by reciting or reading it from beginning to end.

with the former and combining with them by this very simultaneity into a new meaningful arrangement.[23]

So far we have investigated the social relationship between composer and beholder. What we have found to be the outstanding feature of musical communication – that is, the sharing of the ongoing flux of the musical content – holds good whether this process occurs merely in the beholder's recollection,[24] or through his reading the score, or with the help of audible sounds. To believe that the visible signs of musical notation are essential to this process is no more erroneous than to assert, as even Husserl does, that a symphony exists merely in its performance by an orchestra. To be sure, the participation in the process of musical communication by means other than audible sounds requires either a certain natural gift or special training on the part of the beholder. It is the eminent social function of the performer – the singer or player of an instrument – to be the intermediary between composer and listener. By his re-creation of the musical process the performer partakes in the stream of consciousness of the composer as well as of the listener. He thereby enables the latter to become immersed in the particular articulation of the flux of inner time which is the specific meaning of the piece of music in question. It is of no great importance whether performer and listener share together a vivid present in face-to-face relation or whether through the interposition of mechanical devices, such as records, only a quasi simultaneity between the stream of consciousness of the mediator and the listener has been established. The latter case always refers to the former. The difference between the two shows merely that the relationship between performer and audience is subject to all variations of intensity, intimacy, and anonymity. This can be easily seen by imagining the audience as consisting of one single person, a small group of persons in a private room, a crowd filling a big concert hall, or the entirely unknown listeners of a radio performance or a commercially distributed record. In all these circumstances performer and listener

[23] See, for instance, the Brahms song, "Wir wandelten wir zwei zusammen," in the introduction of which the walking together of the two lovers is expressed by the specific musical means of a canon, or the same device used in the Credo of Bach's B-minor Mass for expressing the mystery of the Trinity ("Et in unum").

[24] In this connection, one recalls Brahm's dictum: "If I want to listen to a fine performance of 'Don Giovanni,' I light a good cigar and stretch out on my sofa."

are "tuned-in" to one another, are living together through the same flux, are growing older together while the musical process lasts. This statement applies not only to the fifteen or twenty minutes of measurable outer time required for the performance of this particular piece of music, but primarily to the coperformance in simultaneity of the polythetic steps by which the musical content articulates itself in inner time. Since, however, all performance as an act of communication is based upon a series of events in the outer world – in our case the flux of audible sounds – it can be said that the social relationship between performer and listener is founded upon the common experience of living simultaneously in several dimensions of time.

V

The same situation, the pluridimensionality of time simultaneously lived through by man and fellow-man, occurs in the relationship between two or more individuals making music together, which we are now prepared to investigate. If we accept Max Weber's famous definition, according to which a social relationship is "the conduct of a plurality of persons which according to their subjective meaning are mutually concerned with each other and oriented by virtue of this fact," then both the relationship prevailing between intermediary and listener and that prevailing between coperformers fall under this definition. But there is an important difference between them. The listener's coperforming of the polythetic steps in which the musical content unfolds is merely an internal activity (although as an "action involving the action of Others and being oriented by them in its course" undoubtedly a social action within Weber's definition). The coperformers (let us say a soloist accompanied by a keyboard instrument) have to execute activities gearing into the outer world and thus occurring in spatialized outer time. Consequently, each coperformer's action is oriented not only by the composer's thought and his relationship to the audience but also reciprocally by the experiences in inner and outer time of his fellow performer. Technically, each of them finds in the music sheet before him only that portion of the musical content which the composer has assigned to his instrument for translation into sound. Each of them has, therefore, to take into account what the other has to execute in simultaneity. He has not only to interpret his own part which as such remains necessarily fragmentary, but he has also to anticipate the other player's interpretation of his – the Other's – part and, even more, the Other's anticipations of his own execution. Either's freedom of interpreting the composer's thought is restrained by the freedom granted to the Other. Either has to foresee by listening to the Other, by protentions and anticipations, any turn the Other's interpretation may take and has to be prepared at any time to be leader or follower. Both share not only the inner *durée* in which the content of the music played actualizes itself; each, simultaneously, shares in vivid present the Other's stream of consciousness in immediacy. This is possible because making music together occurs in a true face-to-face relationship – inasmuch as the participants are sharing not only a section of time but also a sector of space. The Other's facial expressions, his gestures in handling his instrument, in short all the activities of performing, gear into the outer world and can be grasped by the partner in immediacy. Even if performed without communicative intent, these activities are interpreted by him as indications of what the Other is going to do and therefore as suggestions or even commands for his own behavior. Any chamber musician knows how disturbing an arrangement that prevents the coperformers from seeing each other can be. Moreover, all the activities of performing occur in outer time, the time which can be measured by counting or the metronome or the beat of the conductor's baton. The coperformers may have recourse to these devices when for one reason or another the flux of inner time in which the musical content unfolds has been interrupted.

Such a close face-to-face relationship can be established in immediacy only among a small number of coperformers. Where a larger number of executants is required, one of them – a song leader, concert master, or continuo player – has to assume the leadership, that is, to establish with each of the performers the contact which they are unable to find with one another in immediacy. Or a nonexecutant, the conductor, has to assume this function. He does so by action in the outer world, and his evocative gestures into which he translates the musical events going on in inner time, replace for each performer the immediate grasping of the expressive activities of all his coperformers.

Our analysis of making music together has been restricted to what Halbwachs calls the musician's music. Yet there is in principle no difference between the performance of a modern orchestra or chorus and people sitting around a campfire and singing to the strumming of a guitar or a congregation singing hymns under the leadership of the organ. And there is no difference in principle between the performance of a string quartet and the improvisations at a jam session of accomplished jazz players. These examples simply give additional support to our thesis that the system of musical notation is merely a technical device and accidental to the social relationship prevailing among the performers. This social relationship is founded upon the partaking in common of different dimensions of time simultaneously lived through by the participants. On the one hand, there is the inner time in which the flux of the musical events unfolds, a dimension in which each performer re-creates in polythetic steps the musical thought of the (possibly anonymous) composer and by which he is also connected with the listener. On the other hand, making music together is an event in outer time, presupposing also a face-to-face relationship, that is, a community of space, and it is this dimension which unifies the fluxes of inner time and warrants their synchronization into a vivid present.

VI

At the beginning of this paper the hope was expressed that the analysis of the social relationship involved in making music together might contribute to a clarification of the tuning-in relationship and the process of communication as such. It appears that all possible communication presupposes a mutual tuning-in relationship between the communicator and the addressee of the communication. This relationship is established by the reciprocal sharing of the Other's flux of experiences in inner time, by living through a vivid present together, by experiencing this togetherness as a "We." Only within this experience does the Other's conduct become meaningful to the partner tuned in on him – that is, the Other's body and its movements can be and are interpreted as a field of expression of events within his inner life. Yet not everything that is interpreted by the partner as an expression of an event in the Other's inner life is meant by the Other to express – that is, to communicate to the partner – such an event. Facial expressions, gait, posture, ways of handling tools and instruments, without communicative intent, are examples of such a situation. The process of communication proper is bound to an occurrence in the outer world, which has the structure of a series of events polythetically built up in outer time. This series of events is intended by the communicator as a scheme of expression open to adequate interpretation by the addressee. Its very polythetic character warrants the simultaneity of the ongoing flux of the communicator's experiences in inner time with the occurrences in the outer world, as well as the simultaneity of these polythetic occurrences in the outer world with the addressee's interpreting experiences in inner time. Communicating with one another presupposes, therefore, the simultaneous partaking of the partners in various dimensions of outer and inner time – in short in growing older together. This seems to be valid for all kinds of communication, the *essentially* polythetic ones as well as those conveying meaning in conceptual terms – that is, those in which the result of the communicative process can be grasped monothetically.

It is hardly necessary to point out that the remarks in the preceding paragraph refer to communication within the face-to-face relationship. It can, however, be shown that all the other forms of possible communication can be explained as derived from this paramount situation. But this, as well as the elaboration of the theory of the tuning-in relationship, must be reserved for another occasion.

MOZART AND THE PHILOSOPHERS

To the memory of Erich Itor Kahn,
musician, philosopher, friend.

Some thirty years ago an outstanding German writer, Friedrich Gundolf, published a book entitled *Caesar: The History of his Glory*. He showed that each century, and even each generation, has formed a different image of the person and character of Julius Caesar, and has interpreted his influence on the destiny of occidental culture in a different way. Not two thousand but hardly two hundred years separate us from Mozart's lifetime, and nevertheless a history of his glory would offer a fascinating topic for an essay in the philosophy of history.

But I have to forego the temptation to demonstrate how each generation has had to rediscover the man Mozart and his work and to reinterpret his position within the main stream of music. My purpose is to examine in a very condensed form the images that three modern philosophers – Hermann Cohen, Søren Kierkegaard, and Wilhelm Dilthey – have formed of Mozart and his art; and these images, as will be shown, are restricted to Mozart's operas. I shall preface that discussion with a few remarks on the relationship between philosophy and music in general, and shall refer briefly to certain views held by the philosophers of the eighteenth century with respect to the operatic art; and I shall close with a consideration of the purely musical means by which Mozart solved the problems of the philosophers in his own way, thereby proving himself to be the greatest philosopher of them all.

I

From the Pythagoreans, from Plato and St. Augustine to Bergson and Santayana, philosophers have concerned themselves with music as one of the ways in which man expresses the basic experience of transcendency constitutive of his place within and his attitude toward the cosmos. Schopenhauer, whose insight into the nature of music still remains unsurpassed in modern occidental thought, summed up his pertinent theory by the statement: "Using common language one might say that music as a whole is the melody to which the whole world furnishes the text." [1] And in the more technical language of his system he explained: "The thing-in-itself, the will, is the subject-matter of any true metaphysics and also the very subject-matter of music: both speak of the same topic in different languages ... We might, therefore, just as well call the world embodied music as embodied will; and this is the reason why music makes every picture, and indeed, every scene of real life and of the world, at once appear with higher significance ... It rests upon this that we are able to set a poem to music as a song, or a perceptible representation as a pantomime, or both as an opera. ... Supposing it were possible to give a perfectly accurate, complete explanation of music, extending even to particulars, that is to say, a detailed repetition in concepts of what it expresses, this would also be a sufficient repetition and explanation of the world in concepts, or at least entirely parallel to such an explanation, and thus it would be true philosophy." [2] To be sure, Schopenhauer's musical ideal, especially in opera, was not Mozart but Rossini. But his statements show clearly the reasons for philosophy's concern with music. Nietzsche, in this respect a true follower of Schopenhauer, said once that he did not care for a philosophy that is not capable of explaining music and love.

What was Mozart's attitude toward philosophy? It can safely be stated that Mozart, in contradistinction to Beethoven, who as a man of wide reading studied Kant, had hardly any knowledge of the writings of philosophers. His education as a prodigy gave him neither time nor opportunity for any occupation with the study of literature in general. Among the few books he left behind at the time of his death there was but one philosophical

---

[1] Schopenhauer, *Philosophische Aphorismen*, Aus dem handschriftlichen Nachlass gesammelt von Otto Weiss, Leipzig, 1924, p. 196.
[2] Schopenhauer, *The World as Will and Idea*, translated by R. B. Haldane and John Kemp, 3 Vols., 6th ed., London, 1907–09, Book III, Section 52, and Book III Supplement, Ch. 34.

work, the *Phaidon* by Moses Mendelssohn, and we do not know
how he obtained it or whether he ever read it. He did, however,
become concerned with certain metaphysical problems, although
in a rather derived form, when, after entering in 1785 one of the
eight lodges of Freemasonry in Vienna, he came into contact with
the man who was leader of that circle, the famous scientist Ignaz
von Born.

It was especially the problem of death which occupied him. In
his last letter to his ailing father, on April 4, 1787, he wrote:
"Since death (properly understood) is the true ultimate purpose
of our life I have for the last two years made myself so well
acquainted with that truest and best friend of mankind that he
has for me not only nothing terrifying any more but much that
is tranquillizing and consoling. And I thank God that he bestowed upon me the good fortune to provide the opportunity
(you understand me) of recognizing death as a key to our true
blessedness." This is a statement of a truly philosophical mind
which has dealt for a lifetime with the melody to which the whole
world furnishes the text.

But was Mozart familiar with the theories of music held by
the philosophers of his day? There is reason to believe that he
became acquainted with them during his stay in Paris in 1778.
His protector, Baron Friedrich Melchior Grimm, was a close
friend of d'Alembert, Diderot, Holbach, and, for a certain time,
Jean Jacques Rousseau. It may be useful to mention briefly
some of the significant views these philosophers of the French
Enlightenment had on music.

Nearly all of them were concerned with this topic. But music
meant to them above all vocal music, and especially opera, and
the very possibility of the operatic form, that is, the combination
of music and drama, attracted their particular interest. They all
took part in the various controversies concerning the meaning of
the operatic form which excited public opinion in Paris during
the second half of the eighteenth century: first, that relating to
the transformation of the traditional French opera style by
Rameau; then the debate between the admirers of the classic
French opera and the Italian *opera buffa*, which started with the
performance of Pergolesi's *La serva padrona* in Paris; and finally
the battle between the supporters of Gluck and those of Niccolò

Piccini, which was at its height during Mozart's second stay with Baron Grimm.

It seems that among the *philosophes* around the *Encyclopédie*, d'Alembert and Diderot had the greatest understanding of musical problems, but without any doubt Rousseau was the most influential. His lifelong relationship with matters of music deserves a separate study. Inventor of a new system of musical notation, earning his livelihood for many years as a copyist of music, Rousseau was also a moderately gifted composer, whose opera *Le devin de village*, for which he wrote also the text, was performed everywhere in Europe (a transformation of its libretto was used by the twelve-year-old Mozart for his "Singspiel" entitled *Bastien and Bastienne*). Rousseau wrote copiously on music – most of the articles in the *Encyclopédie* on this subject are from his pen – and even published a two-volume dictionary of music. In some of his writings he touched on serious problems of the art form of the opera,[3] which should be briefly characterized because they are intimately connected with our main topic.

The role that Rousseau's concept of nature and his postulate of returning to the natural state of man played in his theories of society, government, morals, and language is well known. The same ideas dominated his philosophy of art, and especially of music. To him, as to all the philosophers of the Enlightenment, the arts had to imitate nature. Music imitates human nature – human feelings and sentiments. And what is it that makes music an imitation of nature? It is melody, which plays the same role in music that design plays in painting: melody creates the contour; the chords, the harmony, furnish merely the color. Unity of melody is thus the main principle of naturalness and simplicity in music.

This principle of unity of melody requires, first, that in a duet or trio the melody has to be distributed in succession among the parts, but in such a way that two melodies are never heard simultaneously. Nothing is less natural than to hear two persons speaking at the same time. This idea explains Rousseau's con-

---

[3] In addition to the articles "Opera" and "Recitatif" in his dictionary of music see especially his "Letter on French Music" (1753) and his "Observations Concerning the Italian Alceste by Gluck" (1774); see also Adolphe Jullien, *La Musique et les philosophes du 18ème siècle*, Paris, 1873.

tempt for complicated ensembles and his horror of contrapuntal forms, such as canons and fugues, which he regarded as residues of a barbarian taste. The principle of the unity of melody requires, in the second place, the avoidance of complicated harmonies in the accompaniment, and the restriction of the orchestral part to filling out the contours of the melody and fortifying its expressive values.

Opera is subject, in addition, to the requirement of dramatic plausibility, which again originates in the principle of naturalness. Hence the *recitativo secco*, without any orchestral accompaniment, has to imitate the spoken language carefully in its declamatory style. The accompanied recitative is admissible only if the situation requires the monologue of the actor to be interspersed with pauses and hesitations into which the orchestra cuts in. It remains a curious paradox that Rousseau regarded the duet or an accompanied recitative as against the rules of dramatic plausibility and imitation of nature, but had no objection to the fact that in opera the persons communicate by singing. This paradox is characteristic, however, of the musical theories of all the *encyclopédistes*.

We shall see how Mozart in his way, the way of a pure musician, solved the problems of the *philosophes*, that is, how he achieved unity of melody and dramatic plausibility by his handling of the ensembles, the recitatives, and the orchestra in a manner not even seen by the French theoretician. But I hasten now to examine what Mozart has meant to some modern philosophers.

II

It might be assumed that philosophers, following Schopenhauer's views, would turn to Mozart's music as an embodiment of the universe and an expression of transcendental experience as such. Astonishingly enough, all the thinkers here under scrutiny were concerned merely with Mozart's operas. His other works, his instrumental music, his compositions for the church, above all his most personal confessions – the concertos for pianoforte which constitute a series of self-portraits comparable only to those of Rembrandt – were never in the focus of their interest. To be sure, Dilthey, the only philosopher whose conception of Mozart dealt with some essential elements of his music, was right in stating that Mozart was the greatest dramatic genius of the eighteenth century and has therefore to be considered primarily as a dramatist (Hegel, who made an occasional remark on Mozart in his Lectures on Aesthetics, went so far as to interpret even his instrumental works as a kind of dramatic dialogue). But it can safely be stated that, with the exception of Dilthey, the philosophers were more concerned with the problem of how to find a place for the phenomenon Mozart within their own systems than with Mozart's music itself. This explains their tendency to pay exaggerated attention to the plots of his operas and the characters involved in them.

A striking example of this is a little book by Hermann Cohen, the foremost representative of the German neo-Kantian school, on "The Dramatic Idea in Mozart's Opera Texts." [4] The monograph is clearly intended as a supplement to Cohen's "Aesthetics of Pure Feeling," the third volume of a trilogy which interprets Kant's three critiques. Half of the book deals with general aesthetic considerations; the other half is an interpretation of the five generally known operas by Mozart.

Cohen's first problem was to investigate the nature of the unity of the musical drama. All dramatic art, he held, is based on the unity of action (in Aristotle's sense). Unity of action refers to the unity of will, and this, in turn, refers to the basic problems of ethics. The dramatic poet deals with the great questions of fate and freedom, and he can do so because he uses the medium of language, which, by reason of its conceptual structure, is an instrument fit to deal with dialectical and casuistic problems. But music, lacking any logical or conceptual structure, has to establish the unity of action by using another symbol. This symbol is love, in its various forms.

According to Cohen, love is the action of pure feeling and, even more, it is the only aesthetic action. Music is the expression of pure aesthetic feeling, and for this reason opera, as the amalgamation of drama and music, has to make love the spring of dramatic action. This is possible because all actions, and also all

---

[4] Hermann Cohen, *Die dramatische Idee in Mozarts Operntexten*, Berlin, 1916; see also his paper "Mozarts Operntexte," in *Allgemeine Musikzeitung*, Vol. 33, No. 4, 1912, pp. 60 ff.

conceptual terms of ordinary language, have "feeling suffixes" referring to the manifestations of eros. Thus love became the central theme of Mozart's operas; his problem was to show how all human actions originate in love and terminate in it, and to unify this principle with the ethics of the dramatic action. He succeeded in doing so by maintaining his musical independence and, at the same time, merging the dramatic idea of the plot with the harmonies of his language of love – love of the natural and the human world. For this reason the human voice is the backbone of his operas; everything else is of secondary importance. It was a particular achievement of Mozart's genius to keep the connection between love and the dramatic idea on the level of pure humanity and nevertheless to express on this level the experiences of the transcendent and the divine. He brought the two movements of the beautiful – the sublime and the comic – into a balanced combination attained before him by Shakespeare alone. Mozart was the first who gave the opera in the true sense its dramatic idea, far beyond the historical forms of *opera seria* and *opera buffa*, far beyond also the compositions of a Gluck or a Rameau.

Unfortunately, the whole theory is reduced to absurdity in the second half of Cohen's book, in which he analyzes the plots of five Mozart operas and their main characters in terms of his principles. To give just a few examples, *The Abduction from the Seraglio* represents, in Belmonte, love as a natural right of man which defeats a tyrant, and in Osmin the barbaric love of concupiscence and voluptuousness, as expressed in his sensual entry song and his drinking song "Vivat Bacchus." Don Giovanni combines the problem of Don Quixote with that of Faust; and Elvira – Elvira of all persons! – has to perform the mission of Gretchen in Goethe's *Faust*, who invokes the omnipotence of love, becomes in the final scene the St. John of the marble statue which appears for dinner, and brings Don Giovanni salvation by the mere fact of admonishing him to repent.

To be sure, only a German professor of philosophy could develop interpretations of this kind. And in order to do so Cohen had to make Mozart and Mozart alone responsible for both the selection of the plots and the formulation of their inherent dramatic ideas – as if the Stephanies, Da Pontes, Schikaneders had not existed at all, and as if the selection of the texts had not been more or less a matter of chance. The facts surrounding the genesis of Mozart's operas are a matter of historical record;[5] and these facts alone explain sufficiently Richard Wagner's astonishment at the unconcerned lack of discrimination in Mozart's selection of his libretti, and Beethoven's frequent statements that he never would have been able to set to music such frivolous texts as Mozart used.[6]

Moreover, Mozart did not hesitate to change the dramatic structure of his operas, here inserting an aria for a favorite singer, there leaving out one not suitable for the performer, and even dropping for the Viennese production the last scene of *Don Giovanni*, where the survivors rush in after the hero's disappearance, merely because the opera would have been too long by reason of the numbers added for that performance. And if all this does not sufficiently prove that Cohen's assumption is untenable, we have only to look at the personalities of Mozart's librettists, Da Ponte and Schikaneder, both highly gifted adventurers of the period. Their concept of a good opera text would certainly not have been compatible with Hermann Cohen's theories. Arthur Schurig is right in stating, in his otherwise highly objectionable work,[7] that Mozart as an opera composer could not be represented in a more unrealistic manner.

Hermann Cohen does not mention Kierkegaard's writings on Mozart but certain details point to the assumption that he was familiar with them. In Kierkegaard's *Either-Or*, published in 1843, we find a chapter called "The Stages of the Immediate-Erotic or the Musical-Erotic," which has frequently been considered the most profound interpretation of Mozart.[8] But to give such an interpretation was clearly not Kierkegaard's intention. He used Mozart's music and the characters of his operas merely as symbols for an indirect communication of certain fundamental problems of his own philosophy. W. J. Turner disregards this

[5] See Edward Dent, *Mozart's Operas*, Oxford, 1942.
[6] Richard Wagner, "Oper und Drama, I," in *Gesammelte Schriften und Dichtungen*, Vol. 3, Leipzig, n.d., p. 246; Albert Leitzmann, *Ludwig van Beethoven, Berichte der Zeitgenossen, Briefe und persönliche Aufzeichnungen*, Vol. 1, Leipzig, 1921, p. 48 (report by Ignaz Seyfried), p. 298 (Rellstab), p. 333 (G. v. Breuning).
[7] Arthur Schurig, *Wolfgang Amadeus Mozart*, 2 Vols., Leipzig, 1916.
[8] Søren Kierkegaard, *Either-Or; A Fragment of Life*, translated by D. F. and L. M. Swenson and W. Lowrie, 2 Vols., Princeton, 1949, Vol. 1.

aspect in his otherwise excellent book on Mozart,[9] and therefore comes to an entirely erroneous conclusion concerning Kierkegaard's views. The main problem of *Either-Or* is man's choice between a life on the aesthetic-erotic level and one on the ethical or even religious plane, a problem that Kierkegaard developed fully in later writings. In *Either-Or* he dealt with this problem in a literary form that gave him the possibility of approaching it by means of indirect dialectics.

This is not the place to enter into a detailed analysis of Kierkegaard's technique of indirect communication, so characteristic of him. It must be pointed out, however, that *Either-Or* is one of his pseudonymous – or, as he preferred to say, "polynomous" – writings. Not Kierkegaard but an imaginary Victor Eremita signs as the editor of two sets of manuscripts which he pretends to have discovered by chance in the secret drawer of an antique writing table. The main theme of both sets is the erotic experience in human life. The writer of the first set is a man called simply Mr. *A*. He lives on the aesthetic level, and is the type of the seducer who knows merely the sensual aspects of love. William, the writer of the second set – consisting of letters addressed to *A* – is a family man and stands for the ethical and even religious aspect of love, which only marital life can reveal. It is *A*, the seducer, in trying to express his experience of what he calls the immediate-erotic, who uses Mozart and his operas as symbols. His intent is twofold: first, an *apologia pro vita sua;* and second, a polemic against William. The reference to Mozart and his work is merely a device of the dialectic of indirect communication. Thus we have here an example of the frequently recurrent situation that a symbol, once established, can be used in a different context of meaning as the starting point for another symbolization of a higher degree, the meaning of which supersedes or possibly even annihilates the meaning that the symbol had originally.[10]

But why does *A* choose Mozart's operas as a starting point for symbolizing the various stages of the immediate-erotic, which is

[9] W. J. Turner, *Mozart: The Man and his Works*, New York, 1938, Ch. 19, "Kierkegaard on Mozart and Music"; see also Anna Charlotte Wutzky, "Søren Kierkegaard und Mozart," in *Zeitschrift für Musik*, Vol. 97, 1930, p. 913.

[10] See Alfred Schutz, "Symbol, Reality and Society," in *Collected Papers* I, pp. 287–356.

his main topic? He does so because he takes it as a basic axiom that the immediate-erotic is identical with the musical-erotic. Immediacy, that key word in Kierkegaard's philosophy, is the opposite of reflection. As soon as the erotic experience is reflected upon, it loses its immediacy; it is no longer an aesthetic experience, but turns into an ethical one. Ordinary discursive language presupposes reflection, but music begins where language ends. Music can express the immediate in its immediacy; even more, the erotic experience is, to *A*, the proper subject matter of music because music is a demoniacal element.

A distinguishes three stages of the immediate-erotic experience, but hastens to add that he should speak, instead, of metamorphoses, for all these transformations occur within the realm of immediacy. For that reason, too, these stages or metamorphoses cannot be described by ordinary linguistic means. But they can be explained by symbolic reference to Mozart's music.

The first stage of the immediate-erotic is symbolized by Cherubino, the page in *Figaro* – not, however, the character of the page as he appears on the operatic stage, but the myth of Cherubino as represented by Mozart's music. This mythical Cherubino visualizes the sensual, but the sensual-erotic has not yet been roused to joy and pleasure. The page experiences it in a mood of quiet melancholy; the desire still slumbers, and anticipates its object in an uncertain twilight. Here is the origin of the infatuating, magical, sweet pain of this state, characterized by the music Mozart bestowed upon his page: Cherubino is drunk with love.

The symbol for the second stage is Papageno. The dreaming desire has been roused and, as is always the case, only at the moment of his awakening does the dreamer become aware that he has dreamed and that the dream is over. In Papageno the desire starts on a voyage of exploration. His hilarity, his pulsating joy of life is the pleasure of discovery. This is mirrored in Mozart's music, and Kierkegaard identifies the mythical Papageno with his first aria and the chimes of his magic bells. These are the symbols for his way of life, which could be said to be a continuous twittering. He enchants, he allures, he seduces.

Thus at the first stage the desire dreams, and at the second stage it explores. But at the third it becomes absolutely determined.

This third stage is symbolized by Don Giovanni – and not only by the eponymous hero but by the opera as a whole. In *Don Giovanni* desire is victorious, irresistible, demoniacal, a principle that rules the world, and Don Giovanni is its embodiment. Again the expression of his personality is music, and music alone. A compares Don Giovanni, who is the demoniacal determined as the sensual, with Faust, who is the demoniacal determined as the spiritual.

Don Giovanni hovers between the idea which he represents and his individuality, and this hovering is a particular feature of the medium of music. Only music can express the force of seduction in Don Giovanni in its immediacy; it is inexpressible for ratiocination, for well ordered reflective thought. Don Giovanni does not consciously plan seduction by intrigues and skillful calculations. He desires, and his desire has the effect of seduction. His life sparkles and glistens like the wine he enjoys, and it is the so-called Champagne aria that mirrors the basic mood of the whole opera. This unreflecting passion can be expressed only by music, and only a musician, only Mozart, could do this. Whereas other presentations of the same plot, say that by Molière, merely speak of the seducer, Mozart's art shows us that this seducer exists. Kierkegaard emphasizes that the immanent problem of the opera, in contradistinction to the drama, consists not in the characterizations of the persons and the presentation of the action – for such a purpose the art form of opera is not reflective enough – but in the unity of mood forged out of the plurality of the separate voices. Consequently action in opera is not the action of the characters; it is immediate action.

All the other characters in the opera receive their force from Don Giovanni. His life is the efficient principle for the life of all the others, his passion makes all the others move. It is echoed by the earnestness of the Commendatore, the ire of Elvira, the hatred of Anna, the gravity of Octavio, the anxiety of Zerlina, the confusion of Leporello. And all this is performed by musical means. Take, as an example, Elvira's first scene. She stands in the foreground, Don Giovanni and Leporello in the background. The setting can be grasped by the eye of the beholder, the musical situation by his ear. But the unity of the situation is affected by the harmony of Don Giovanni's and Elvira's voices, and the beholder should not see Elvira and Don Giovanni together in the unity of a spatial situation. He should hear Don Giovanni in Elvira's singing.

Even in the overture Mozart circumscribes the central role of Don Giovanni and therewith the whole realm of the opera. Don Giovanni's life is not a life of despair. It exhibits the full power of the sensual, which is born in anxiety, but this anxiety is nothing else than the demoniacal lust for life. He dances over the abyss and jubilates in the short time that is given to him. Mozart always interprets him as representing an ideal – life, power, lust – that is, as an ideal over against a reality. He dissolves him into music; he immerses him in a world of sounds. And it is the basic mood of the opera, not the changing situations, which gives it its dramatic importance.

The basic mood and not the changing situations: this is the conclusion necessarily reached by *A*, the man living on the aesthetic stage, who tries to express in indirect communication his immediate-erotic experience by taking Mozart's operatic characters as starting points for a symbolization on a higher level. Let us not forget, he emphasizes, that what acquires symbolic functions is not the "real" Cherubino, the "real" Papageno, the "real" Don Giovanni as they appear on the operatic scene, but the mythical ones, the "ideas" of their natures. That is why, from his point of view, each of these mythified characters represents a basic mood, and why the changing situations in which these characters are placed are irrelevant.

It seems to me that this statement touches on one of the most serious questions of Mozart interpretation, one that has hardly received the attention it deserves. This is the question whether we are entitled, as is generally assumed, to interpret the persons in the plots of Mozart's operas as unified personalities with consistent characteristics – an interpretation that would certainly be valid in regard to Beethoven's *Fidelio* or Wagner's operas. The discussion of this question will occupy us presently, after a brief examination of Dilthey's pertinent views, which, in my opinion, come closest to an understanding of Mozart as a dramatic genius.

Dilthey starts his essay on Mozart [11] with a comparison of

[11] Wilhelm Dilthey, *Von deutscher Dichtung und Musik: Aus den Studien zur Geschichte des deutschen Geistes*, ed. by Herman Nohl and Georg Misch, Leipzig, 1933, pp. 275–95.

Gluck's musical drama with the Italian form of opera. Gluck subordinated the musical forms to the dramatic idea. The unity of action and, therewith, the principles of mimetic vigor and declamatory expression prevail in his operas; dramatic action is always imitation of real action, only intensified and transplanted to a higher level. In the Italian type of opera, however, music is the natural expression of mental life. The persons of the play think in sounds, and sounds are their language. Thus music obtains a dominant position, and as a result the opera of the Italian type transcends the realm of the drama: it becomes entirely detached from the reality of life and develops its particular style by using forms that are specific for the world of sounds. Arias, duets, ensembles, and the strict separation of the musical forms from one another (the so-called "numbers") – so incompatible with the continuous flux of dramatic life – have their justification in the fact that a world detached from reality derives its inner unity from the structure of music.

Mozart made opera the strongest form of the dramatic art by accepting the Italian principle of musical construction and developing it with the aid of the contrapuntal supremacy of German music, that is, by means of an orchestral art evolved in symphonies and chamber music. He built characters, actions, and situations on purely musical principles. A character is expressed in the lower regions of sentiment, in the recitative. It enters into relations to other characters whereby the inner life is intensified until it leads to actions in the well circumscribed forms of the interchange of musical speech and the simultaneity of duets, trios, and the like. The intensified state of feeling, originating in action, manifests itself in the aria. Thus the main characters are led through these well determined forms and reveal in these changing relations of life the inner context of their temperaments, habits, and traits. These aspects of the personality become more accessible in the opera than in the spoken drama.

Also the interrelations of the persons with one another in the dramatic actions of the plot are revealed by a set of musical means unattainable to the mere word. First, the mood of each scene finds a powerful support in the orchestra, which may prepare it in the introduction and sustain it through all the changing occurrences on the stage. Second, there is the specific operatic possibility of having the persons speak in simultaneity. Mozart used this device by having each person express his individuality and at the same time interweaving all of them into the unity of the musical form. By these means the wealth of life is made accessible to the beholder in a single step: being impelled to blend the diversified characters into a harmonious whole, he experiences the world in terms of more or less typical relations of basic modes of conduct of human beings. And in the third place, Mozart assured the continuity of the dramatic process by his technique of presenting the typical attitudes of each of his main characters toward life in most diversified situations. Although these attitudes are modified again and again in manifold variations, they nevertheless remain the same. In this connection Dilthey spoke of a "modulation" of attitudes and personal traits within a single individuation of life.

These musical principles of constructing his characters explain Mozart's relative independence of his texts. He succeeded in expressing in a rich differentiation precisely those moments of the dramatic occurrence to which the text alludes in a merely fragmentary and rather trivial way. Mozart's dramatic ingenuity originated in his temperament, which was capable of surrendering itself in an entirely objective manner to any situation, to any human being, and even to any event. His was a mimetic vivacity of the highest degree, mirrored also in his letters and his outer appearance. Dilthey believed that he must have been an excellent imitator. Any situation and any human being had for Mozart from the outset a musical voice, and he grasped the musical kernel in any experience. Thus originated in him that fundamental feeling for the fulness of existence which is specific for a dramatist of his kind. In this respect he was similar to Shakespeare. He was born not in order to set the world right but merely to express musically what exists in it. Nothing human was strange to his genius; he showed his full greatness precisely where the text revealed the diversity of life. He had to choose themes reaching from the transcendental world to the lowest region of sensual life, he had to create masters and servants, he had to show noble feelings and low motives, and he had to combine all of them. Only then was he himself.

III

Dilthey thus attempted to explain Mozart's dramatic genius in terms of musical forms. Like Kierkegaard and Cohen he assumed, however, that the main dramatic purpose of Mozart was to construct by musical means individually unique personalities – characters in this specific sense – and to show the "modulations" of their basic attitudes and traits in changing situations of life or in various interrelations with one another. He assumed that in spite of all modifications and variations these characters remained fundamentally "the same." This view is more or less shared by most of the interpreters of Mozart, by romantic writers such as E. T. A. Hoffmann and Moerike as well as by modern musicologists such as Abert, Dent, Einstein, and Levarie. I submit, however, that in each of Mozart's operas the persons of the play are represented by musical means as "acting out of character." In substantiating this I must restrict myself to a few examples.

For three acts of *Figaro* we enjoy Susanna's scintillating extroversive personality and the wit and inventiveness of the intrigues she initiates. Then, in the fourth act, precisely at the moment when her scheme of playing tricks on both Figaro and the Count is about to succeed, she sings the famous aria in F-major "Deh vieni, non tardar," which is the deepest expression of the feelings of a young woman who expects her lover. Listening to this aria we forget what Susanna has meant to us so far; we forget even the context in which this scene stands in the construction of the plot. It is just a delightful night in spring and here is a girl – any girl – who is looking forward to meeting the man she loves. Commentators have tried in different ways to explain the inconsistency between this aria and Susanna's general attitude toward life. Tovey sees in the aria an ironic dramatic tension, whereas others point out that Susanna's real figure is concealed in this scene by the fact that she is wearing the Countess' dress.[12] But is not the "character" of the Countess also full of contradictions? Her two deeply emotional arias are sincere prayers for regaining

[12] Donald Francis Tovey, "Opera," in *Encyclopaedia Britannica*, 14th ed., Vol. 16; Siegmund Levarie, *Mozart's La Nozze di Figaro*, Chicago, 1952, p. 209; Arthur Schurig (cited above, note 7) Vol. 2, p. 88; Hermann Abert, *W. A. Mozart*, 2 Vols., Leipzig, 1923, Vol. 2, pp. 352ff.

her husband's love, and nevertheless at the same time she enters with considerable gusto into a highly doubtful conspiracy with her servants against the Count. How to explain that Papageno, immediately after the clownish encounter with Monostatos, joins Pamina, whom he meets for the first time, in a duet that is a serious and profound meditation on the mystery of the togetherness of man and woman? Are Elvira's arias consistent with one another and merely "modulations" of a basically unchanged personality? Is the fickleness of the leading characters in *Così Fan Tutte* compatible with the feelings expressed in the enchanting canon at the wedding banquet during which only the seriously hurt Guglielmo goes his own way?

All these difficulties disappear if we abandon the assumption that Mozart, by musical means, intended to construct individual characters, unique personalities who grow and develop in the pursuit of their aims and have to meet their comic or tragic destiny. In order to understand Mozart's dramatic intent we have to forget what we have learned from Beethoven and Wagner. We have to consider that Mozart's operas are first of all *plays*, in the true sense of that word as delineated by Huizinga,[13] that is, playful representations of the fullness of life, with all its tragic and comic aspects.

Certainly Mozart deals with both these aspects. Socrates, at the end of the Symposium, compels Aristophanes and Agathon to acknowledge that the genius of comedy is the same as the genius of tragedy, and that the true artist in tragedy is an artist also in comedy. Mozart was such a true artist, and his *dramma giocoso* fulfills Socrates' postulate, as do also the various movements of his great compositions in the symphonic form. Nevertheless, as a dramatist he shows the tragic and the comic not in the destiny of the individual but in a succession of diversified and frequently inconsistent *situations*. It is always the situation, and not the individual character, which Mozart builds up in terms of musical forms. Frequently the situations themselves are only typified occasions for displaying typical attitudes on the part of the participants. In a certain sense it could be said that we would not be surprised if Susanna's aforementioned aria were

[13] J. Huizinga, *Homo ludens*, New York, 1950, pp. 2, 28.

allocated to Zerlina or Dorabella or Pamina: they all are sisters under the skin.

The structural principle of Italian opera consists in a splitting up of the musical process into a set of well circumscribed musical forms – arias, duets, ensemble, the so-called "numbers" – which are interspersed by recitative or even by spoken dialogue. This technique leads in itself to the dissolution of the plot into a string of more or less self-contained situations, in which the persons of the play are involved and within which they have to find their bearings. Musicologists are right in stating that, in general, "the recitative interprets musically the action," whereas "the aria expresses the reflections, feelings, or resolves of the principal character, which are the consequence of the action just preceding." [14] The skill of the librettist and, above all, of the composer appears in the handling of the manifold problems arising from this particular feature of the "number opera."

Any student of the operas produced by Mozart's contemporaries will easily recognize the extent to which Mozart's genius surpassed the techniques of a Paisiello or Martìn or Spontini. Mozart does not merely communicate to us, the beholders, the objective meaning that the situation has within the context of the plot (and even a dramatist of the stature of Gluck does only this). He shows us, in addition, the different meanings that the same situation has to each of the characters involved in it. He makes us understand that to each of them the presence and the behavior of the others are elements of his own situation; and he reveals to us the specific springs of action by which each character acts within and reacts to the situation. This situation itself may be just a typified frame for the events on the stage, and even the attitude of each of the persons involved therein may be merely a typified one. Yet in Mozart's hands such a typified situation becomes unique and concrete, individual and atypical by the particular meaning it has for each of the participant persons.

And this is precisely the condition in which each of us finds himself in everyday life. I am always involved in a situation which – to use a term of modern sociologists – I have to define,

---

[14] D. J. Grout, "Opera, VIII," in W. Apelt, *Harvard Dictionary of Music*, Cambridge, Mass., 1947, p. 510.

and which, in spite of its typicality, has to me and each of my fellow - men a unique and particular meaning. My interrelationships with my fellow - men, their interpretations of my situation and mine of theirs, codetermine the meaning this situation has for me. This complicated texture of meanings is constitutive for our experiencing the social world. It could rightly be said that *Mozart's dramatic art is rather a representation of the basic structure of the social world than an imitation of nature.* By purely musical devices he not only illuminates from within the meaning in terms of which each of the characters on the stage defines the situation, but also succeeds in letting us, the beholders, participate in this process.

What are these musical devices? Dilthey refers rightly to Mozart's handling of the recitatives, his treatment of the orchestra, and his use of the vocal ensemble; and we remember that these three elements of the operatic art were also of particular interest to the French philosophers of the eighteenth century. Dilthey even mentions the deeper reasons for their importance: their function is to build up the unity of the art form of the opera in complete detachment from the reality of everyday life. We have now to discuss very briefly the relationship of the events on the operatic scene to reality as established by the use of these three elements.

The action on the stage takes place before our eyes in outer space and in outer time. Music, however, is a process that goes on in the dimension of inner time, within the *durée*, as Bergson calls it. In listening to music we immerse ourselves in the continuous flux of our consciousness, and participate simultaneously and immediately in the ongoing musical process – with our feelings, emotions, and passions – in an attitude that Nietzsche has called the Dionysiac. The main problem to be solved by the operatic composer is the translation of events in outer time and space into events within the flux of inner time: in order to be expressed by music the disconnectedness of the former has to be brought into the continuum of the latter. This problem can be solved in different ways. In the Wagnerian type of opera the beholder is never released from the continuous flux of inner time in which the uninterrupted musical process immerses him. The technique of the leitmotif and its metamorphoses imbues the

actual musical occurrences with recollections of past and anticipations of future events.

With very few exceptions Mozart, however, does not transgress
the actual Here and Now determined by the situation at hand.
He makes no attempt to establish within each of the "closed"
numbers a context either with what precedes the situation or
with what follows it. The events of the plot are to him merely
occasions for letting his persons say just what they have in their
hearts. In his operas full musical treatment is reserved for defining the culminating situations by the characters involved in
them: for the arias and the ensembles. For communication of
the intervening events the recitative suffices. But Mozart's recitatives by no means follow Rousseau's advice that the declamatory
style of spoken language be taken as model. They give us the
inflection, the speech melody, of everyday conversation, but
exactly in doing so they communicate the emotional fringes
around the conceptual kernel, the "feeling suffixes" of the words,
as Hermann Cohen called them. And Mozart frequently applies
a particular technique in order to lead the listener from the
twilight region of the recitative into the depth of the *durée*:
gradually the speech melody of the unaccompanied recitative
becomes intensified by the addition of the orchestra in the
accompanied one, and the passionate expressive content
of the latter leads to the *arioso*, until the whole process culmi-
nates in the fully developed musical form of the aria or the
ensemble.

This leads us to the second feature of the art form of Mozart's
operas: the role of the orchestra. Mozart's contemporaries rightly
regarded his treatment of the orchestra as an innovation in the
operatic art. The role of the orchestra in opera is to a certain
extent comparable to that of the chorus in Greek tragedy: the
orchestra is the interpreter of and commentator on the events on
the stage. It offers to the beholder an objective interpretation
of the meaning of the happenings back of the footlights. In doing
so it performs a double function. On the one hand, it separates
the reality of the world of the stage from the reality of daily life,
which is that of the beholder in the stalls; on the other hand, it
amalgamates the flux of the inner *durée* of the listener with the
inner events of the characters on the stage into the single unified

stream of the ongoing musical process. Thus the listener participates in immediacy in the feelings, emotions, and thoughts of the
dramatis personae: the orchestra reveals to the listener more
about their inner life than they manifest by their actions, gestures, and words.

Mozart was fully aware of this function of the orchestra, as is
evident from a passage in his well known letter to his father
(September 26, 1781), concerning his work on *The Abduction
from the Seraglio:* "Let me now turn to Belmonte's aria in A-
major, 'O wie ängstlich o wie feurig.' Would you like to know
how I expressed it – and even indicated the throbbing heart? By
the two violins, playing octaves ... You feel the trembling – the
faltering – you see how his throbbing breast begins to swell; this
I have expressed by a crescendo. You hear the whispering and the
sighing – which I have indicated by the first violins with mutes
and a flute playing in unison."

Dilthey merely touched on this problem in stating that the
orchestra creates and sustains the *mood* of the particular scene.
Mozart's orchestra performs an additional function: with unfailing surety he uses this device for bringing about a simultaneity
of the fluxes of inner time, that is, a simultaneity between the
stream of consciousness of the persons on the stage and that of
the beholder. He thus establishes a community of intersubjectivity between the two, since both participate in the same flux of
inner time.

And this establishment of an intersubjective community, now
between the various *dramatis personae*, is the secret of Mozart's
powerful treatment of the ensembles, the third distinctive feature
of his operas. To be sure, every dramatist places his characters
in a community of space and time, and makes them share a
common situation to which they react in a particular way as they
act and react upon one another. But the dramatist can present
their diversified actions and reactions only in succession, and
therefore in isolation. To show them in simultaneity is the privilege of the musical drama. Yet Mozart does more: he uses this
specific device of the art form of opera in order to present in
immediacy the intersubjective relations in which his characters
are involved. In spite of their diversified reaction to the common
situation, in spite of their individual characteristics, they act

together, feel together, will together as a community, as a We. This does not mean, of course, that they act, feel, or will the same, or with equal intensity. On the contrary, ensembles such as the admired first Finale of *Figaro* clearly show many groupings of the *personae* involved, both in cooperation and in antagonism. Nevertheless, even in antagonism they are bound together in an intersubjective situation of a community, in a We.

I submit that Mozart's main topic is not, as Cohen believed, love. It is the metaphysical mystery of the existence of a human universe of pure sociality, the exploration of the manifold forms in which man meets his fellow - man and acquires knowledge of him. The encounter of man with man within the human world is Mozart's main concern. This explains the perfect humanity of his art. His world remains the human world even if the transcendental irrupts into it. The sacred realm of *The Magic Flute* or the supernatural occurrences in *Don Giovanni* belong themselves to the human world. They reveal man's place in the universe as experienced in human terms.

I started with a brief presentation of Schopenhauer's philosophy of music, and in closing I may quote one of his most profound insights. In *The World as Will and Idea* (Book III, Section 52) he refers to Leibniz' famous definition of music:[15] "Musica est exercitium arithmeticae occultum nescientis se numerare animi" – music is a hidden arithmetical activity of a mind that does not know it is counting. And Schopenhauer proposes to sum up his own conception of music in another definition: "Musica est exercitium metaphysices occultum nescientis se philosophari animi" – music is a hidden metaphysical activity of a mind that does not know it is philosophizing.

If Schopenhauer is right, and I believe he is, then Mozart was one of the greatest philosophical minds that ever lived. Goethe, in his unerring perspicacity, recognized Mozart's genius, and the words he spoke to Eckermann (March 11, 1828) are still the greatest tribute paid to him: "What else does genius mean but the productive force which brings about new deeds that can stand forth before God and Nature and for this very reason have

---

[15] Leibniz' letter to Christian Goldbach, April 1712, in G. E. Guhrauer, *Leibniz*, Breslau, 1846, Vol. I, appendix p. 66.

consequences and last? All the works of Mozart are of this kind;
they contain a creative power which will remain effective from
generation to generation without being exhausted and con-
summated in times to come."

SANTAYANA ON SOCIETY AND GOVERNMENT

After some thirty years of strenuous work Santayana, at the age of 88, has published *Dominations and Powers*, which, as its subtitle indicates, contains his "Reflections on Liberty, Society and Government." This book is a kind of last will and testament of a man who may rightly contend that he has lived in the truest sense of the word a philosophic life. At its end he reverts to problems discussed by him some forty years ago in the second volume of the *Life of Reason*, but now these problems reappear in an entirely changed atmosphere. They are placed in the general setting of an elaborate and closely interconnected system of thought, detached from the vantage point of the "judicial moralist," which, in the author's own words, prevailed in the earlier work.

His present "tractatus ethico-politicus" will be analyzed in the following pages without any reference to other writings of this great thinker. This procedure, imposed by limitations of space, is obviously not meant to involve any unfairness to the work under scrutiny and its author. On the contrary, it is believed that this book is one of the few by this philosopher which furnish their own scheme of interpretation.

I

We have to deal here with a typical masterwork of old age. Goethe defined old age as a gradual withdrawal from the realm of appearances. Many works of art and philosophy, created by a genius at the end of a long life, show traits proving the truth of Goethe's insight – the last operas by Verdi, the last paintings by Titian, the last philosophic writings by Plato, the last poetic works by Goethe himself. These productions of old age, in all their concreteness and individuality, do not deal with the concreteness of the phenomena and appearances pertaining to the reality of the world of action; nor are they concerned with the individuality of autobiographical or historical persons and places. This withdrawal from appearances is perfectly compatible with another aspect of history, as formulated by Goethe in another statement. He confessed that in his advanced years everything, even his own life and thought, became to him historical. He felt that the world of his thought had acquired a symbolic character, that new dimensions were revealed to him. These dimensions cannot be directly communicated; the secret pattern that transforms the cosmos of personal experiences into a universe of a great tradition common to all creative minds of earlier generations can merely be suggested by hints and allusions, by "clues dispersed in the book."

In literature in the broadest sense, the necessity of using symbols and relations resisting precise communication determines the style of masterworks of old age. Its outstanding feature in the present case is the aphorism, the pithy maxim, which, as the Greek root of the term indicates (apo-horizo), detaches its meaning from its horizon. Yet this horizon, consisting of the fringes around the conceptual kernel of the proposition, is precisely the undisclosed pattern to be explored. "As we grow older," says T. S. Eliot, "the world becomes stranger, the pattern more complicated." And he continues: "Old men ought to be explorers. Here and there does not matter."

These general characteristics of the creative work of old age hold especially good for the work of a philosopher who has succeeded in leading a "bios theoretikos," a life of pure contemplation in the sense of Plato and Aristotle. If such a philosopher deals with the social world he does not want to change it, he does not have to offer reforms; his aim is not to fight for a good cause or to defeat a bad one. He is just the detached and disinterested observer of the comedies and dramas of the social life, interested in their foundation in human nature and conduct, interested also in their moral implications, but not in their concrete result as far as political ends and means are concerned. On the contrary, the possibility of political ends and means as

such, whatever their particular content might be, becomes philosophically questionable and problematic. Not a system of ends,
or of means for their practical realization, has to be established
by the thinker, but a theoretical system which, widely used, may
teach the politician – any politician – where he comes from and
where he is going.

For this reason the many reviewers who have reproached Santayana for a lack of understanding of liberalism, of American
leadership, of Soviet Russia's policies, for refraining from any
remark relating to fascism, and so on, have, I believe, missed
the point entirely. All these categories vanish when we consider
the theoretical position intentionally chosen by Santayana, and
if they are referred to in some chapters, they are used only as
illustrations for general insights, as a means of indirect communication of the hidden pattern. We have to read this book as a
work full of wisdom, based on not always adequate knowledge,
and sovereignly disdaining nearly any and all information. This
feature implies both its glory and its shortcoming. It combines
the deepest insight into the resting of all social and political
life on the nature of man, with a curious misunderstanding of
the functions of the modern economic system (which is sometimes
interpreted in the ways of the French Physiocrats of the
eighteenth century), and with historical errors. Yet there is not
a single page that does not reveal the highest craftsmanship in
philosophizing, let alone an unsurpassed beauty of diction and
style.

The form of the work is one that can be found in certain
movements of the late chamber music of Beethoven and Brahms:
it consists of variations on an undisclosed theme. This theme
is here Aristotle's concept of an "episteme politike," a political
science, as clearly described in the preface of his *Nicomachean
Ethics* and carried out in his *Politics*, thus originating a great
tradition of political thinking handed down to us over the centuries. Yet there are hidden allusions to the works of other
philosophers participating in this great tradition, allusions that
belong to the technique of indirect communication mentioned
before. An example of this technique is the title of the book
itself. Although I have not found the name of St. Thomas
Aquinas mentioned in the book, the antithesis of "Dominations"

and "Powers" becomes understandable only in connection with the theory of the Doctor Angelicus.

The book, in the beginning, refers the reader to a passage in St. Paul's Epistle to the Colossians (i, 16), in which it is stated that the invisible God created all things that are in heaven and that are in earth, visible and invisible, whether they be thrones or dominions or principalities or powers. This sentence and several other scriptural passages (for example, Isaiah vi, 2; Ezekiel x, 15, 20; Ephesians i, 21) are the origin of the Angelology, developed by St. Augustine, Dionysius the Pseudo-Areopagite, and St. Gregory the Great, a development codified and brought into a system by St. Thomas Aquinas. This system, according to Gilson,[1] distinguishes three stages or hierarchies of angels, each consisting of three orders. According to St. Thomas angels are intelligences without a body, placed in the Realm of Creatures between the Divinity (Trinity) and Men. The angels of the first stage know the intelligible essences, inasmuch as they proceed from the first universal principle, which is God: the Seraphim consider Divine knowledge; the Cherubim consider His Goodness; the "Thrones," symbols of judiciary power, consider the disposition of Divine judgments.

The angels of the second stage – the important one for our topic – know the intelligibles in so far as they are subject to the most universal of created causes. Their proper object is, therefore, the general ordering of means in view of the end. The three orders of this group [2] are:

1. Dominations, that is, authority: they order what others have to execute; they appoint those things which have to be done.

2. Virtues: they impart to the general causes the necessary energy to preserve them from failure in the accomplishment of their operations.

3. Powers, whose office is to protect the order of Providence from evil influences attempting to disturb it. They have to order how that which has been commanded or decided can be carried out by others.

For the sake of completeness it may be mentioned that the

---

[1] Étienne Gilson, *The Philosophy of Saint Thomas Aquinas*, London, 1939, Chapter VIII.

[2] *Summa Theologica*, Q. 108 a.8.

angels of the third stage know the intelligibles as applied to particular things and as dependent on particular causes, and are thus
directly charged with the ordering of human affairs. Of their
three orders one is the Principalities, concerned with the common
and general good of nations, cities, and kingdoms, with the passing of temporal supremacy to this nation rather than to that,
with the conduct of princes and nobles, and the like. The two
others are the archangels, messengers occupied with the truth of
faith, and the simple angels, who are guardians of men.

This is the celestial hierarchy from which Santayana, without
giving a particular account of it, borrows his Dominations and
Powers. He does not mention Virtues in the title of his book, but
he hopes that "the reader may feel them always silently hovering
over the pages." [3]

II

To Santayana the distinction between Dominations and
Powers is a moral, not a physical, one. All Dominations involve
an exercise of power, but not all Powers are Dominations. The
distinction arises from the point of view of a given person or
society, with initial interests of its own but surrounded by uncontrollable circumstances. These circumstances are divided into
two classes: things favorable or neutral, and things fatal, frustrating, or inconvenient. The latter, when inescapable, become
Dominations.

With this basic statement the purpose of the investigation has
been established. This purpose is a philosophical anthropology,
in the continental European sense, that is, a science of man –
not a science of primitive culture which, in contradistinction to
anthropology, is called in Europe ethnology. Such an endeavor
requires a basic philosophical position. Santayana calls himself
a naturalist and materialist, but these terms are used by him with
a particular meaning. To be a naturalist means to him to recognize that mankind is a race of animals living in a material world,
that fellow-men exist, that reported historical facts exist, that,
briefly, man has an "animal faith" in the physical theater of life.
Of course spirit exists too. But spirit is not the *cause* of order

[3] Santayana, *Dominations and Powers*, p. 3.

in the world: life and spirit are the results of order. Santayana understands under "matter" the principle of natural existence, or our "being in the world." [4] Matter determines, for any ideal form, its relations in space and time, its duration and disappearance. Spirit is a merely possible locus for surveying the universe, to be actualized and individuated only as particular material tensions meet and form a center for further diffusion of energy. By reacting on things distant, past, or future, the animal organism evokes spirit.

Though Santayana calls himself a materialist he expressly rejects both vulgar interpretations of materialism; according to the one, nothing exists except sensations, and according to the other, nothing exists except matter. Matter is always recondite in nature, and to be a materialist is, therefore, to be fundamentally a naturalist. Not the development of any theory of matter or of substance or of atoms is his purpose; he has to begin with "the natural assumption made by children and poets that he is living in an existing and persisting world in which there are rocks and trees, men and animals, feelings and dreams." In this view Santayana meets other important philosophers of our century. To William James and Bergson mind is not detachable from the world of matter, but is its product; to Husserl all operations of the mind and even logic refer to and are even founded upon the "Lebenswelt," the world we are living in. Thinkers so different as Heidegger and Whitehead start their interpretation of the universe from men's living within the world, the world of matter and of things at hand, the world surrounding and including our physical and mental existence. But the naive belief in the world as taken for granted is the focal point of view of the theories of two other thinkers: of Piaget, who in his recent "genetical epistemology" starts from the natural assumptions made by children with respect to the existing and persisting world and of Max Scheler, to whom the analysis of the relative natural aspect of the world, that is, the world taken for granted within a culture at a particular moment of its development, is the point of departure for his philosophical anthropology and sociology.

If we stretched the concept of naturalism as far as Santayana does, all the aforementioned philosophers could be considered

[4] *Op. cit.*, p. 12.

naturalists. But they could not be interpreted – always in Santayana's sense – as materialists. The philosophic naturalist has
stopped to observe how the rocks and trees, men and animals,
feelings and dreams, which can be found in the existing and
persisting world, change, grow, pass into one another. These
observations may lead him to the belief that something continuous runs through them, makes them up, causes them to
appear. Yet these appearances are not parts of the material
object, since they change with the distance, position, and condition of the observer, and since there are illusions and dreams
of nonexisting objects. If upon examination and in the practice
of the arts the naturalist thinks this theory verified, if, although
denying immaterial agencies, the naturalist does not deny that
material agencies may be *at the same time* animated by ideal motives, such as moral or religious purposes, the naturalist has become a materialist.

According to Santayana, for a materialistic philosopher in his
sense, dealing with human affairs, the subject of investigation
is man, with an unexplained human nature and an unexplained
personal character, but subject to contagion, training, and
teaching.[5] In investigating the particular form of Dominations
and Powers manifested in the field of politics, the philosopher
need not trouble himself with truths deeper than conventional
truths, his contact with facts need not go deeper than the contacts
that other people have had with them, or may have on other
occasions: as far as historical facts are concerned, he is com-
posing a drama *as it might have been lived.* Students of Max
Weber's methodological writings will easily recognize in this
formulation of Santayana's the basic postulate for the forming
of correct ideal-typical constructs of social events – that is, adequacy of meaning and causal adequacy.

To be sure, the materialistic philosopher, investigating the
causes of historical events, will have to assume that the causes
are all physical, since history goes on in a material world which
existed before all history began and, by its biological development, made history possible. Like any sort of creatures, human
beings, and therewith every form of societal life and of government, spring out from the Earth – this term understood as the

[5] *Op. cit.,* p. 28.

infinite possibilities of Being reduced at each point by previous local accidents to a particular arbitrary form. Yet in politics we may assume as roughly constant the physical order of nature and of human nature. To Santayana – in contradistinction to Marx and others – a materialistic interpretation of politics need not be especially climatic or economic or Malthusian. All these categories are Circumstances, important in letting loose or suppressing the various instincts and powers of human nature.[6] On the contrary, the agent – and also the patient – in politics is the psyche, the instincts, needs, passions, or interests, which are the springs of action of any animal, to which Powers and Dominations have to be referred. The "psyche" is not to be interpreted as a spirit separable from the body; it is the life of the body, as the naturalist observes it.[7] Psyches change with the circumstances, and individual passions and feelings may determine human actions. The interplay between the psyche and the circumstances is the origin of Powers and Dominations. Again this position recalls a theory of Max Scheler's: the theory of real factors and ideal factors in societal life, the latter developing independently of the former in accordance with their intrinsic particular laws, but the former having the function of a sluicegate, without which the stream of ideal factors can never materialize in the reality of the world of natural things or, in Santayana's language, in the world of circumstances.

III

It has seemed essential to describe carefully the particular meaning of Santayana's materialistic-naturalistic position, because this key concept is at the foundation of his study of society and government on three different levels, the generative, militant and rational orders.

The first Powers and Dominations occur in the generative order which is the order of growth, custom, and tradition. The helplessness of human children and their prolonged immaturity create the Dominations of parental authority first, and of custom later, leading thus to the biological units of the family and the

[6] *Ibid.*, p. 5.
[7] *Ibid.*, p. 14.

social units of the tribe. But as soon as the natural growth of the
human family is disturbed or disrupted, and the dominance of
a different social unit is substituted for it, complications may
arise within traditional society by creating factions or demanding
reform or by the superimposition of a wider influence or allegiance. The characteristic of such a change is that it is deliberate:
the new social order is no longer biological but is voluntarily
imposed, because potentialities in the psyche now come to consciousness before they are habitually realized in action. There
is therefore a contrast, and often a conflict, between the new
prompting at work and the traditional convention.

This conflict constitutes the militant order of society, which
includes all voluntary associations that cross the generative order
of society: not only military bands but all political parties, religious sects, and parasitical arts. Under the latter term Santayana
understands every art that does not contribute directly or indirectly to supplying mankind with food, since it is the principle
of his exposition that man lives originally by bread alone. Yet
even agriculture requires instruments; clothes, furniture, and
shelter are needed, and trades must exist to furnish the necessi-
ties of life and to defend it. The trades require special skill and
special knowledge, and differences of age, sex, natural gifts, tastes
and manners will create other criteria of excellence, other forms
of happiness, besides the virtue of laboring in order to eat, sleep,
and breed. The choice of what necessary and optional arts shall
be allowed to develop, and the measure of their proportions,
determine the economic order of society. But since many of
these arts, in a material sense, are parasitical within the meaning
of the definition just given, and are nevertheless most important
for human happiness, Santayana calls this order rather the
rational order.

The three orders – the generative, the militant, and the
rational – are, as we may say in the established terminology of
the social sciences, ideal-typical constructs; that is, they are interwoven in reality, and while the first may exist without the second
and third, as in the vegetable kingdom, the other orders cannot
exist without the first, and in human history the second and
the third are present throughout. The construction of the three
orders is only a methodical device adopted in order to study

Powers and Dominations within each of them, as well as to mark
the Domination which each order exercises over the rest. To
be sure, it is in the militant order that the interplay of Dominations and Powers appears most clearly, but the generative
order remains fundamental throughout, lending body to all Dominations and Powers apparently moral. And, conversely, nothing
human, especially in politics, can be justly appreciated without
remembering the rational order, or implicitly appealing to it.

The plan of the further investigation is thus clearly established.
The great outlines of these analyses will be traced in the following pages, with no attempt to enter into the many details which
constitute the remarkable wealth of this book.

IV

Santayana starts his analysis of the generative order of society
with a description of the birth of liberty in the newly born child.
The child's first cry reveals a wonderful power: he can make
noises that he hears. He can also move his limbs, and agitation is
his second free act. He sees light, but from the outset this light
is unequally distributed; a point, perhaps a spark, will be automatically fixed by the child's eyes and followed if it moves. Then
something philosophically momentous happens to the child: he
is not merely seeing but is looking. He distinguishes the spark
from the darker field, he can repeat this movement after the
spark has disappeared, can reawaken the image of the spark,
retain a fixed term in thought to mark a lost fact in nature: he
proves, thus, to be endowed with intelligence, spontaneity, and
initiative.

All these are manifestations of what Santayana calls the
"primal will" as manifested in each creature. Under primal will
he understands "the universal movement of nature in so far as
running through a cycle or trope it precipitates a result that
seems to us a consummation. When this will in man *foresees* and
desires some consummation, perhaps impossible, it is will in the
psychological sense." [8] Yet primal will in man (as in each
creature) is impotent, since the needs felt, that is, the conditions

[8] *Op. cit.*, p. 41, footnote; although different in terminology this theory converges
with G. H. Mead's interpretation of action.

to be fulfilled before some good can be obtained, are separated
from the good itself by some "unfulfilled prerequisite to possess
it." This is the fatal source of spiritual suffering. Primal will is
not coextensive with the entire automatism of nature. Will
envelops this automatism, and though it does not imply intelligence or premeditation, it does imply eagerness to act. But action
requires adjustment between will and opportunity. By education
the child is taught to conform to the nature of things, the will
of other persons, the customs and habits of the social environment. Conformity is the method of successful action and
art, but it involves in a certain sense the loss of liberty, or at
least the loss of the illusion of a vacant liberty, which might
permit the will to act freely without a definite impulse in an
existing world.

   This vacant liberty has to be distinguished from logical liberty,
or the contingency of existence itself, that is, the insight that
the order of the universe is not a necessary one, has the fundamental character of chance, may change at any moment but may
also remain free to be constant. The psyche, which demands
freedom from some particular obstacle, is itself a mode of existence in the midst of the contingent order of nature, and, if
craving for changes, is at least consistent in this craving. Logical
freedom thus includes both freedom to change and not to change.
A stupid misinterpretation of logical freedom – although, as Santayana says, sometimes, a stupid but learned one – induces the
belief that everything must necessarily happen as the men of
science or the philosophers of history explain that it happens,
according to physical or dialectical laws. Yet the so-called laws
are rash generalizations, the theories of science are hypothetical,
and even if known laws were universally valid for our known
world this fact would be itself contingent. Another prejudice
is the conviction of people who are sure that there is absolute
contingency in their deliberate choices, that it was they that
made the decisions, and not motives of measurable weights and
pressing circumstances that made the decisions for them. But
self-consciousness is not self-knowledge, and what comes to
consciousness in different minds comes from different depths and
represents wider or narrower fields of acquaintance. Both prejudices, the scientific and the practical one, lead to the ghost of

a "liberty of indifference" which, although fervidly claimed, is just a specter of vital liberty.

All this refers to the life of spirit, when spirit ignores its station in the material world. Under spirit Santayana does not understand any separate power, soul, person, or deity, but only the awakened inner attention that suffuses all actual feelings and thoughts; it is not an individual category, but life, in so far as it reaches pure actuality in feeling or thought. To be sure, spirit is always incarnated, and seems, therefore, to be imprisoned and captive in the toils of time, place, person, and circumstances. Yet, in reality, incarnation is the cause of the existence of spirit, and the necessary prior occasion to any selection of images, feelings, wishes, or ideals that spirit may encounter. Spirit has not to choose to be or not to be, has not to choose this or that fortune. Given existence, given fortune in which the spirit is captive, the problem for it is to digest, to refine, to dominate that existence. Thus the inner liberty of the spirit will be not vacant but vital; for it will be the very vitality of its body and of its world, here and now actualized and become conscious.

In this realm of vital liberty there opens a chasm between the demands of the natural powers of primal will and the path open to action. This conflict is manifested in the various forms of servitude. There is first the necessary servitude which originates in the fact that spirit, even in its most extroverted acts such as sensation or perception, reaches a conclusion, defines an image, intuits an essence as a term for retrospection and reasoning, whereas the flux of nature has flowed on. The necessary servitude of the spirit is thus a double one: servitude to the changing world of things, which conditions the life of the animal psyche; and servitude to the animal psyche, which conditions the life of the spirit. This necessary servitude is servitude to heredity and physical endowment, to the non-ego as body and as things.

But there is another kind of servitude, namely servitude to society as the non-ego represented by fellow-men, the servitude of the child to the parents, of the adult to the language, mores, manners, morals, religions of the crowd, to family, country, party. In so far as primal parental and sexual bonds are concerned, this servitude, too, is a necessary one; but servitude to custom is to a certain extent voluntary – the tavern, the morning paper, the novel, the game of bridge. Yet slavery in all forms, including the modern slavery to machinery, belongs to the perfect order of society in which, in this sense, all men, even their leaders, must be slaves in soul and body. Custom, even if open to preferential choosing, becomes authoritative and even sacred, and it is only one step from preferences of the tribe, expressed in imperious maxims, to the systematic use of force by a chieftain, boss, or prophet, and to the establishment of law and government. But government has traits of the militant order of society: all government is a modification of war, a means of using compulsion, although without shedding so much blood. It is a special organ of society, with a life of its own, always an evil and sometimes also a good, as war is.

This drama of primal will, psyche, and spirit in the various realms of vacant, contingent, and vital liberty, undergoing the various forms of necessary and voluntary servitude, is one of the constituent factors of the genetic order of society. The other is technology in the broadest sense of the word, the dependency of man on his tools, even if these are only a heavy stick or a pointed stone to bring the world within his reach and under his domination. Technology has here to be understood in the sense of *techné:* the arts of practicing agriculture or breeding animals as well as the production of tools and weapons for war, hunting, and fighting. It is the ultimate and fatal function of mechanical arts to make primal will in man irresponsible. The power of making tools expands the range and multiplies the instruments of the psyche, but the tool-maker or commodity-maker obtains power over society when society has begun to think these wares indispensable. He directs their interests. The economic arts are rooted in the indiscriminate impulse – hidden in the human psyche – to grasp, to keep, and to swallow. All arts are Powers in danger of becoming Dominations, because they are rivals and each tends to monopolize the energies of life.

Economic arts are based on a system of instruments: the first layer of instruments being the bodily organs, the second layer consisting of tools of any kind, the third of images and moral relations used in the way of a recipe in the broadest sense. The particular systems of instruments and their use create the ethos of the particular occupation, such as being a farmer, nomad, seaman.

Within this generative order of society, economic arts are first of all those concerned with the economics of food production. Its corollary in terms of social organization is the family group, which is also an economic and a political unit. Patriarchal government may lead to ideal monarchy, defined as government by a single psyche, by the organizing principle of a living soul. Its chief offices, as in all government, are the administration of justice and the waging of war. Santayana describes in detail the inherent vicissitudes but also the moral values of monarchical government and government in general. To him all government is an imposition and an evil, yet however irrational may be the will that animates it, it is at least an art in method and in the use of means to its ends. Politics and morals are both the names for the human physiognomy that natural life acquires, or for the natural conditions that cause that moral physiognomy to change. This holds good for all sets of instruments and for all economic arts. They may, however, change their meaning. To make an axe in order to fell a tree is an economic art; but the use of the axe to kill a wild beast or an enemy transforms it into a weapon that is an instrument in the arts of defense and destruction. It belongs to the militant order of society.

V

In distinguishing the militant order of society Santayana means to separate, in the sphere of politics and morals, the love of reforming the world from the total mutation that the world is always undergoing. To be sure, all action, all economic art exert force and have effects; but this alone does not render them militant. Existence itself is essentially a blind and involuntary war, as Heraclitus has seen, and construction involves destruction of the state of things that preceded. But when in a human psyche the master passion that would like to be absolute and to dominate the whole world becomes hostility and hatred to all dissenting forms of existence, then war becomes intentional, and the spirit of such a war is what Santayana calls militancy.

For this reason militancy is not absent, morally, from what

politically passes for peace. In polite society there is militancy among rival leaders and factions; in families and between friends there is unreasonable insistence on dominating one another; even in each individual there is often a civil war in which a new passion militates against an old circle of interests. Religion may become militant if wicked leaders of the people flout as nonsense the truths enounced by the prophet. Knowledge in its perverted form of sophistry becomes militant, imposing its images upon common sense if these images contradict the animal faith in reality which is reenacted in every perception and expectation and verified in every successful action or piece of work.

The politician becomes militant by a curious phenomenon of mirage: everything in his mind represents the real world, except his politics. Not one political philosopher has dared to chart the ocean on which he sails, or what he knows are the waves of opinion on the surface. If the politician could obtain unanimity of opinion he would sail safely forever. Yet ideas are essences, not "pictures in animals";[9] they are therefore not loaded with zeal or capable of self-propaganda. What we call the contagious force of an idea is the force of the people who have embraced it. The secular arm might stop peoples' mouths, yet the ideas remain unrefuted. The politician, becoming militant, feels that he has to mark beforehand the path that reason shall be allowed to follow, employing eloquence, personal ascendancy, education of children, and propaganda for adults. Propaganda consists in intentionally controlling the movement of ideas by social agencies. Propaganda should not be confused with propagation. The latter is something natural, comparable to the harmonious relationship between the seed and the soil. The former – propaganda – is something artificial, and is characterized by its appeal to irrelevant interests. For example, propaganda has it that religion has to be maintained because it is good for morality, sport to avoid ill health, an army to avoid war. The thoughts to be conveyed are not allowed to recommend themselves, and mere cold facts would miss the fire. Propaganda must be speculative, based on loudness, repetition, eulogy, personal influence, affections, self-interests, and vilification of all other things.

[9] *Op. cit.*, p. 198.

War itself has changed its meaning. In earlier periods its true function was the maintenance of the rights and liberties of some social organization, a state or city or family or even an individual. War was an appeal to God to give justice. This, says Santayana, was the spirit of chivalry, which made war an incidental duel fought under accepted rules. Chivalry is now thoroughly dead. Fanatical or materialistic wars appear more rational; they look to radical and final issues. Our one preoccupation is to be safe. We talk not of justice but of interests; we need our neighbor's land or colonies or markets, or at least a strip along the border. We are dreadfully crowded, insecure, and unhappy, but we believe that we would be better off if only more people spoke our language and were governed by our government.

This state of affairs gives rise to several forms of abusing domination. There is the *Realpolitiker*, from Machiavelli to Nietzsche, who assumes that it is better to be a wicked prince than no prince at all, and who takes it for granted that to survive is a mark of excellence. There is the sentimental bandit who is cruel only in order to dry the people's tears. There is the tyrant who imposes absolute government established by revolution, and not sanctioned by the previous law of the state, upon a society not in its entirety ready for the change. There are the various forms of political criminals or madmen. There is finally the anarchist who wants to bring about in the world the law of freedom as he understands it: think as you like, say what you think, do what you choose – forgetting that if there were nothing in the free mind but this law of freedom, the law would remain inapplicable because that empty mind would never know what to like or what to think.

So far we have dealt with factions as constitutive elements of the militant order of society. Another set of such elements can be found in the various forms of enterprise, which is also a form of militancy but without moral provocation and without enemies. Enterprise is less social than factional in its inspiration, but society may be more affected by it in the end. It is militancy in so far as it desires to improve the world. In economically advanced countries enterprise is chiefly economic. The peddler, the merchant, the shopkeeper, the banker, the capitalist – briefly, the middleman in trade – imposes by missionary work, that is, by advertisement and propaganda, the commercial mind first upon the urban, then upon the suburban and rural populations. Commerce has influence on religion, puritanism being a tradesman's religion; on metaphysics, favoring shallow enlightenment by reducing the universe to what can be found, weighed, measured; on philosophy, favoring positivism, reducing liberty to liberty of opinion and personal safety; on science; and even on the arts. Commerce, always as Santayana sees it, does not produce wealth but indirectly produces luxury. It has turned industry from a liberal art into a militant process of making as much money as possible, and the effect is the reversal of the moral order by turning means into ends, by creating the dominance of the producers in universal economy.

A third form of militant enterprise is created by the organizational form of government itself, namely bureaucracy. The substance of modern government is the man in office, with his particular governmental mind expressed in a particular phraseology, in legal duties and the established mechanism of his chores. Members of the government acquire, besides imitative imagination, a corporate instinct of self-preservation. This creates in the body of public officials a parasitical little organism in a large one. Domination develops as an art, the militant art of imposing a precise regimen on others. One of the many means of this art is the creating of artificial allegiances – to the nation, the country, the government – which supersede the natural allegiances originating in the generative order of society, such as those to the home and the family.

VI

As mentioned before, the three orders of society – the generative, the militant, and the rational – are ideal-typical constructs for the particular purpose of disentangling the problems of Dominations and Powers on each level. Strictly speaking, militancy itself is a strand in the generative order of society, the integrity of a part asserting itself and seeking to dominate the blind drift of the rest. It may seem that reason enters the political arena as an aggressor, and plays therein an eminently militant part. But a rational order of society must be imposed upon society by art, by express institutions and laws, and the agent whereby these institutions are imposed can never be reason itself but must be some militant enthusiasts in whom the idea of a rational society has become an obsession. The primary force in establishing a rational order of society is thus a purely vegetative growth in the psyche, as rationality itself can be interpreted as a secondary habit in the animal psyche.

Reason in itself is something internal to spirit but, like spirit itself, it cannot escape nature. Reason is a faculty of seeing identity, affinity, contrast, or irrelevance between essences present together in direct intuition. It is not a new force in the physical world, but a new harmony in vital forces, a conjunction and mutual modification of impulses or impressions in a man or a society, a life led in the light or the shadow of the past and the possible. A rational order of society would liberate all human interests, especially those that, being ideal, do not materially disturb one another and can be pursued together.

To be sure, morals, opinions, and all judgments about right and wrong are relative inasmuch as they arise in psyches, and express the capacity and inevitability of such opinions and judgments at each moment in each psyche. They are but psychological transcripts of biological processes which are self-transcendent, relevant to their occasion and relative to the organ that produces them under the stimulus. To be sure, vices and virtues frequently take masks of all kinds. But in all this relativity and in all these masks is contained some degree of truth and virtue. In politics the element of rationality is explicit, and the whole is carried on in conventional terms of interests, claims, and wrongs, the nature and ground of which seem to be self-evident: in a political debate or election nobody questions the value of victory for his own party or his own opinion. Society breeds uniformity, and superstition to defend it, and the mechanical domination of usage, if socially approved, passes for authority. Yet the more a custom or opinion flourishes, the less rational authority it has.

What, then, makes an action rational? Santayana answers that what makes an action rational is the material possibility of carrying it out successfully – in one word, Circumstances. Action well adapted to circumstances is rational. Yet this would require at each step perfect knowledge of the circumstances, whereas knowledge can never be complete, nor can it be summed up adequately, especially since other people figure as elements in circumstances, as centers of life on their own account, which cannot be rationally grasped by their fellow-men. Men are necessarily unequal, biologically, historically, and morally. Earlier times considered God to be the power governing the universe of circumstances. Liberalism has tried to grasp the diversity of life rationally, but nothing was rationalized by the liberal regime except the mechanism of production.

If all men had been born similar in capacity, government would never have arisen among them. Authority and government have the function of establishing an adequate defense against the pressure of the stronger and more militant group upon the more peaceful one. The pressure that government exerts on an individual is less brutal than that which nature exerted on him in the jungle. Absence of control may remain the ideal of enterprise in its active faith, but control becomes useful in preserving the fruits of enterprise.

The power of facts as such does not constitute authority. Public opinion and the public itself are conceptual fictions, and refer always to private opinions and private feelings which get their particular flavor by my finding that the alter ego thinks and feels as I do. Merely this "spell of unanimity" makes that which everybody thinks, or that which the majority are likely to think, a standard of solidity which in turn might become a domination.

The political form of the rational order in society is democracy. There are several forms of democracy: the spontaneous democracy of brotherly identity of impulse and interest belonging to the generative order of society; the absolute democracy, defined as power exercised by the proletariat for its own benefit, based upon the fictitious assumption of a possible unanimous vision of the world by all men; and the restricted democracy, based upon the principle of majority, universal suffrage, and representative government.

In analyzing the idea of representative government Santayana gives an outstanding example of the possiblity and even the necessity of referring concrete forms of social institutions to the principles of philosophical anthropology. He starts with the fact that only generated organisms can live and think. Human society is not a generated organism; it forms a colony of units, and its so-called life is only the resultant of the lives of the individuals forming it. The successive phases and passions of a society have to be referred to the actual life in particular psyches, with their changing needs within a world to supply or deny them. Mind, being the faculty of reviving naturalized reactions, memories, and habits, and of establishing relations among them, can arise only in individual living beings; and occasional aggregates, such as governments and societies, cannot be rationally guided except by the mind of some individual. Reason is a species of insight by which essential relations are seen to obtain between ideal terms, and therefore it cannot arise before animal sensibility has offered such terms to actual attention. The spontaneous cooperation of irrational impulses in diverse individuals, for instance under the influence of sexual or parental passion, creates an ingrained bent in one person to bring about the existence, welfare, or safety of another. Such an ingrained bent is called by Santayana "morally representative." A suitor prevailing over hesitation in the lady and a parent teaching a child are judged to represent morally the true interest of the woman or the child. Government is a machinery contrived for the survival of the individuals belonging to that particular society, and therefore it is justified biologically. Elected magistrates and legislators have to represent society not officially but morally, in the sense just outlined.

If only official representation were intended, the representative could be designated by drawing lots. The task of morally representing the unaided individual is taken over by the party, rather than by its elected members. When the nation to be governed has never had moral unity, or has lost it, the government cannot be rational, for it does not supply to its rulers a guiding purpose; and unless a political prophet can impose a faith of his own, that government must be by politicians. Yet in all circumstances a moral dilemma besets a representative officer. If he is merely an instrument executing instructions, issued by the peoples who have elected him, he is not an officer of government at all, but only a servant of the government. A certain initiative must be left to a representative. Moreover, an elected representative is elected by a majority of votes; a large minority would have given him contrary instructions. This is a congenital defect of government by election: a party is not the whole people, and if a representative is bound to express only the will of the party he is not a fair representative of a truly self-governing people.

Here starts the actual function of a parliament: it gives the opportunity for discussion and persuasion; it relieves tyranny because it ventilates grievances; it serves the useful purpose of conciliating the governed. In a democracy everyone votes, but it is not yet clear whether each is expected to vote in the interest of his "country" or only of his own person and trade. Democracy, in choosing its agents, is faced by a dilemma: shall representatives be expected to voice the opinions or advance the schemes of their electors, or shall they be trusted, in view of their acknowledged gifts, to serve their electors by serving the best interests of all who are affected? Is a parliament a central exchange for demands, or is it an elite commissioned to govern justly? Americans, says Santayana, expect a government to govern the country by governing the people. Yet in history most governments that have really dominated their territories have governed the people by governing the country.

But who are the people? The inhabitants of a region or of the globe? Are they the population subject to the jurisdiction of the particular government? Are resident foreigners or tourists part of the people? Are the interests of the people their actual interests as they understand them, or have purposes pursued in the past history of a nation to be taken into account? And if the people misunderstand their "true interest" has good government to make itself representative of the people's "higher self"? Santayana feels that we must look to the generative order of society to see what "the people" may signify in fact: there we find that people is a civilized tribe united by blood, language, and religion. If a mixed population in a given territory tends to segregate rather than to merge (as whites and colored in the United States) it will become two peoples (which would not necessarily prevent them from living side by side under the same government).

In a democracy the people, however defined, is not only the object of government but also its agent. The operations of the government are necessarily a part of the people's life and history.

The public participates emotionally in the fortunes of its government, makes itself spiritually an accomplice to its deeds. They obey the decrees issued, thus showing agreement. Yet the idea of government by the people remains elusive and ambiguous because it is by deputy only that the people can steadily govern. There are two possibilities: either a man selected for his eminence to represent the people may care more for the general interest and understand the people better than does the average citizen supposed to direct him; or by transformation of the class of deputies into professional politicians, and by the growth of special party interests in the governing class, government may cease to be even indirectly government by the people and may become either an oligarchy or a bureaucracy. Thus self-government by the people can never be fully realized, and always runs the danger of turning into a domination.

Parliamentary democracy has found a protection in the principle of compromise. Compromise is always established between will and fate, at least in the economic arts. In politics it prevails between will and other wills, not between will and physical circumstances. Compromise extends to morals the rational procedure of the economic arts, executed in the service of primal will. There are two stages in this rational cooperation with circumstances: one political, when we change only the method or the instrument by which we meant to achieve an end; the other, deeper one, occurs when we suspend a given aim, substituting another no less compatible with primal will and vital liberty. Yet the basic supposition of democratic government is acquiescence by both the people at large and the agents of the government. Custom is the greatest source of acquiescence; the menace of brute force is another. Acquiescence expresses always an adjustment already made or in the making to normal conditions, not favorable in themselves yet impossible to disregard if action is to be successful.

Success in the moral sense will depend upon two things: whether the government sees what is truly the good of the people; and whether it can secure it in the circumstances then prevailing. Yet the criterion of what is good for the people lies within the people itself, that is, in its will, in the demands and potentialities of its nature, not within its consciousness. Whose good has a government to pursue? Obviously, the good of all, those within its jurisdiction whom it can actually control, tax, imprison, execute, or forcibly enroll for military service. More difficult is the question what good the people, or special classes among them, will derive from being thus governed. The generative order of society proceeds not toward an ultimate goal but through a concourse of tentative actions frequently clashing with one another. In the individual, spirit (Kant's transcendental unity of apperception) may lighten this war in the psyche by reason. Society, however, is many-centered, and there is no living seat for observation or judgment except those individuals themselves.

A social order approaching rationality can be attained only by institutions that can sanction verbal laws by force. This control can be exercised either by government, with explicit laws sanctioned by military force, or by natural contagion, cooperation, or suasion. Both have their sources in the two authorities which, by their interplay, determine the forms of morals: the authority of things that permit, prevent, reward, or punish our actions; and the authority of primal will within us, which chooses our path and discriminates between success and disaster in our careers. Government is the rational art of minimizing the conflicts of primal irrational wills with one another and with the forces of nature. In other words, a rational government is one that speaks to its people in the name of the nature of things, and acts by that authority. The first principle of rationality in government is that it should protect and encourage vital liberty in whatever form. Like a physician, such a government would impose only a legal diet enabling us to escape or to overcome the assaults that natural accidents make upon us. All else a rational government would leave to the special genius of each free society and each free individual. Such a government would be autocratic but not totalitarian, for it would speak for the material conditions imposed by nature on the realization of any ideal, without dictating to any person or society what this ideal should be.

Thus the circle is accomplished: we are living in a world wherein our behavior has causes and consequences that recede in all directions until they become irrelevant to our interests; but at closer quarters they can be traced in terms of the sensations and ideas that events excite in us. Knowledge of the world and

of what is possible in it will not solve for us the question of what
is our true good. There is therefore another sphere, that of
potential goods, which each man may evoke according to the
warmth and richness of his imagination. It follows from the
evolution of the psyche through plants and animals that its
treasure is different at each stage. In man it is alien domination
that makes any one mistake his vocation. But existence imposes
limitation even on the imagination and the will. Wisdom lies
not in pronouncing what sort of good is best but in understanding
each good within the lives that actually enjoy it as it actually is
in its physical complexion and its moral essence.

VII

With these words Santayana dismisses the reader. He leaves
him in a state of bewilderment as well as of admiration. Admiration is due to his truly philosophical craftsmanship in organizing the problems of a philosophical anthropology around the
existential experience of the human situation within the world;
admiration is due also to the consistency with which social and
political life is described in terms of a drama of will, psyche, and
spirit oscillating between the vacant, the indifferent, and the
vital forms of liberty, and the forms of necessary and voluntary
servitude. But with bewilderment we confront the thesis that man
lives originally by bread alone, and that all arts not contributing
directly or indirectly to food supply are merely parasitical even
though they are important for human happiness. We understand
perhaps better than any other generation Santayana's thesis of
the enslavement of mankind by technology, of the self-alienation
of the spirit by its bondage to the means which have become
omnipotent and ends in themselves. But when we read that
modern economic enterprise has become a domination, since the
"middleman in trade" imposes militancy on the generative order,
or when we read that democracy is not capable of solving the
political problem unless it looks to the generative order of society, we feel that something must be basically wrong in Santayana's point of departure.

It seems to me that the root of this shortcoming lies in the
metaphysical assumption that the generative order of society is

the paramount social reality upon which all the other orders are founded. This, in turn, is due to the attempt to deal with man from the point of view of a naturalist and materialist who is not satisfied with an analysis of the world as taken for granted but aims at founding life, psyche, and spirit, in brief, human nature, upon the physical order of nature. But, to quote Kurt Riezler, man, who asks such questions, "is himself the reality to be questioned, and thus carries the entire burden of the question. He cannot learn from the atom what he is, though in the conceptual mirror of physics he may entirely 'consist of atoms.' " [10]

In his *Dialogues in Limbo* Santayana includes two colloquies between Socrates and the Stranger on self-government. The basic theme is an old oracle which reads, "Right government rests on the will of the governed." And at the end of the dialogue Socrates interprets this oracle as follows: "There is no right government except good government; good government is what benefits the governed; the good of the governed is determined not by their topmost wishes or their ruling passions but by their hidden nature and their real opportunities; and only knowledge discovering the hidden nature and these real opportunities, and speaking in their name, has a right to rule in the state or in the private conscience."

[10] Kurt Riezler, *Man: Mutable and Immutable*, Chicago, 1950, p. 311.

EQUALITY AND THE MEANING STRUCTURE
OF THE SOCIAL WORLD

I. INTRODUCTION

The subject of the present paper is the theoretical analysis of various aspects of the notion of equality in the common-sense thinking of concrete social groups. The general idea of equality in the philosophical or religious sense is not within the scope of our investigation, and therefore is intentionally omitted. It is sufficient for our purpose to acknowledge that all common-sense aspects of equality are merely secularizations of more or less clearly conceived ethical or religious principles which are just taken for granted beyond question. Consequently, no attempt has been made at referring the common-sense notion of equality to the idea of the dignity of man, to the relation of the soul to God, or to the Right of Nature.

Our main thesis is that the meaning which the common-sense notion of equality has for a particular social group is as such an element of the system of typifications and relevances approved by it, and so of the sociocultural situation as taken for granted by it at any moment of its history. The common-sense aspects of equality – as distinguished from the philosophical and theological idea of equality – have thus a relational character; they depend upon the structure of the system of relevances, and it is submitted that a shift in this structure is mirrored in changes of the aspects of equality.

It is also hoped that an analysis of the relationship between equality and the system of references will, on the one hand, eliminate some of the equivocations which obfuscate the notion of equality – first of all, the confusion of homogeneity with equality – and, on the other hand, show why we speak in different contexts of social equality, political equality, equality before the law, and equality of opportunity; or why the more subtle language of Greek philosophy could distinguish equality in several domains of relevances such as *isotimia* or equal respect for all, *isonomia* or equality before the law, *isogoria* or equal freedom of speech and hence of political action, *isokratia* or equality in political power, *isopsephia* or equal right to vote, *isopoliteia* or equality of civil rights, *isodaimonia* or equality in fortune and happiness, *isomoiria* or participation in a partnership with an equal share.

The analysis of equality is, however, complicated by the fact that its meaning is different when interpreted by members of the group under scrutiny (in-group) in terms of its own system of typifications and relevances; when interpreted by members of other groups (out-groups) in terms of theirs; or, finally, when interpreted by the social scientist who inquires into either or both. This is just a special case of the principal ambivalence of the meaning of all social phenomena which many social scientists, and especially Max Weber, have clearly pointed out. In Weber's unfortunate – but generally accepted – terminology, we have to distinguish between the *subjective meaning* a situation has for the person involved (or the one a particular action has for the actor himself), and the *objective meaning*, that is, the interpretation of the same situation or the same action by anybody else. The terminology is unfortunate because the so-called objective meaning – or better, meanings – are again relative to the observer, partner, scientist, etc. Yet, by reason of terminological discipline we shall use the terms subjective and objective meaning in this paper in accordance with these definitions.

It can easily be shown that, strictly speaking, subjective and objective meanings can never coincide, although institutionalizations and standardizations of social situations and interaction-patterns make possible their assimilation to an extent sufficient for many practical purposes. We shall encounter the dichotomy of subjective and objective meaning on various levels and in connection with various problems: the ways of life of a group as seen by in-group and out-group; the definition of the individual's personal situation within the group by himself and by the group; the notion of "group" itself as defined by its members and by outsiders; the formation of domains of relevances; the dialectic of prejudices; the concepts of discrimination and minority rights;

the rank order of discriminations; equality aimed-at and to-be-granted; and, finally, the concepts of opportunity and chance.

This brief outline of the paper also determines its organization. In a first section we shall deal in a rather abbreviated way with the system of socially approved typifications in terms of which the common-sense experience of man living his everyday life within it interprets the social world and its organization. It will be shown that these typifications are themselves organized in domains of relevances which form, in turn, a system and are elements of what Max Scheler called the relative natural conception of the world (*relativ natürliche Weltanschauung*) of the particular group. The qualifier *relativ*, let it be said, should distinguish this concept from the idea of a general State of Nature as assumed by Hobbes, Locke, Rousseau, and the ancient and modern theoreticians of a Right of Nature.

Starting from certain teachings of Plato and Aristotle it will be shown in the second section that only elements pertaining to the same domain of relevances ("homogeneous" elements) can be compared in terms of equality or inequality, whereas elements pertaining to different domains of relevances ("heterogeneous" elements) cannot be compared without leading to logical or axiological contradictions.

A third section will deal 1) with the self-interpretation of the social group, 2) with the interpretation by the out-group of the system of typifications and relevances prevailing in a particular group, and 3) with the interpretation of both by the social scientist, the philosopher, and the theologian. This will give us the opportunity for some brief remarks on the interrelationship of the several interpretations.

The fourth section comprises a detailed study of some significant examples of the dichotomy between subjective and objective interpretation. A first subsection deals with the problem of group membership, which can be defined by the individual or imposed from outside. The concepts of imposed group membership and imposed systems of relevances are keys for the analysis of particular problems of the subjective and objective implications of equality. These will be studied in a second subsection. Although a systematic treatment is not possible, we shall nevertheless find occasion to examine certain decisions of the Supreme Court of the United States relating to the Fourteenth Amendment, documents prepared by the Secretary General of the United Nations on discrimination and protection of minorities, and passages from Gunnar Myrdal's *An American Dilemma*, and to study them within the conceptual framework developed in the preceding sections. The final subsection, (C), is concerned with the objective and subjective meaning of the notion of opportunity.

II. THE SOCIAL WORLD AS TAKEN FOR GRANTED AND ITS STRUCTURIZATION

We start from an examination of the social world in its various articulations and forms of organization which constitute the social reality for men living within it. Man is born into a world that existed before his birth, and this world is from the outset not merely a physical but also a sociocultural one. The latter is a preconstituted and preorganized world whose particular structure is the result of an historical process and is therefore different for each culture and society.

Certain features, however, are common to all social worlds because they are rooted in the human condition. Everywhere we find sex groups and age groups, and some division of labor conditioned by them; and more or less rigid kinship organizations that arrange the social world into zones of varying social distance, from intimate familiarity to strangeness. Everywhere we also find hierarchies of superordination and subordination, of leader and follower, of those in command and those in submission. Everywhere, too, we find an accepted way of life, that is, a conception of how to come to terms with things and men, with nature and the supernatural. There are everywhere, moreover, cultural objects, such as tools needed for the domination of the outer world, playthings for children, articles for adornment, musical instruments of some kind, objects serving as symbols for worship. There are certain ceremonies marking the great events in the life cycle of the individual (birth, initiation, marriage, death), or in the rhythm of nature (sowing and harvesting, solstices, etc.).

Social scientists have frequently tried to classify the various activities of men found in all social organizations by establishing a list of basic needs which have to be satisfied by the functions of the body social. These needs, it is assumed, motivate the action of individuals and determine the organizational and institutional framework within which such activities take place. Nearly all of these lists include the so-called biological needs for food, shelter, and sex; some also include the need for common protection against the forces of nature, against evil spirits or outer enemies. Others stipulate certain psychological needs as basic and general: for example, the wish for recognition by fellow-men, or the wish to proceed to ever new experiences.

In the present state of the social sciences all these lists of needs believed to be basic and general seem at best to be more or less aptly formulated heuristic devices and, as such, are doubtless useful. Yet neither studies in social or individual psychology nor in cultural anthropology can establish the criteria for deciding which needs and motives have to be considered as "basic" and universal. Without such criteria it is impossible to formulate a sound theory of the equality of men grounded on the equal needs of mankind. Only an examination of the human condition in general, of the place of man in the cosmos – in other words, only a fully developed philosophical anthropology – could teach us the elements necessary for the solution of this problem. It appears from his last writings that Scheler had planned such a study. Our task in the present paper is not to embark upon an enterprise of this kind. We shall restrict ourselves to a general description of some features of social reality as experienced by man living his daily life among his fellow-men within it.

Thus, the social world into which man is born and within which he has to find his bearings is experienced by him as a tight knit web of social relationships, of systems of signs and symbols with their particular meaning structure, of institutionalized forms of social organization, of systems of status and prestige, etc. The meaning of all these elements of the social world in all its diversity and stratification, as well as the pattern of its texture itself, is by those living within it just taken for granted. The sum-total of the relative natural aspect the social world has for those living within it constitutes, to use William Graham Sumner's term, the folkways of the in-group, which are socially accepted as the good ways and the right ways for coming to terms with things and fellow-men. They are taken for granted because they have stood the test so far, and, being socially approved, are held as requiring neither an explanation nor a justification.

These folkways constitute the social heritage which is handed down to children born into and growing up within the group; and by a process of acculturation the approaching stranger who wants to be accepted by the group has, in the same way as the child, not only to learn the structure and significance of the elements to be interpreted, but also the scheme of interpretation prevailing in and accepted by the in-group without question.

This is so, because the system of folkways establishes the standard in terms of which the in-group "defines its situation." Even more: originating in previous situations defined by the group, the scheme of interpretation that has stood the test so far becomes an element of the actual situation. To take the world for granted beyond question implies the deeprooted assumption that until further notice the world will go on substantially in the same manner as it has so far; that what has proved to be valid up to now will continue to be so, and that anything we or others like us could successfully perform once can be done again in a like way and will bring about substantially like results.

To be sure, what has been beyond question so far and remained unquestioned up to now may always be put in question: things taken for granted then become problematical. This will be the case, for example, if there occurs in the individual or social life an event or situation which cannot be met by applying the traditional and habitual pattern of behavior or interpretation. We call such a situation a crisis – a partial one if it makes only some elements of the world taken for granted questionable, a total one if it invalidates the whole system of reference, the scheme of interpretation itself.

For our purpose, it will be necessary to investigate somewhat more fully the structure of common-sense knowledge that man living his everyday life within the group has of its folkways, and also the manner in which he acquires such knowledge. This common-sense knowledge is by no means identical with that of the social scientist. Modern sociologists dealing with the social system as such describe a concrete social group, for example, as a structural-functional context of interlocked social roles and status relations, of patterns of performance and significance.

Such patterns, in the form of expectations adhering to these roles and status relations, become motivational for the actual and future actions of the incumbents to fulfill the functions prescribed by the position occupied by them within this system. Talcott Parsons says, for example:

A role ... is a sector of the total orientation system of an individual actor which is organized about expectations in relation to a particular inter-action context, that is integrated with a particular set of value-standards which govern interaction with one or more alters [fellow-men] in the appropriate complementary roles.[1]

In the monograph which Parsons and Edward A. Shils contri-buted to the volume, *Toward a General Theory of Action*, we read:

For most purposes *the conceptual unit of the social system is the role*. The role is a sector of the individual actor's total system of action. It is the point of contact between the system of action of the individual actor and the social system. The individual then becomes a unity in the sense that he is a composite of various action units which in turn are roles in the relationships in which he is involved. ...

What an actor is expected to do in a given situation both by himself and by others constitutes the expectations of that role ...

In each specific situation institutionalization exists when each actor in the situation does, and believes he should do, what the other actors whom he confronts believe he should do.[2]

This is not the place to enter into a critical discussion of some of the notions used in this highly ingenious conceptual scheme. For our purpose the few sentences just quoted give a sufficient picture of the views taken by an influential school of modern social scientists. But it will be useful to remember that what the sociologist calls "system," "role," "status," "role expectation," "situation," and "institutionalization," is experienced by the individual actor on the social scene in entirely different terms. To him all the factors denoted by these concepts are elements of a network of typifications – typifications of human individuals, of their course-of-action patterns, of their motives and goals, or of the sociocultural products which originated in their actions. These types were formed in the main by others, his predecessors

---

[1] Talcott Parsons, *The Social System*, Glencoe, 1951, pp. 38 ff. Quoted by per-mission of the Macmillan Company, New York.

[2] Talcott Parsons and Edward A. Shils, "Values, Motives, and Systems of Actions," *Toward a General Theory of Action*, edited by Parsons and Shils, Cambridge, Massa-chusetts, 1951, pp. 190, 191, 194. (author's italics). Quoted by permission of Harvard University Press.

or contemporaries, as appropriate tools for coming to terms with things and men, accepted as such by the group into which he was born. But there are also self-typifications: man typifies to a certain extent his own situation within the social world and the various relations he has to his fellow-men and cultural objects.

The knowledge of these typifications and of their appropriate use is an inseparable element of the sociocultural heritage handed down to the child born into the group by his parents and his teachers and the parents of his parents and the teachers of his teachers; it is, thus, socially derived. The sum-total of these various typifications constitutes a frame of reference in terms of which not only the sociocultural, but also the physical world has to be interpreted, a frame of reference that, in spite of its inconsistencies and its inherent opaqueness, is nonetheless sufficiently integrated and transparent to be used for solving most of the practical problems at hand.

It should be emphasized that the interpretation of the world in terms of types, as understood here, is not the outcome of a process of ratiocination, let alone of scientific conceptualization. The world, the physical as well as the sociocultural one, is experienced from the outset in terms of types: there are mountains, trees, birds, fishes, dogs, and among them Irish setters; there are cultural objects, such as houses, tables, chairs, books, tools, and among them hammers; and there are typical social roles and relationships, such as parents, siblings, kinsmen, strangers, soldiers, hunters, priests, etc. Thus, typifications on the common-sense level – in contradistinction to typifications made by the scientist, and especially the social scientist – emerge in the everyday experience of the world as taken for granted without any formulation of judgments or of neat propositions with logical subjects and predicates. They belong, to use a phenomenological term, to prepredicative thinking. The vocabulary and the syntax of the vernacular of everyday language represent the epitome of the typifications socially approved by the linguistic group.

But of what does the process of typification consist? If we call an animal a dog we have already performed a kind of typification. Each dog is a unique individual and as such different from all other dogs, although he has in common with them a set of characteristic traits and qualities. By recognizing Rover as a dog and calling him so, I have disregarded what makes Rover the unique and individual dog he means to me. Typifying consists in passing by what makes the individual unique and irreplaceable. In so far as Rover is just a dog, he is deemed to be equal to all other dogs: a doglike behavior is expected of him, a particular way of eating, of running, etc. But even looking at Rover as an individual in his uniqueness, I may find that today he behaves in an extraordinary way. It is typical for him to greet me when I return home. Today he is rather lethargic and I fear he may be ill. Even my notion of the individual and unique Rover already involves a typification of what I believe to be his habitual behavior. And even the ill Rover has his typical way of being ill. (The problem of typification was studied by Husserl in his *Erfahrung und Urteil*, but the question of whether the ill Socrates as a whole is like Socrates in health taken as a whole had already been discussed in Plato's *Theaetetus*, 159 B). On the other hand, I may look upon Rover as a mammal or an animal, or simply as an object in the outer world.

How is it possible to subsume the same individual object under any of the typifications which can be arranged in a gamut reaching from the typical behavior of the ailing Rover all the way to the characteristics typical of an object in the outer world? Or, in other words, what are the motives for positing – under certain conditions – certain traits as equal (or, as we prefer to say, "homogeneous") in all the objects falling under the same type; and under other conditions for disregarding the particular traits by which the typified objects differ from one another?

The answer is that all typification consists in the equalization of traits relevant to the particular purpose at hand for the sake of which the type has been formed, and in disregarding those individual differences of the typified objects that are irrelevant to such purpose. There is no such thing as a type pure and simple. All types are relational terms carrying, to borrow from mathematics, a subscript referring to the purpose for the sake of which the type has been formed. And this purpose is nothing but the theoretical or practical problem which, as a consequence of our situationally determined interest, has emerged as questionable from the unquestioned background of the world just taken for granted. Our actual interest, however, is the outcome of our actual biographical situation within our environment as defined by us.

The reference of the type to the problem for whose solution it has been formed, its *problem-relevance* as we shall call it, constitutes the meaning of the typification. Thus a *series of types* of concrete unique objects can be formed, each emphasizing certain aspects which the object has in common with other objects because these aspects alone are relevant to the practical or theoretical problem at hand. Each problem requires, thus, another kind of typification.

This statement, however, is not to be interpreted in the sense that only one particular type can be formed for the solution of each particular problem under scrutiny. On the contrary, numerous types can be formed and frequently have to be formed for the solution of one particular problem. The well circumscribed problem can be said to be the locus of all possible types that can be formed for the sake of its solution, that is, of all problem-relevant types. We may also say that all of these types pertain, by the very fact of their reference to the same problem, to the same *domain of relevance*.[3]

The expression "the same problem" is, however, an abbreviation. More accurately, one should speak of a domain of relevances as being constituted by a set of interrelated problems. For it must be kept in mind that there is no such thing as an isolated problem. Any problem is a problem within a context; it carries along its outer horizons that refer to other problems, and it has its infinite inner horizons whose implications can – at least potentially – be made explicit by ever new inquiry. The determination of the conditions under which a problem has to be deemed sufficiently solved, *i.e.*, of the point at which further inquiry may cease, is an element of the formulation of the problem itself. This, incidentally, involves the drawing of a demarcation line between problem-relevant features and all the other elements in the field under scrutiny, considered as mere "data." Data are thus, for the time being, unquestioned facts which until further notice need not be called in question. However, it is

---

[3] By the term "relevance" is meant always "problem-relevance" as previously defined. There are also other forms of relevance which, however, are not dealt with in the present paper.

precisely the system of problem-relevances that establishes the boundaries between the typical and what has been passed by in the typification. (The dangerous fallacy of confusing the untypified with the atypical is frequent.)

Since the system of problem-relevances depends, in turn, upon the interests originating in a particular situation, if follows that the same object or event may turn out as relevant or irrelevant, typified or untypified, and even typical and atypical, in relation both to different problems to be solved and different situations within which the object or event emerges, that is, in relation to different interests. To illustrate the last case: if parents observe that their child acts in a "strange," *i.e.*, atypical way, a psychologist may comfortingly inform them that it is "typical" for children of that age to behave as their child does. Parents and psychologists simply use different systems of relevances and therewith different types for interpreting the same event.

Thus, the field of everyday experience is at any particular moment structured into various domains of relevances, and it is precisely the prevailing system of relevances that determines what has to be assumed as being typically equal (homogeneous) and what as being typically different (heterogeneous). This statement holds good for all kinds of typifications. In the social world as taken for granted, however, we find, as our preceding analyses have shown, a socially approved system of typifications called the ways of life of the in-group. It likewise constitutes a particular structure of domains of relevances which also are taken for granted. Its origin can easily be understood: the world taken for granted by the in-group is a world of a common situation within which common problems emerge within a common horizon, problems requiring typical solutions by typical means for bringing about typical ends.

Each of these problems determines what is problem-relevant and what is not. In this manner socially accepted domains of common relevances are circumscribed, though that does not necessarily mean that their system is fully integrated or that they do not overlap. They may be, and frequently are, inconsistent and sometimes even in conflict with one another. Nor is the system static. On the contrary, it changes, for example, from generation to generation, and its dynamic development is one of the main causes for changes in the social structure itself.

A system of relevances and typifications, as it exists at any historical moment, is itself a part of the social heritage and as such is handed down in the educational process to the members of the in-group. It has various important functions:

1. It determines which facts or events have to be treated as substantially – that is, typically – equal (homogeneous) for the purpose of solving in a typical manner typical problems that emerge or might emerge in situations typified as being equal (homogeneous).

2. It transforms unique individual actions of unique human beings into typical functions of typical social roles, originating in typical motives aimed at bringing about typical ends. The incumbent of such a social role is expected by the other members of the in-group to act in the typical way defined by this role. On the other hand, by living up to his role the incumbent typifies himself; that is, he resolves to act in the typical way defined by the social role he has assumed. He resolves to act in a way in which a businessman, soldier, judge, father, friend, gangleader, sportsman, buddy, regular fellow, good boy, American, taxpayer, etc., is supposed to act. Any role thus involves a self-typification on the part of the incumbent.

3. It functions as both a scheme of interpretation and as a scheme of orientation for each member of the in-group and constitutes therewith a universe of discourse among them. Whoever (I included) acts in the socially approved typical way is supposed to be motivated by the pertinent typical motives and to aim at bringing about the pertinent typical state of affairs. He has a reasonable chance, by such actions, of coming to terms with everyone who accepts the same system of relevances and takes the typifications originating therein for granted. On the one hand, I have – in order to understand another – to apply the system of typifications accepted by the group to which both of us belong. For example, if he uses the English language, I have to interpret his statements in terms of the code of the English dictionary and English grammar. On the other hand, in order to make myself understandable to another, I have to avail myself of the same system of typifications as a scheme of orientation for my projected action. Of course, there is a mere chance, namely, a mere

likelihood, that the scheme of typifications used by me as a scheme of orientation will coincide with that used by my fellow-man as a scheme of interpretation; otherwise misunderstandings among people of goodwill would be impossible. But at least as a first approximation we take it for granted that we both mean what we say and say what we mean.

4. The chances of success of human interaction, that is, the establishment of a congruency between the typified scheme used by the actor as a scheme of orientation and by his fellow-men as a scheme of interpretation, is enhanced if the scheme of typification is standardized, and the system of pertinent relevances institutionalized. The various means of social control (mores, morals, laws, rules, rituals) serve this purpose.

5. The socially approved system of typifications and relevances is the common field within which the private typifications and relevance structures of the individual members of the group originate. This is so, because the private situation of the individual as defined by him is always a situation within the group, his private interests are interests with reference to those of the group (whether by way of particularization or antagonism), his private problems are necessarily in a context with the group's problems. Again, this private system of domains of relevance might be inconsistent in itself; it might also be incompatible with the socially approved one. For example, I may take entirely different attitudes toward the problems of rearmament of the United States in my social role as a father of a boy, as a taxpayer, as a member of my church, as a patriotic citizen, as a pacifist, and as a trained economist. Nevertheless, all these partially conflicting and intersecting systems of relevances, both those taken for granted by the group and my private ones, constitute particular domains of relevances; all objects, facts, and events are homogeneous in the sense that they are relevant to the same problem. But are they therefore equal, or at least equal in some respect? Or are they merely treated as equal although they are not? And is the opposite of this concept of equality inequality – or merely differentiation?

The attempt to answer these questions leads us to a new dimension of our inquiry.

III. THE CONCEPT OF EQUALITY
AND THE STRUCTURE OF RELEVANCE

The preceding section has shown how the social world as taken for granted in common-sense thinking is articulated in various domains of relevances, each constituted by a set of problem-relevant types. Typification consists in disregarding those individual features in the typified objects, facts, or events which are irrelevant to the actual problem at hand. In a certain sense it could be said that all objects falling under the same type are "equal" or at least deemed equal. For instance, we think of people as Frenchmen or Germans, Catholics or Protestants, aliens or neighbors, Negroes or Orientals, men or women, as speaking English or Russian, and as being wealthy or poor. Each of these terms designates a type, and all individuals falling within such a type are considered as being interchangeable with respect to the typified trait.

This is certainly one meaning of the highly equivocal term equality. But in order to avoid semantic confusion it might be better to call all objects, facts, events, persons, traits, falling in the same type and so pertaining to the same domain of relevance, *homogeneous*. Elements, however, pertaining to different domains of relevances will be called *heterogeneous*. We propose to reserve the terms equality and inequality for the relationship of elements pertaining to the same domain of relevance.

We must always bear in mind that even within a homogeneous domain there are differences in degrees of excellence of the typified traits and characteristics, and differences with respect to traits and characteristics which are not within the focus of the type formed and can be called "so far untypified elements." To seize upon them would require the formation of additional types, either subtypes of the same order, or even of types of a different order. The type "soldier," for example, includes generals as well as privates, the type "college student" seniors and freshmen, and among them students of various aptitudes and scholarly achievements. Equality and inequality in this sense refer to various degrees of excellence in performance, achievement, and status – but only of homogeneous elements, that is, only elements belonging to the same domain of relevances are comparable in this respect. The discussion of problems of equality and inequality is frequently obscured by the fact that these terms are applied to relationships between heterogeneous elements.

Aristotle, in a famous passage in his *Politics* (1282b 15–1283a 20), has discussed these problems and some interrelated ones that are of immediate interest to us. The passage deals with the problem of justice and points out that all men think justice to be a sort of equality:

But there still remains a question: equality or inequality of what? Here is a difficulty which calls for political speculation.

It would be wrong, Aristotle maintains, to say that persons of superior excellence in whatever respect should have offices of state. If this were a valid qualification, then the complexion or height of a man or any other advantage would be a reason for him to claim a greater share of political rights. But height cannot be measured against wealth, nor can both be measured, against freedom. And since no such comparison can be made, it is evident that if some be slow and others swift, that is no reason why the one should have more and the other fewer political rights. It is in gymnastic contests that such excellence is rewarded, whereas the rival claims of candidates for office can be based only on the possession of elements which enter into the composition of the state.

If we translate these observations of Aristotle into the terminology of this paper, we may say that equality and inequality are relational notions and have to be defined in terms of the domain of relevances to which they pertain. Only within each of these domains of relevances can degrees of merit and excellence be distinguished. Moreover, that which is comparable in terms of the system of one domain is not comparable in terms of other systems, and for this reason the application of yardsticks not pertaining to the same domain of relevances leads to logical or axiological (moral) inconsistencies.

This view clearly appears to have been Aristotle's, for in the passage just referred to he gives a further illustration and develops another idea of the highest importance for our further investigation:

When a number of fluteplayers are equal in their art, there is no reason why those who are better born should have better flutes given to them;

for they will not play any better on the flute, and the superior instrument should be reserved for him who is the better artist.

Then, after a solemn warning to the reader, ("If what I am saying is still obscure it will be made clearer by what follows.") Aristotle continues:

For if there were a superior fluteplayer, who was far inferior in birth and beauty, *although either of these may be a greater good than the art of flute-playing, and may excel fluteplaying in a greater ratio than he excels the others in his art,* still he ought to have the better flute given to him, unless the advantages of wealth and birth contribute to fluteplaying, which they do not.

Not only is it clearly stated here that the privileges of birth and of wealth are elements heterogeneous to the domain of relevance of flute-playing, but from this passage it also appears that there exists a certain order of ranks among the domains of relevances themselves, and that, even if birth or beauty or wealth are higher goods than the art of fluteplaying, excellence in flute-playing has, nevertheless, to be determined in terms of the domain of relevance to which this artistic activity pertains.

The domains of relevances are, thus, themselves arranged in an order of superiority and of inferiority; and their order differs from group to group. This can be clearly seen from another passage in Aristotle [4] in which the problem of equality is discussed in connection with his notion of distributive justice. The question is, how a certain good, let us say a reward, should justly be distributed between two persons. According to Aristotle, four terms are involved here: the two persons and the two parts into which the good should be divided. The distribution is just if the good is divided in a ratio C : D, equal to the ratio of merit between the two persons A and B.[5]

This is, of course, the same idea as that of Plato's geometrical equality (*isótēs geometrikē*), which is developed in *Laws* VI, 757 A, in contradistinction to the *isótēs arithmetikē*, which is merely the equality of the rules of measures, weight, and number, that leads, for example, to using the equality of the lot for elections in a democracy (this term to be understood as it was used by Plato). Thus, says Plato:

[4] Aristotle, *Nicomachean Ethics*, 1131a 14–1131b 24.
[5] W. D. Ross, *Aristotle*, London, 1945, p. 210.

To unequals equals become unequal, if they are not harmonized by measure.

But Aristotle continues, and this is a decisive point for our problem:

Merit is, however, estimated differently in different states; in democracy freedom is the standard and all freemen are deemed equal; in oligarchy the standard is wealth or noble birth; in aristocracy, virtue.

This means that the order of domains of relevances prevailing in a particular social group is itself an element of the relative natural conception of the world taken for granted by the in-group as an unquestioned way of life. In each group the order of these domains has its particular history. It is an element of socially approved and socially derived knowledge, and frequently is institutionalized. Manifold are the principles that are supposed to establish this order. In Plato's *Laws* (631 C, 697 B, 728 E, 870), for example, all the details of the proposed legislation are derived from the order of goods: the divine ones (wisdom, temperance, courage, justice) and the human ones (health, beauty, strength, wealth); or the things in which every man has an interest have their specific rank: the interests about money have the lowest, next come the interests of the body, and of the highest rank are the interests of the soul (*Laws*, 743 E). And Plato comes to the conclusion that a law must be wrong in which health has been preferred to temperance, or wealth to both.

But this is just one example of the many principles in accordance with which the domains of relevances can be ranked. Aristotle's statement that merit is differently estimated in different states, contains an important element of modern sociology of knowledge. We have to recall Max Scheler's findings that in any culture the highest rank is accorded to one of the three types of knowledge distinguished by him – knowledge for the sake of domination (*Beherrschungswissen*), knowledge for the sake of knowing (*Bildungswissen*) – knowledge for the sake of salvation (*Heilswissen*) – and therewith to one of the three types of men of knowledge: the scientist-technician, the sage, the saint. The social acceptance of this rank-order determines the whole structure of the particular culture. Finally, Aristotle's statement recalls the concepts of modern anthropology (Linton) and sociology (Parsons-Shils) of ascription and achievement as basic determinants of status and role expectations within the social system.

Quite independently, however, of the particular principle according to which the order of the various domains of relevances has been established in a particular group, certain general statements as to their formal structure can be made:

1. The various domains of relevances are not commensurable one with another; they are essentially heterogeneous. It is impossible to apply the criteria for excellence valid in one domain of relevances to another domain.

2. Both the relevance structure which constitutes the particular domains of relevances and the order of these domains itself are in continuous flux within each group. This is a main factor in the dynamics of the notions of equality and inequality accepted by a particular group. These concepts change, either a) if for one reason or another the relevance structure which demarcates a *particular* domain of typification is no longer taken for granted beyond question but becomes questionable itself, a fact that might lead to a permeation of a particular domain of relevance by a heterogeneous one; or b) if the *order* of the domains of relevances ceases to be socially approved and taken for granted.

3. Since, however, the domains of relevances and their order are themselves elements of the social situation, they might be defined in different ways in accordance with their subjective and objective meaning. This, however, leads us to another aspect of our problem.

IV. THE VARIOUS INTERPRETATIONS OF THE WORLD TAKEN FOR GRANTED

Father, Mother and me,
Sister and Auntie say
All the people like us are We
And everyone else is They.
And They live over the sea,
While We live over the way.
But – would you believe it? – They look upon We
As only a sort of They! [6]

---

[6] Rudyard Kipling, "We and They," *Debits and Credits, Verse, Inclusive Edition,* copyright 1926 by Rudyard Kipling, reprinted by permission of Mrs. George Bambridge, London.

The system of typifications and relevances forming part of the relative natural conception of the social world is one of the means by which a group defines its situation within the social cosmos and, at the same time, becomes an integral element of the situation itself. The terms "situation" and "definition of the situation" are, however, highly equivocal. W. I. Thomas has already shown that a distinction has to be made between the situation as defined by the actor or the group within it, and the situation, as defined by outsiders. This distinction coincides more or less with that made by Sumner between the in-group or We-group and the Others-group or out-group, and is also at the foundation of Weber's concepts of subjective and objective interpretation.

In this section we propose to investigate the various meanings the world as taken for granted has 1) from the point of view of the in-group, 2) from the point of view of the out-group, 3) from the point of view of the social scientist, and 4) from that of the philosopher. In the following section, V, we shall proceed with the application of the dichotomy of subjective and objective interpretation to a series of problems closely connected with the subject of equality.

1) The self-interpretation of the world taken for granted by the in-group

Sumner has coined the technical term "ethnocentrism" as the name for the view of things in which one's own group is the center of everything and all others are scaled and rated with reference to it:

Each group thinks its own folkways the only right ones, and if it observes that other groups have other folkways, this excites its scorn. Opprobrious epithets are derived from these differences. "Pig-eater," "cow-eater," "uncircumcised," "jabberers," are epithets of contempt and abomination.[7]

Ethnocentrism requires, however, some justification. As Eric Voegelin [8] has pointed out, any society considers itself as a cosmion, a little cosmos, which is illuminated from within and

---

[7] William Graham Sumner, *Folkways: A Study of the Sociological Importance of Manners, Customs, Mores, and Morals*, New York, 1906, p. 13.

[8] Eric Voegelin, *The New Science of Politics, An Introduction* (Charles R. Walgreen Foundation Lectures), Chicago, 1952, pp. 27 ff., 53 ff.

which requires symbols connecting its order with the order of the cosmos. R. M. MacIver in his remarkable book, *The Web of Government*, speaks in this connection of the "central myth" governing the ideas of a concrete group and of the rationalization and institutionalization of such a myth. Others speak of dominating ideologies (Mannheim) or residua (Pareto).

This central myth in the sense of MacIver, that is, the scheme of self-interpretation, belongs itself to the relative natural conception of the world which the in-group takes for granted. For example, the idea of equality might be referred to an order of values ordained by Zeus, or originating in the structure of the soul; it might be conceived as reflecting the order of the cosmos, or the Right of Nature, as revealed by Reason; it might be held as sacred, and connected with various ideas of taboo. Any change in this order is subject to particular sanctions: it is supposed to disturb the order of the cosmos, entail the revenge of the gods, and bring disaster to the group as a whole.

It has to be taken into consideration that the self-interpretation of the group, its central myth, as well as the forms of its rationalization and institutionalization, is subject to changes in the course of history. A good example is the change in the meaning of the notion of equality in the political ideas of the United States from the Declaration of Independence ("We hold these truths to be self-evident, that all men are created equal") to the wording of the Fifth and Fourteenth Amendments and the various interpretations given by the United States Supreme Court to these amendments, leading to the "separate but equal" doctrine and the latter's recent abolishment.

2) *The out-group's interpretation of the world taken for granted by the in-group*

The members of an out-group do not hold the ways of life of the in-group as self-evident truths. No article of faith and no historical tradition commits them to accept as the right and good ones the folkways of any group other than their own. Not only their central myth, but also the processes of its rationalization and institutionalization are different. Other gods reveal other codes of the right and the good life, other things are sacred and taboo, other propositions of the Right of Nature are assumed.[9] The outsider measures the standards prevailing in the group under consideration in accordance with the system of relevances prevailing within the natural aspect the world has for his home-group. As long as a formula of transformation cannot be found which permits the translation of the system of relevances and typifications prevailing in the group under consideration into that of the home-group, the ways of the former remain ununderstandable; but frequently they are considered to be of minor value and inferior.

This principle holds good, although in a slighter degree, even in the relationship between two groups that have many things in common, that is, where the two systems conform to a considerable extent. For example, Jewish immigrants from Iraq have considerable difficulty in understanding that their practices of polygamy and child marriage are not permitted by the laws of Israel, the Jewish national home. Another example appears in the discussions in the French National Assembly of 1789, after Lafayette submitted his first draft of the Declaration of Human Rights modeled after the American pattern. Several speakers referred to the basic differences between American and French society: the situation of a new country, a colony having severed its relationship with its motherland, cannot be compared with that of a country which had enjoyed its own constitutional life for fourteen centuries. The principle of equality would have an entirely different function and meaning in the historical setting of both countries; the equal distribution of wealth and the equal way of life in America permit the application of equalitarian phraseology that would have the most disastrous consequences if applied to the highly differentiated French society.[10]

It is, however, important to understand that the self-interpretation by the in-group and the interpretation of the in-group's natural conception of the world by the out-group are frequently interrelated, and this in a double respect:

a. On the one hand, the in-group feels itself frequently mis-

---

[9] T. V. Smith, *The American Philosophy of Equality*, Chicago, 1927, p. 6, has pointed out that Locke used the State of Nature and Equality to overthrow tyrants, Hobbes to enthrone the "mortal God."

[10] Eric Voegelin, "Der Sinn der Erklärung der Menschen- und Bürgerrechte von 1789," *Zeitschrift für öffentliches Recht*, Vol. 8, 1928, pp. 82–120.

understood by the out-group; such failure to understand its ways of life, so the in-group feels, must be rooted in hostile prejudices or in bad faith, since the truths held by the in-group are "matters of course," self-evident and, therefore, understandable by any human being. This feeling may lead to a partial shift of the system of relevances prevailing within the in-group, namely, by originating a solidarity of resistance against outside criticism. The out-group is then looked at with repugnance, disgust, aversion, antipathy, hatred, or fear.

b. On the other hand, a vicious circle [11] is thus set up because the out-group, by the changed reaction of the in-group, is fortified in its interpretation of the traits of the in-group as highly detestable. In more general terms: to the natural aspect the world has for group A belongs not only a certain stereotyped idea of the natural aspect the world has for group B, but included in it also is a stereotype of the way in which group B supposedly looks at A. This is, on a major scale – i.e., in the relationship between groups – the same phenomenon which, in respect to relations between individuals, Cooley has called the "looking-glass effect."

Such a situation may lead to various attitudes of the in-group toward the out-group: the in-group may stick to its way of life and try to change the attitude of the out-group by an educational process of spreading information, or by persuasion, or by appropriate propaganda. Or the in-group may try to adjust its way of thinking to that of the out-group by accepting the latter's pattern of relevances at least partially. Or a policy of iron curtain or of appeasement might be established; and finally, there will be no other way to disrupt the vicious circle but war at any temperature. A secondary consequence might be that those members of the in-group who plead for a policy of mutual understanding are designated by the spokesmen of radical ethnocentrism as disloyal or traitors, etc., a fact which again leads to a change in the self-interpretation of the social group.

These are merely possible illustrations of the way in which the interpretation by the out-group of the natural aspect of the world

---

[11] On the problem of the vicious circle of prejudices, see R. M. MacIver, *The More Perfect Union*, New York, 1948, esp. pp. 68–81; also, United Nations, Memorandum of the Secretary-General on *The Main Types and Causes of Discrimination*, Document E/Cn 4/ Sub 2/ 40/ Rev. of June 7, 1949, sections 56 ff.

prevailing in the in-group changes the latter. A complete typology cannot be established on the ground of theoretical deliberations, but a wide field seems open here for badly needed empirical research. Such research would also have to consider the particular personal types involved – for example, the stranger who wants to be accepted by the approached group, the convert, the renegade, the marginal man, and also the various attitudes developed by the in-group toward these types. In all these situations, major problems of equality and equal opportunity are involved.

3) Interpretation of the order of relevances by the social scientist

This is not the place to enter into such a highly complicated subject matter, which has in any case been dealt with elsewhere.[12] We want merely to point out that the social scientist *qua* theoretician has to follow a system of relevances entirely different from that which determines his conduct as an actor on the social scene. The scientific situation, that is, the context of scientific problems, supersedes his situation as man among his fellow-men within the social world. The problems of the theoretician originate in his theoretical interest, and many elements of the social world that are scientifically relevant are irrelevant from the viewpoint of the actor on the social scene, and *vice versa*. Moreover, the typical constructs formulated by the social scientist for the solution of his problem are, so to speak, constructs of the second degree, namely, constructs of the common-sense constructs, in terms of which everyday thinking interprets the social world.

4) Interpretation of the order of relevances from a philosophical, mythical, or theological basic position

In all these interpretations the system of relevances prevailing in a given social group is not investigated as a matter of fact but from the point of view of a principle of higher order. Doubtless such a point of view is indispensable for the development of a philosophy of equality and the foundation of ethics. But all these topics are intentionally excluded from the present paper.

---

[12] *Cf.* Alfred Schutz, "Common-Sense and Scientific Interpretation of Human Action," in *Collected Papers* I, pp. 3–47 and "Concept and Theory Formation in the Social Sciences," *loc. cit.*, pp. 48–66.

It is, however, worthwhile to refer – without entering into all the intricacies of the problem – to the influence of philosophical ideas upon the self-interpretation of the group, and *vice versa*. This is the vast domain of a sociology of knowledge which understands its task. It can easily be seen that philosophical or theological systems have a considerable influence on the meaning structure of the world taken for granted. The most valuable contribution to the development of such a theory was again made by Scheler in his study on the interrelationship of material factors (*Realfaktoren*, such as race, geopolitical structure, political power relationships, conditions of economic production) and ideas (*Idealfaktoren*).

According to this philosopher, an idea or a philosophy or even a scientific concept can become effective within the social reality only if the *Realfaktoren* – corresponding in our terminology to the structure of the social group as interpreted by the group itself – are ready for it. The *Realfaktoren* open and close, so to speak, the sluice gates through which the stream of *Idealfaktoren* has to pass. On the other hand, the blind material factors can be guided and directed by the ideal factors. If according to Comte the history of the material factors is characterized by a *fatalité modifiable*, the stream of ideal factors exhibits a *liberté modifiable*, namely, a freedom that is conditioned in its translation into social reality by the resistance of the material factors.

An illustration may be drawn from the history of the concept of equality. Equality based on the idea of a Natural Right can originate only after philosophy has discovered the concept of Nature.[13] To derive equality from a divine law presupposes that the underlying theology is accepted by the respective society and taken for granted. Only the idea of the progress of reason, developed from Hobbes to Rousseau, makes possible the assumption of an original state of nature in which all men are free and equal. And only the particular administrative and political structure of the Roman Empire led the Roman jurists to the dialectic of the *jus naturale* and the *jus gentium*.[14]

---

[13] Leo Strauss, *Natural Right and History*, Chicago, 1953.
[14] Sir Henry Sumner Maine, *Ancient Law*, New York, 1906, pp. 48 ff. and 76.

V. SUBJECTIVE AND OBJECTIVE INTERPRETATION

In the following sequence we propose to deal with the categories of subjective and objective interpretation under three principal headings:

A. subjective and objective meaning of the concept "social group"
B. subjective and objective meaning of equality
C. subjective and objective meaning of equal opportunity.

A) Subjective and objective meaning of the concept "social group"

Our presentation so far has suffered from a very serious shortcoming. We have been using terms such as "social group," "in-group," "out-group" in a rather uncritical way, without examining the meaning of group membership for the individuals forming the group, on the one hand, and for outsiders, on the other. Sumner's distinction between We-group and They-group can be clarified only by referring it to the basic antithesis of subjective to objective meaning. In other words, the term "group" itself has an entirely different meaning for those who say *"We* Protestants," *"We* Americans," etc., from the one it has for those who say *"the* Catholics," *"the* Russians," *"the* Negroes."

The problem under scrutiny has been obscured by the well known elemental division of groups into voluntary and involuntary ones, the stock-in-trade concepts of sociology. I cannot choose my sex and race, nor my place of birth, and, therewith, the national group into which I was born; neither can I choose the mother tongue I learned or the conception of the world taken for granted by the group with which I was indoctrinated during childhood. I cannot choose my parents and siblings, or the social and economic status of my parental family. My membership in these groups and the social roles I have to assume within them are existential elements of my situation which I have to take into account, and with which I have to come to terms.

On the other hand, I may choose my spouse, my friends, my business partners, my occupation, change my nationality and even my religion. I may voluntarily become a member of existing groups or originate new ones (friendships, marital relations), determine at least to a certain extent the role I want to assume within them, and even make some efforts to attain by my achievements that kind of position and status within them toward which I aspire.

This distinction between involuntary – or better, existential – and voluntary groups is legitimate and useful for many purposes. But although it refers to the distinction between the subjective and the objective meaning of the group, it does not coincide with it.

1) Subjective meaning of group membership

The subjective meaning of the group, the meaning a group has for its members, has frequently been described in terms of a feeling among the members that they belong together, or that they share common interests. This is correct; but unfortunately, these concepts were only partially analyzed, namely, in terms of community and association (MacIver), *Gemeinschaft* and *Gesellschaft* (Toennies), primary and secondary groups (Cooley), and so on.

We do not intend to follow these lines of investigation, not because we doubt their importance but because we believe that precisely the feeling of "belonging together" and the "sharing of common interests" from which they start requires further analyses in terms of common-sense thinking (as distinguished from conceptions in the social sciences).

The investigations of the first section of the present paper are of some help here: the subjective meaning the group has for its members consists in their knowledge of a common situation, and with it of a common system of typifications and relevances. This situation has its history in which the individual members' biographies participate; and the system of typification and relevances determining the situation forms a common relative natural conception of the world. Here the individual members are "at home," that is, they find their bearings without difficulty in the common surroundings, guided by a set of recipes of more or less institutionalized habits, mores, folkways, etc., that help them come to terms with beings and fellow-men belonging to the same situation. The system of typifications and relevances shared with the other members of the group defines the social roles, positions, and statutes of each. This acceptance of a common system of relevances leads the members of the group to a homogeneous self-typification.

Our description holds good for both a) existential groups with which I share a common social heritage, and b) so-called voluntary groups joined or formed by me. The difference, however, is that in the first case the individual member finds himself within a preconstituted system of typifications, relevances, roles, positions, statuses not of his own making, but handed down to him as a social heritage. In the case of voluntary groups, however, this system is not experienced by the individual member as ready - made; it has to be built up by the members and is therefore always involved in a process of dynamic evolution. Only some of the elements of the situation are common from the outset: the others have to be brought about by a common definition of the reciprocal situation.

Here a highly important problem is involved. How does the individual member of a group define his private situation within the framework of those common typifications and relevances in terms of which the group defines its situation? But before we proceed to an answer, a word of caution seems indicated.

Our description is a purely formal one and refers neither to the nature of the bond that holds the group together, nor to the extent, duration, or intimacy of the social contact. It is, therefore, equally applicable to a marriage or a business enterprise, to membership in a chess club or citizenship in a nation, to participation in a meeting or in Western culture. Each of these groups, however, refers to a larger one of which it is an element. A marriage or a business enterprise, of course, takes place within the general framework of the cultural setting of the larger group and in accordance with the way of life (including its mores, morals, laws, and so forth) prevailing in this culture, which is pregiven to the single actors as a scheme of orientation and interpretation of their actions. It is, however, up to the marriage or business partners to define, and continuously redefine, their individual (private) situation within this setting.

This is obviously the deeper reason why, to Max Weber, the

existence of a marriage or a state means nothing but the mere chance (likelihood) that people act and will act in a specific way – or, in the terminology of this paper, in accordance with the general framework of typifications and relevances accepted beyond question by the particular sociocultural environment. Such a general framework is experienced by the individual members in terms of institutionalizations to be interiorized, and the individual has to define his personal unique situation by using the institutionalized pattern for the realization of his particular personal interests.

Here we have one aspect of the private definition of the individual's membership situation. A corollary to it is the particular attitude that the individual chooses to adopt toward the social role he has to fulfil within the group. One thing is the objective meaning of the social role and the role expectation as defined by the institutionalized pattern (say, the office of the Presidency of the United States); another thing is the particular subjective way in which the incumbent of this role defines his situation within it (Roosevelt's, Truman's, Eisenhower's interpretation of their mission).

The most important element in the definition of the private situation is, however, the fact that the individual finds himself always a member of numerous social groups. As Simmel has shown, each individual stands at the intersection of several social circles, and their number will be the greater the more differentiated the individual's personality. This is so because that which makes a personality unique is precisely that which cannot be shared with others.

According to Simmel, the group is formed by a process in which *many* individuals unite *parts* of their personalities – specific impulses, interests, forces, – while what each personality really is, remains outside this common area. Groups are characteristically different according to the members' total personalities and those parts of their personalities with which they participate in the group.[15] Elsewhere,[16] Simmel speaks of the consciousness of degradation and oppression felt by the individual in the descent of the whole ego to the lowlands of the social structure,

[15] *Cf.* Kurt H. Wolff, *The Sociology of George Simmel*, Glencoe, 1950, pp. 202–203
[16] *Ibid.*, p. 283.

an insight which will be of considerable consequences for our later investigations.

It must further be added that in the individual's definition of his private situation the various social roles originating in his multiple membership in numerous groups are experienced as a set of self-typifications which in turn are arranged in a particular private order of domains of relevances that is, of course, continuously in flux. It is possible that exactly those features of the individual's personality which are to him of the highest order of relevance are irrelevant from the point of view of any system of relevances taken for granted by the group of which he is a member. This may lead to conflicts within the personality, mainly originating in the endeavor to live up to the various and frequently inconsistent role expectations inhering in the individual's membership in various social groups. As we have seen, it is only with respect to voluntary, and not to existential group membership that the individual is free to determine of which group he wants to be a member, and of which social role therein he wants to be the incumbent. It is, however, at least one aspect of freedom of the individual that he may choose for himself with which part of his personality he wants to participate in group memberships; that he may define his situation within the role of which he is the incumbent; and that he may establish his own private order of relevances in which each of his memberships in various groups has its rank. This freedom is probably the deeper meaning of the "unalienable right to the pursuit of happiness" and will be referred to in the following under this label. And this in spite of the fact that this term was interpreted by philosophical radicals not in relation to the whole personality of man but only in relation to material welfare and pleasure.[17]

2) Objective meaning of group membership

So far we have discussed the subjective meanings of the group from the point of view of those who consider themselves members of it and speak of one another in terms of "We." The objective meaning of group membership is that which the group has from

---

[17] Cf. David Thomson, *Equality*, Cambridge, 1949, pp. 22 ff.

the point of view of outsiders who speak of its members in terms of "They." In objective interpretation the notion of the group is a conceptual construct of the outsider. By the operation of *his* system of typifications and relevances he subsumes individuals showing certain particular characteristics and traits under a social category that is homogeneous merely from his, the outsider's, point of view.

It is of course possible that the social category constructed by the outsider corresponds to a social reality, namely, that the principles governing such typification are considered also by the individuals thus typified as elements of *their* situation as defined by *them* and as being relevant from *their* point of view. Even then, the interpretation of the group by the outsider will never fully coincide with the self-interpretation by the in-group, and this was the case studied in the previous section.

It is also possible, however, that people considering one another as heterogeneous may be placed by the outsider's typification under the same social category, which then is treated as if it were a homogeneous unit. The situation in which individuals are placed in this way by the outsider is of his, but not of their definition. For this reason the system of relevances leading to such typification is taken for granted merely by the outsider, but is not necessarily accepted by the individuals who may not be prepared to perform a corresponding self-typification.

The resultant discrepancy between the subjective and the objective interpretation of the group remains relatively harmless, so long as the individuals thus typified are not subject to the outsider's control. The American way of life is not disturbed by the fact that foreigners identify it with the pattern presented by Hollywood films. Nor has the image won from the reading of French novels or comedies any influence on real French family life. If, however, the outsider has the power to impose his system of relevances upon the individuals typified by him, and especially to enforce its institutionalization, then this fact will create various repercussions on the situation of the individuals typified against their will.

Strictly speaking, nearly all administrative and legislative measures involve the placing of individuals under imposed social categories. Tax laws group them into income classes, draft laws into age groups, rent laws into various categories of tenants. This kind of imposed typification will hardly achieve the effect that those subjected to it consider themselves members of a We-group, although those concerned may, for example, form a protective committee.

From the subjective point of view such typifications are of minor importance for two reasons. First, they annihilate neither the boundaries of the domains of relevances nor their order, both being accepted by the individuals falling under the imposed category as an integral element of their situation. In our example, individuals defined by law as taxpayers, draftees, and tenants consider these categories merely as differentiations within the domain of relevance constituting the "group" of law-abiding citizens, a domain accepted by them and preserved in its homogeneity. Secondly – and this is the more decisive point – only a very small part, and a very superficial one, of the personality of the individual concerned is impinged upon by this kind of imposed typification. That feeling of degradation or oppression, which Simmel said emerges if the whole ego has to descend to the lowlands of the social stratum, is not involved. The integrity of the personality remains intact, and the individual's right to the pursuit of happiness is only insignificantly impaired.

Entirely different is the situation if the imposed typification breaks the integrity of the personality asunder by identifying the whole, or broad layers, of the individual's personality with the particular trait or characteristic typified. To be sure, man is frequently willing to identify his whole personality with a particular trait or characteristic of his, provided that *on his own terms* he acknowledges this trait as being of high relevance to him. Then, he even experiences this kind of self-typification as one of the highest forms of self-realization.

But if he is compelled to identify himself as a whole with that particular trait or characteristic which places him in terms of the imposed system of heterogeneous relevances into a social category he had never included as a relevant one in the definition of his private situation, then he feels that he is no longer treated as a human being in his own right and freedom, but is degraded to an interchangeable specimen of the typified class. He is alienated from himself, a mere representative of the typified traits and characteristics. He is deprived of his right to the pursuit of happiness.

This may even lead to a complete breakdown of his private order of domains of relevances – that is, to a crisis as this term was defined in section I. What has been unquestioned so far looms now as highly questionable, while heretofore subjectively problem-irrelevant factors become vitally relevant to the now imposed problems. To cite just a few examples: persons who believed themselves to be good Germans and had severed all allegiance to Judaism found themselves declared Jews by Hitler's Nuremberg laws and treated as such on the ground of a grandparent's origin, a fact up to that time entirely irrelevant. Refugees from Europe, who believed they had found a haven in the United States, discovered themselves placed, after Pearl Harbor, in the category of enemy aliens, by reason of the very nationality they wanted to abandon. A change in rules or definitions established by a Senatorial committee turns loyal civil servants into security risks. The whole problem of guilt by association and collective responsibility comes under this heading of imposed typification.

It is submitted that the feeling of degradation caused by the identification of the whole, or broad layers, of the individual's personality with the imposed typified trait is one of the basic motives for the subjective experience of discrimination, which has to be treated in the following subsection.

B) Subjective and objective meaning of equality

In the second section of the present paper we examined the relationship between the concept of equality and the structure of relevances. Guided by an analysis of Aristotle's and Plato's pertinent views, we found that in any society not only a particular set of domains of relevances, but also a particular order of these domains is taken for granted; each domain consists of a collection of homogeneous elements. We came to the conclusion that the relational terms "equality" and "inequality" are applicable only to homogeneous elements, that is, to elements belonging to the same domain of relevances, because heterogeneous elements – elements pertaining to different domains – cannot be compared with one another.

The fact that equality can prevail only within the same domain of relevances, explains why we can speak of separating political equality, equality before the law, equality in wealth, equality of opportunity, religious or moral equality, etc., or even apply the more refined distinctions of the Greek vocabulary enumerated in the Introduction. And from the very fact that domains of relevances are defined and ordered by each social group in a different way, it follows that the content of the concept of equality is also an element of the relative natural conception of the world taken for granted by the particular social group. (Here, as everywhere in this paper, we intentionally disregard concepts of equality based on philosophical or religious principles). To give an example for our present culture: the Universal Declaration of Human Rights of the United Nations (art. 2) proclaims moral and juridical equality, that is to say, it is equality in dignity, formal equality in rights and equality of opportunity, but not necessarily material equality as to the extent and content of the rights of all individuals.

Our analyses in sections III and IV (A) have, however, shown that it cannot be sufficient to refer equality just to the structure of relevances and the natural conception of the world prevailing in a particular group, because both of these terms are again equivocal. The natural conception of the world prevailing in a group may be interpreted on various levels (self-interpretation, interpretation by outsiders, by scientific, and by philosophical thinking). And the term "group" itself can be stated in subjective and in objective terms. Our present endeavor is to find the subjective and objective elements in the notion of equality. We have, however, to restrict ourselves to the analysis of a few examples. A systematic treatment of this highly involved problem, that opens a tremendous field to empirical research, is of course far beyond the scope of this paper.

1) Subjective and objective constitution of homogeneous domains of relevance

Our first question is whether a particular homogeneous domain of relevances, in which in a concrete case the problem of equality or inequality emerges, has been constituted by subjective interpretation of group membership, or whether this homogeneity refers to typifications imposed by outsiders.

Let us begin with an example. If the Daughters of the American Revolution deny to Marian Anderson the use of their concert hall in Washington, D.C., because she is a Negro, such an act will rightly be considered a discriminatory one, originating in the fact that by imposed typification all persons subsumed under the category Negro are treated equally. Color of skin, we may say, has "nothing to do" with a singer's art as, in Aristotle's example, wealth has nothing to do with the excellence of fluteplaying. But is this statement in such generality true? Could Marian Anderson sing Negro Spirituals in her unsurpassed way if she did not share with her fellow Negroes this specific cultural heritage, this specific conception of the world of which the Spirituals are a partial expression? Seen from this angle, does not the pertinence to a race *have* something to do with artistic excellence? And is an imposed typification in this sense discriminatory in the pejorative connotation of this word?

Our example shows, first, that the constitution of a domain of relevance as such may originate in an imposed typification. Second, in more general terms, the example confronts us with the highly important question of whether the imposition of a typification alone, that is, the subsumption of individuals under a particular social category by an outsider, involves as such an unequal treatment of the kind that is commonly called discriminatory. In other words, is discrimination the necessary consequence of the imposition of a scheme of typifications or relevances in objective terms?

Doubtless this is not the case, and the definition given in the study of the United Nations,[18] to be discussed presently, will corroborate this statement. No United States citizen will feel discriminated against because Switzerland considers him an alien and denies him participation in the political life of Switzerland. But another example will bring us closer to the heart of the problem involved here. We borrow it from Morroe Berger's excellent study.[19]

The example in question deals with the interpretation of the

---

[18] *The Main Types and Causes of Discrimination, op. cit.* See footnote 11.
[19] Morroe Berger, *Equality by Statute*, New York, 1952, pp. 53ff.

so-called equal protection clause of the Fourteenth Amendment to the Constitution of the United States by a decision of the Supreme Court (Plessy *v.* Ferguson, 163 U.S. 537, 1896). This was the beginning of the famous "separate but equal" doctrine. The Supreme Court (Justice Henry B. Brown) maintained in this decision that the principle of equality of the races before the law does not abolish distinction based on color, nor does it involve the enforcement of social – as distinguished from political – equality, nor the commingling of the races on terms unsatisfactory to either:

> If inferiority is inferred from it, it is not by reason of anything found in the act but solely because the colored race chooses to put that construction upon it ... Legislation is powerless to eradicate racial instincts ... If one race be inferior to the other socially the Constitution of the United States could not put them on the same plane.

It would be easy to dismiss this statement as the poor attempt at justifying racial prejudice that it is, if it were not of a particular theoretical interest for the way it reveals the dialectic hidden in the unclarified term "prejudice" itself. The Court takes the position that to deny to the colored race equal access to public opportunities (this term is MacIver's in *The More Perfect Union*) does not establish that the individuals included in this imposed typification – that is, in the objective sense – are inferior. Merely the interpretation of the imposed typification in terms of the scheme of relevances of the typified group – in the subjective sense, therefore – gives birth to such an inference. And such a "construct" is obviously the outcome of an act of bad faith on the part of the colored race ("the colored race *chooses* to put that construction upon it").

Here we meet again the "looking-glass effect" noted in another context in section III (B): the system of relevance of the typifying group also contains a stereotype of the system of relevances which is not only supposed to be accepted by the typified group, but is actually imposed upon it. The imposition of social categories both creates the "group" and invests it with a fictitious scheme of relevances that can then be manipulated at will by the creator of the type. Gunnar Myrdal rightly says, in *An American Dilemma:*

It keeps coming to me that this is more a white man's problem than it is a Negro problem ... The real problem is not the Negro but the white man's attitude toward the Negro.[20]

On the other hand, the imposed system of relevances has indeed repercussions upon the system of relevances of those it is inflicted upon. Even under the assumption that separation was not meant to involve an inferiority in the colored race, segregation is taken as an insult by the Negro and he becomes sensitive about it. His being treated as a type induces self-typification with an inverted sign. Even if he never intended to travel by sleeping car, the principled denial of its use becomes to him relevant in his own terms. He has a new problem to grapple with.

In more general terms, we may state that the imposition of a system of typifications and relevances does not in itself necessarily lead to discrimination. This objective interpretation of group membership has to be supervened by another element, namely, the afflicted individuals' subjective experience: by the very imposition of the typification they become alienated from themselves and are treated as mere interchangeable representatives of the typified traits and characteristics. Thus, discrimination presupposes both imposition of a typification from the objective point of view and an appropriate evaluation of this imposition from the subjective viewpoint of the afflicted individual.

We shall presently proceed to a more detailed study of this dialectical situation. Here we want only to add that the reduction of this highly involved problem to questions of prejudices can, it seems to us, be of but limited help. The category "prejudice" itself belongs exclusively to the sphere of objective interpretation. In common-sense thinking only the other fellow has prejudices. *I* can never be prejudiced because *my* beliefs are well founded, *my* opinions taken for granted, and *my* faith in the rightness and goodness of *our* ways – whatever this may mean – unfailing. It is submitted that progress toward a better theoretical understanding of social tensions could be expected, if social scientists and philosophers were prepared to abandon for a time their well meant idea that discrimination and other social evils originate exclusively in prejudices that would disappear as if touched by a

---

[20] Gunnar Myrdal, *An American Dilemma*, New York, 1944, p. 43.

magic wand, as soon as we informed the evildoers that they are cherishing prejudices.

We had better courageously face the fact that prejudices are themselves elements of the interpretation of the social world and even one of the mainsprings that make it tick. Prejudices are rationalizations and institutionalizations of the underlying "central myth" upon which the self-interpretation of the group is founded. It makes little sense to tell the Negrophobe in the South that in terms of biological science there is no such thing as a Negro race.

Nevertheless, in order to avoid any misunderstanding, I wish to emphasize that the preceding remarks refer merely to the danger of jettisoning further *theoretical* investigation of problems such as discrimination as soon as the magic formula, "They originate in prejudices," has been invoked. Quite another question is that of the strategy by which the evil of social tensions can be at least diminished. This educational goal can in my opinion be reached only by a slow and patient modification of the system of relevances which those in power impose upon their fellow-men. And MacIver, in *The More Perfect Union*, has clearly shown how this might be accomplished, despite his use of the *notion* of prejudice.

2) Discrimination and minority rights, subjectively and objectively interpreted

Two excellent publications prepared by the Secretary-General of the United Nations [21] corroborate our findings. In investigating the main types of discrimination, the first of these documents (secs. 30–32) starts from the concept of equality as formulated by the United Nations in the Universal Declaration of Human Rights, quoted earlier, and points out that equality does not exclude two classes of differences which are generally considered admissible and justified: a) differentiations based on conduct imputable to the individual – examples: industriousness-idleness, decency-indecency, merit-demerit; and b) differenti-

---

[21] *Cf.* the previously mentioned document, *The Main Types and Causes of Discrimination and Definition and Classification of Minorities,* Document (E/Cn 4/ Sub 2/ 85/ 27 of December, 1949).

ations based on individual qualities that in spite of not being imputable to the individual have a social value – examples: physical and mental capacities, talent, innate ability, and the like.

These two classes refer, therefore, to personal traits or characteristics which, in Aristotle's terminology, correspond to degrees of excellence and merit. On the other hand, moral and juridical equality excludes any differentiation based on a) *grounds which are not imputable to the individual,* and which *should* not be considered as having any social or legal meaning: such as color, race, or sex; and b) grounds of social generic categories such as language, political or other opinion, national or social origin, property, birth, or other status.

This division is justified from the viewpoint of the scheme of reference underlying the classification. Its language is clearly that of ethical-political postulates, in terms of the order of domains of relevances as established and socially approved by the cultural setting the United Nations represents. It is not stated that the grounds mentioned in class (a) – which in our terminology refer to existential groups – *do* not have any social meaning; but it is postulated that they *should* not have any. The term "imputable," frequently used in this classification, has obviously to be understood in the same sense. Differentiations in accordance with class (b) however, are, even from this viewpoint, admittedly "socially generic" categories. The unfavorable treatment of individuals as mere specimens of such categories by an imposed system of relevances is not compatible with the meaning of equality as defined by the United Nations.

The following definition of discrimination suggested by the document (sec. 33) clarifies this point:

Discrimination includes any conduct based on a distinction made on grounds of natural or social categories which have no relation either to individual capacities or merits, or to the concrete behavior of the individual person.

This definition would be too broad (*cf.* our example of the treatment of United States citizens as aliens by Switzerland) if it were not qualified in a following section (37) to the effect that:

Discrimination might be described as unequal and unfavorable treatment either by denying rights or social advantage to members of a particular social category; or by imposing special burdens on them; or by granting favors exclusively to the members of another category, creating in this way inequality between those who belong to the privileged category and others.

Moreover, it is especially stated (sec. 38) that:

... discrimination is not merely a subjective attitude [of course, the term subjective is used here in another sense than that of this paper] but is conduct outwardly manifested.

Accepting the distinction frequently made by contemporary sociologists between a) interindividual relations that are established between two persons as such through the affinities of their peculiarly personal characteristics (sec. 20), and b) social relations proper, that are established on account of a particular role each plays in his capacity as a member of a special social group (sec. 22), the document states that practices characterized as discriminatory belong only to the type of human relations mentioned under (b), namely, social relations.

Discriminatory acts originate from prejudices (sec. 39), and there is a mutual interaction between prejudice and discrimination (sec. 41). A social group prejudice is defined (sec. 43) as:

a way of feeling, a bias of disposition, consisting of a commonly shared attitude of hostility, contempt, or mistrust, or of devaluation of the members of a particular social group, because they happen to belong to that group.   .

Summing up, it is stated (sec. 50) that many people have acquired a habit

of looking upon the members of other social categories not as individuals, but as members of groups: as whites or blacks, as nationals or foreigners, as men or women, as members of the upper or lower class; as Protestants, Catholics, or Jews; as workers or employers. *They are viewed in the light of the alleged attribute (real or supposed) of their group* with all the distortions inspired either by bias or self-interest ... Such *prejudices are accepted without examination or even serious thought, simply because they have become part of the environment of the group.*

It would be plainly repetitive to show in detail the correspondence of these findings with our theory of subjective and objective group membership and of imposed systems of relevances and typifications. Discrimination is based on an objective interpretation of group membership.

But all this is only half the story. The United Nations Commission on Human Rights has not only to make suggestions regarding the elimination or restriction of discrimination but also regarding the protection of minorities, and the second of the two documents mentioned deals with the definitions and classification of minorities. According to this document (sec. 45), the term "minority" should normally be applied to

groups whose members share a common ethnic origin, language, culture or religion, and are interested in preserving either their existence as a national community or their particular distinguishing characteristics.

Elsewhere in the same document (sec. 39), it is stated that

members of such a minority feel that they constitute a ... group or subgroup which is different from the predominant one.

The document distinguishes very clearly (sec. 5) between a) minorities whose members desire equality with dominant groups in the sense of nondiscrimination alone, and, b) those whose members desire, *in addition*, the recognition of special rights and the rendering of certain positive services. Minorities in category (a) prefer to be assimilated by the dominant group; minorities in category (b) feel that even full realization of the principle of non-discrimination would not place their group in a position of *real equality* – but only of *formal equality* – with respect to the dominant group.

Minorities, so the document states (sec. 48), are social realities which are dynamic rather than static, and change under the influence of varying circumstances. For example, as many sociologists and political scientists have pointed out, a minority group that becomes satisfied with its relationship toward the predominant group tends to become more and more assimilated by the latter. If, however, the members of a minority group feel that the rule imposed by the predominant group prevents them from maintaining their particular distinctive characteristics, or inhibits the development of their aspirations for the future, the group's relationship toward the predominant one tends to become more and more strained.

It can clearly be seen that the problem of minorities is a problem of *subjective* interpretation of group membership and of the subjective aspects of the system of typifications and relevances valid within it. This appears also from the position taken by the document on the question of individual membership in a minority. For example, should a member who is not religious be considered as a member of a religious minority? The only answer possible, according to the document (sec. 59), is that the subjective decision of the individual is the governing factor. Each individual should be able to decide voluntarily whether or not he belongs to a specific minority.

Summarizing this subsection, it can be stated that both the problem of formal equality in terms of abolishing discrimination, and the problem of material equality in terms of minority rights, originate in the discrepancy between the objective and subjective definition of a concrete group situation.

3) The order of domains of relevances, subjectively and objectively interpreted

Here we can restrict ourselves to a quotation from Myrdal which speaks for itself:

The white man's rank-order of discriminations:
  1. Intermarriage
  2. Social equality
  3. Segregation
  4. Political rights
  5. Equality before the law
  6. Economic equality
The Negro's own rank order is just about parallel, *but inverse,* to that of the white man. The Negro resists least the discrimination on the ranks placed highest in the white man's evaluation and resents most any discrimination on the lowest level.[22]

4) Equality aimed-at and equality to-be-granted

Still another aspect of the meaning of equality in subjective and objective interpretation remains to be mentioned.

[22] Myrdal, *op. cit.*, pp. 60–61.

Equality, in any connotation, means something different to group A or its individual members aspiring to obtain a position equal to another group B, and to group B with which the first one, A, aspires to become equal, or by which it desires to be treated on an equal footing.

It was Simmel who analyzed this problem in his remarkable studies on the development of the ideas of equality and freedom in the eighteenth and nineteenth centuries, and in the chapter of his sociology dealing with superordination and subordination. Typically speaking, says Simmel, nobody is satisfied with the position he occupies with respect to his fellow-men, and everybody wishes to attain a position that is in some sense more favorable.[23] Equality with the superior is the first objective that offers itself to the impulse toward one's own elevation – and, characteristically enough, equality with the immediate superior. Yet this equality is merely a point of transition. Myriad experiences have shown that once the subordinate is equal to the superior this condition, which previously was the essential aim of his endeavor, is merely a starting point for a further effort, the first station on the unending road to the most favored position. Wherever an attempt is made at effecting equalization, the individual's striving to surpass others comes to the fore in all possible forms on the newly reached stage. But, says Simmel, it makes a characteristic difference whether this attempt at winning cherished values is to be obtained by means of abolishing what he calls the "sociological form" (and what we should call the prevailing system of relevances and their order) or whether it is to be obtained *within* this form, which is thereby preserved.

Doubtless the meaning of equality is a different one for those who are aspiring to an equal position with the superior, whether a superordinate individual or a "predominant" group, and for those in the privileged position who are required to grant equal treatment.

An example can be seen in the analysis of the two types of minorities mentioned in subsection 2. To minority groups of the type (a), assimilation is the kind of equality aimed-at. To those of type (b), however, *real* equality is the kind aimed-at; that is, obtaining special rights such as the use of their national languages

[23] Simmel, *op. cit.*, p. 275.

in schools, before the courts, etc. The history of the cultural struggle of national minorities in the old Austro-Hungarian monarchy is an excellent instance of the point in question. The predominant group may interpret equality-to-be-granted as *formal* equality, and may even be willing to concede full equality before the law and full political equality, and yet resist bitterly any claim to special rights. Another instance is the different interpretation of the rank-order of discrimination by white man and by Negro.

Of particular significance for the twofold interpretation of equality under scrutiny is, however, Simmel's previously noted observation that it makes a characteristic difference whether tensions of this kind can be solved by shifts within the prevailing common system of relevance, or whether this system itself must be abolished. The first attitude is characteristic of conservative thinking, the second, of revolutionary thinking. Those in the privileged position will interpret equality-to-be-granted in terms of the former, while those who aim at obtaining equality frequently interpret it in terms of the latter. Albert Salomon closes his book, *The Tyranny of Progress*, with this statement:

It is the specific postulate of our contemporary scene to be liberal in order to remain conservative. We can secure the continuity of our social and intellectual worlds as conservative reformists.[24]

And R. H. Tawney, comparing the inequalities of the industrial age with those of the old regime in his book, *Equality*, comes to the following conclusion:

The inequalities of the old regime had been intolerable because they had been arbitrary, the result not of personal capacity but of social and political favoritism. The inequalities of industrial society were to be esteemed, for they were expressions of individual achievement or failure to achieve. So it was possible to hate the inequalities most characteristic of the 18th century and to applaud the inequalities of the 19th century. The distinction between them was that the former had their origin in social institutions, the latter in personal character ... *La carrière ouverte aux talents* [25] was the formula of reconciliation (between revolutionaries and conservatives) which had overthrown the class system of the old regime

[24] Albert Salomon, *The Tyranny of Progress*, New York, 1955.
[25] The American equivalent of this slogan coined by Napoleon is "From log cabin to White House."

in France and supplied a satisfactory moral title to the class system which succeeded it.[26]

Equal opportunity, the career open to talents, is again, however, capable of subjective and objective interpretation.

C) Subjective and objective meaning of equal opportunity

The difficulty of analyzing the notion of equal opportunity consists in the fact that not only, as we have seen, does the term equality have different meaning in subjective and objective interpretation, but the term "opportunity" also permits of a twofold interpretation. We start with an analysis of the notion of opportunity in the objective sense and are obliged to recall the quotations from the writings of Parsons and Shils in section I of this paper in order to reconsider how modern sociologists interpret the social system.

In the objective sense a social group is a structural-functional system formed by a web of interconnected interaction processes, social roles, positions, and statuses. Not the concrete individual or the concrete person, but the role, is the conceptual unit of the social system. Each role carries along a particular set of role expectations which any incumbent of the role is expected to fulfill.

In our terminology these role expectations are nothing but typifications of interaction patterns which are socially approved ways of solving typical problems, and are frequently institutionalized. Consequently, they are arranged in domains of relevances which in turn are ranked in a particular order originating in the group's relative natural conception of the world, its folkways, mores, morals, etc.

We may express the same idea in terms of institutionalization by interpreting the social system as an interlaced network of positions, each defined by a socially approved typification of particular interaction-patterns. These typifications also establish the requirements of the position, its authority and duty, to which any incumbent of this position, whoever he may be. has to live up. They also determine the abilities. skills, or fitness – in brief, the

[26] R. H. Tawney, *Equality*, New York, 1931, p. 122.

competence and qualifications – each incumbent is supposed to have in order adequately to fulfill his functions. The conclusion would naturally follow that only qualified persons should be eligible for such positions.

The postulate of equal opportunity in the objective sense is mostly stated in the form of the slogan, "The career open to the talents." In this form it means, however, something more: not only competent persons should be eligible, but *all* competent persons, regardless of any other criteria, should be equally eligible, it being understood that among all the *eligible* persons the best qualified should obtain the position. The French Declaration of Human Rights of 1789 postulates that

all are equally eligible for all honors, places, and employments, according to their different abilities without any distinction other than that created by their virtues and talents.

This postulate corresponds to Aristotle's notion of distributive justice, that award should be granted according to merit. But Aristotle had already stated that the concept of "merit" is different for each society. In our terminology we should say it is the relative natural conception of the world that determines, or at least codetermines, the competences and qualifications everyone eligible for a position has to possess. The reference of the definition of these qualifications to the natural conception of the world prevailing in the particular group leads frequently to the consequence that elements are included in the definition which have no, or merely a remote connection with the proper fulfillment of the particular position. It is, for instance, characteristic of the present American scene that the qualifications required for certain jobs exclude from eligibility, as they do not in other countries of the West, persons over thirty-five years of age.

But there is another reason why equal opportunity in the objective sense, that is, the exact correspondence of highest qualifications for any given position, is impossible; and it was again Simmel, who emphasized this point. Any social order, says Simmel,[27] requires a hierarchy of superordination and subordination of positions, even if only for technical reasons. There

[27] Simmel, *op. cit.*, p. 76.

are, however, always more persons qualified for superior positions than there are superior positions. A good many factory workers could as well be entrepreneurs, or at least foremen; a large number of common soldiers have officer qualifications; there are far more persons qualified for leadership than there are leaders needed. The postulate that any talent develops freely, *i.e.*, that it finds the position commensurate with it, is frustrated by the incommensurability between the quantity of superior competence available and its possible use.

Simmel's argument is doubtless to the point. Nevertheless, Tawney has rightly shown [28] that the postulate of equal opportunity does not disregard the fact that only few can take part in the competition. Rightly interpreted, the postulate requires merely that no one is forever forbidden to enter it, and that no handicap is imposed on those who do.

So far, we have examined the objective meaning of equality of opportunity in the sense of the slogan, "The career open to all." But there is also equality of opportunity for education or the development of ability and talent; equality of opportunity for sharing the benefits of culture; MacIver's concept of equal access to public opportunities, and finally, Tawney's [29] highly interesting statement that equality means not the absence of violent contrasts of income and condition, but equal opportunities for becoming unequal. We cannot enter into detailed discussion of all these notions in the objective sense, but in so far as the concepts involved are not merely subcategories of discrimination, our analysis of the objective meaning of opportunity is applicable, with slight modifications, to all of them. In all these cases objective opportunity is determined by socially approved typifications of social roles, role expectations, and positions.

Consideration must next be given to the subjective meaning of opportunity, that is, the meaning this notion has for the individual who in objective terms would be eligible to avail himself of an opportunity. Such an individual experiences what we have defined in the objective sense as an opportunity, as a possibility for self-realization that stands to his choice, as a chance given

[28] Tawney, *op. cit.*, p. 123.
[29] *Ibid.*, p. 123.

to him, as a likelihood of attaining his goals in terms of his private definition of his situation within the group.

This subjective chance [30] exists, however, from the subjective viewpoint of the objectively qualified individual, only under certain conditions:

1. the individual has to be aware of the existence of such a chance;
2. the chance has to be within his reach, compatible with his private system of relevances, and has to fit into his situation as defined by him;
3. the objectively defined typifications of role expectations have to be, if not congruent, then at least consistent with the individual's self-typification, in other words, he has to be convinced that he can live up to the requirements of his position;
4. the role for which the individual is eligible has to be compatible with all the other social roles in which he is involved with a part of his personality.

It can readily be seen that opportunities which are equal from the objective point of view may be, and in a strict sense must be, unequal in terms of the subjective chances of the particular individual, and *vice versa*. This is so because, merely from the *objective* viewpoint, social roles constitute the conceptual unit of the social system that can be typified and defined in terms of role expectations and competence. Moreover, merely from the objective viewpoint, everyone with equal qualifications can be deemed an equally eligible incumbent of the role.

From the *subjective* viewpoint, however, the individual does not look at himself as an eligible incumbent of a social role but as a human being who is involved in multiple social relations and group memberships, in each of which he participates with a part of his personality. Hence, even if it made sense to assume that equal subjective chances correspond to objectively equal opportunities, the individual human being would weigh the

[30] We prefer to keep this technical term coined by Max Weber despite the fact that the English translators Talcott Parsons and M. Henderson, have rendered it for reasons explained by them by "probability" and sometimes by "likelihood." (Max Weber, *The Theory of Social and Economic Organization*, New York, 1947, p. 100 n. 21).

chances in terms of his personal hopes, anxieties, and passions, which are his alone.

Strictly speaking, therefore, equal opportunity exists merely from the objective point of view. The subjective chances are unequal and as we learned from Plato (section II *supra*), to unequals equals become unequal.

Nevertheless, the ideal of equal opportunity in the objective sense is worthwhile fighting for. It should not, however, be so interpreted that the effect of its realization would be to provide "an equal start for everyone." Most of the authors dealing with this problem have referred to many factors that make an equal start impossible: differences of wealth, the pressure of mere material surroundings such as housing, sanitation, etc., economic conditions (such as the fact that only few men can devote their energies to education until manhood without being compelled to compete early for employment, or the inequality of access to information, particularly to financial information), are among them. Perhaps inequality of leisure time should be added to this catalogue.

As Crane Brinton has pointed out in his article on equality, equality of opportunity understood in these terms would be possible only if the social environment were altered:

... and this can hardly be done except by collective action. The logical conclusion to be drawn from the principle of equality of opportunity is not *laissez faire* but collectivism. The still numerous believers in this form of equality are, however, rarely logicians.[31]

But the ideal of equality of opportunity may mean something else, although something far more modest. It should assure to the individual who finds himself in the human bondage of his various group memberships the right to the pursuit of happiness, as we have defined this notion at the end of Section IV (1), and, therewith – in terms of his own definition – the maximum of self-realization which his situation in social reality permits.

[31] Crane Brinton, "Equality," *Encyclopedia of the Social Sciences*, Vol. 3, New York, 1937, pp. 574–580.

SOME EQUIVOCATIONS IN
THE NOTION OF RESPONSIBILITY

Our discussion of the problem of responsibility was mainly concerned with the question: On what grounds might a person be held answerable or accountable by law or from a moral point of view for something he did or omitted to do? The consequence of responsibility, in this sense, is the affliction of punishment, if we take this term in a sense broad enough to include reprehension, criticism, and censure. But even if used in this sense the notion "to be responsible" may mean two different things: on the one hand, a man is responsible *for* what he did; on the other hand, he is responsible *to* someone – the person, the group, or the authority who makes him answerable.

This distinction between "being responsible *for*" and "being responsible *to*" becomes of particular importance if another equivocation of the notion of "responsibility" is taken into account, namely, that between its use in terms of the third (or second) person and in terms of the first person. I submit that the notion of "responsible" is an entirely different one if used in a proposition of the type "This person is responsible for this and that" and in a proposition of the type "I feel responsible for this and that (e.g., for the proper education of my children)." Furthermore, I submit that these two notions of responsibility cannot fully coincide and that any philosophical analysis of the problem of responsibility must remain incomplete without taking into account its subjective aspect.

In using the expression "the subjective aspect" for the notion "feeling responsible" in terms of the first person, we adopt an unfortunate, but by now generally accepted, terminology of the social sciences, viz., the distinction between the subjective and the objective meaning of human actions, human relations, and human situations. It was Max Weber who made this distinction the cornerstone of his methodology. Subjective meaning, in this sense, is the meaning which an action has for the actor or which a relation or situation has for the person or persons involved therein; objective meaning is the meaning the same action, relation, or situation has for anybody else, be it a partner or observer in everyday life, the social scientist, or the philosopher. The terminology is unfortunate because the term "objective meaning" is obviously a misnomer, in so far as the so-called "objective" interpretations are, in turn, relative to the particular attitudes of the interpreters and, therefore, in a certain sense, "subjective."

To elaborate on the difference between the subjective and the objective meaning of responsibility would require a rather lengthy analysis. We have to restrict ourselves to some scanty remarks. If I feel merely subjectively responsible for what I did or omitted to do without being held answerable by another person, the consequence of my misdeed will not be reprehension, criticism, censure, or other forms of punishment inflicted upon me by someone else, but, regret, remorse, or repentance – or, in theological terms, contrition and not attrition. The resulting states of grief, anguish, or distress are marks of the true sense of guilt which is phenomenologically something entirely different from the "guilt-feeling" in psychoanalytic terminology. It is the outcome of the feeling of being responsible for something done or left undone and of the impossibility of restoring the past. Orestes in Aeschylus' *Eumenides* was not redeemed before the goddess reconciled the Furies, although the judges of the Aeropagus had placed an equal number of white and black balls into the urn. In our times, we find certain eminent scientists suffering under a deep–rooted sense of responsibility for having cooperated in the production of atomic weapons, in spite of the honors bestowed upon them by a grateful government. On the other hand, the law might hold me answerable for an act which my personal sense of responsibility motivated me to perform (Antigone's conflict is an example). And here the distinction between being responsible for something and being responsible to someone appears in a new light. I may agree with the Other's verdict that I am responsible for a particular state of affairs but maintain that I feel accountable for my deed merely to God or my conscience but not to my government.

These are merely examples for the complicated underlying dialectic of the subjective and the objective meaning of responsibility. But the same dialectic underlies the meaning a norm has for the norm-giver and the norm-addressee. Any law means something different to the legislator, the person subject to the law (the law-abiding citizen and the lawbreaker), the law-interpreting court and the agent who enforces it. Duty has a different meaning as defined by me autonomously and as imposed on me from outside. The whole question of determinism in law and ethics will have to be answered in a different way if formulated in subjective or objective terms.

The preceding remarks dealt with the dialectic of the subjective and objective meaning of laws, values, morals, and responsibility merely from the point of view of the individual. But the same dialectic recurs on the level of group relations. Adopting Sumner's classical distinction between in-group and out-group, it can be said that "responsibility," for example, has a different meaning if an in-group acknowledges responsibility for its acts and holds some of its members responsible, or if an out-group makes the in-group and its members responsible for misdeeds. It is one thing if, in the Nuremberg trials, the Nazi leaders were held responsible by the Allied Powers, and quite another thing if they were held answerable by the German people.

TIRESIAS, OR OUR KNOWLEDGE
OF FUTURE EVENTS

I

Tiresias was blinded early in life because he saw Athena naked, but the gods comforted him by the gift of seercraft. This is one of the many forms of the myth handed down to us through the centuries.

Though Tiresias cannot see what actually happens, he has knowledge of things to come. Yet without any power to bring them about or to prevent them, he remains an impotent onlooker of the future. "A fearful thing is knowledge, when to know helpeth no end," says Tiresias in Sophocles' *Oedipus, King of Thebes*.

Does Tiresias, the seer, as distinguished from Tiresias, the helpless blind man, live in the present at all? The images of future things pass through his stream of consciousness, they are integral elements of it. But strictly speaking, merely the acts of his seeing belong to his vivid present; what he sees will materialize in another present, which now still belongs to the future. Tiresias, incapable of seeing his actual surroundings, visualizes a world in which he does not live and in which he has never lived. Moreover, none of his fellow-men lives, or has ever lived, in this world, which is neither that of his contemporaries nor that of his predecessors. Later on some of his contemporaries or their offspring will live or will have lived in it. Actually, however, they do not know that they will do so; they did not pay the price for seercraft by becoming blind to their present. Tiresias' knowledge is thus his private one, for the time being inaccessible to his fellow-men. If it is intersubjective at all, it does not refer to other subjects' present or past experiences, by which it could be verified or falsified within a universe accessible to all. Only other people's future experiences, once having been lived through, will prove the truth or falsity of what the seer states.

Nevertheless, these visions of his are not phantasms but experiences of a reality to be. His is neither a blind belief in what will happen nor a mere guess at what might happen. His judgments are affirmations of future real events, not in terms of probability or likelihood but in terms of certainty. This holds good even in cases in which such judgments have the hypothetical form of "if ... then" statements. Consulted by Odysseus in limbo – for he kept his seercraft after death – Tiresias forecasts for him and his men a safe return to Ithaca if, and only if, they refrain from hurting the herds of Helios on the isle of Thrinacia.

But how is it possible that Tiresias looks at the future in terms of "if ... then" occurrences? Of what structure is his knowledge of future events? Does he live through the onrolling phases of the future happenings, unaware of their outcome, building them up step by step, as the onlooker in the theater follows the events on the stage, not knowing how the play will end or even what the next scene will be? If this is the way in which the consciousness of Tiresias experiences the future – as an ongoing flux of becoming – how is it that he can grasp in a single glance the outcome of the adventures that wait for Odysseus? And up to what point will Tiresias follow the ongoing flux that has no end? What delimits his field of consciousness?

It may be objected that Tiresias looks at future happenings not with the attitude of a spectator in the theater but rather with that of the playwright, who has preconceived the outcome of the play in one single vision and then develops the phases of the plot by which the final situation is brought about. But the dramatic author is sovereign in his microcosm. He can arrange things and events therein arbitrarily; he is their omnipotent creator. The seer does not create anything; the events are not of his making, and they escape his influence. If this knowledge of the future events is similar to that the playwright has of the outcome of the drama, how does he come to know of the chain of events leading to the final state of affairs?

Or – a third possibility – does Tiresias look at the future event as if it were a fact that occurred in the past, the genesis of which he has to tell? In this case he would turn to the envisioned future situation as a ready-made accomplished one, in a kind of anticipated retrospection. He would proceed like a historiographer, except that the latter explains the present situation by events looked at in terms of the past tense or the present perfect tense, or a past situation by events looked at in terms of the pluperfect tense, whereas the seer explains the future situation by events looked at in terms of the future perfect tense. If this were true Tiresias would not prophesy what *will happen* but what *will have happened.* In a certain sense his forecasting would be a vaticination after the event (*vaticinium ex eventu*), for, although in reality the event is still in the future at the time of the vaticination, the seer anticipates it as if it were a past one.

But let us compare the structure of Tiresias' vision of future events, for example of Odysseus' homecoming, with his genuine vaticinations after the event, for instance, in Sophocles' tragedy, his revelation to Oedipus concerning his past, up to then unknown to everyone but soon to be confirmed by eyewitnesses. In the latter case Tiresias discloses facts that have indeed happened in the past. They happened as they happened, and not otherwise; they may be open to various interpretations as to their meaning, but statements relating to the "matters of fact" as such are either true or false. What might have been an empty anticipation before, or while the event was materializing, has by its very occurrence either been fulfilled or not. Oedipus is or is not the son of Laius and Jocasta, and Tiresias' assertion that he is their son is not a hypothetical one. On the other hand, his prophecy of Odysseus' future adventures has the form of an "if ... then" statement. How would this be possible if our assumption were correct that Tiresias envisions the future in an anticipated retrospection? Disregarding Tiresias' conceivable wish not to discourage Odysseus by revealing to him the full truth, do we have to assume that the seer's knowledge of future events is incomplete? Does he not foresee that Odysseus' friends *will* persuade him to land on the island of Thrinacia, that evil winds *will* prevent them from leaving the island before all their food is consumed, and that they *will* hurt Helios' cattle, so that all the misfortunes conditioned by this fact must necessarily occur?

But if Tiresias' knowledge of the future occurrences is a mere fragmentary one, how does it come that certain things to be are known to him, even in terms of hypothetical possibilities, while others, as for example the materialization of such a possibility, are hidden to him? Or is his knowledge of the future not homogeneous? Do some portions stand out in full clarity while others are indistinct? Does perhaps William James' well known distinction between "knowledge about" and "knowledge of acquaintance" also apply to Tiresias' knowledge? In either case the question arises: What makes his knowledge of the future selective, and how does this mechanism of selection operate? To be sure, even the god at Delphi or Dordona gives his oracles frequently in the form of "if ... then" statements. But the god can interfere with the events to come; he can guide and steer them. Tiresias cannot. He is the mere onlooker of happenings beyond his control, and his knowledge is "a fearful thing that helpeth no end."

To sum up, any attempt to conceive how the mind of a fictitious seer might know future events confronts us with the following alternatives. On the one hand we may assume that his consciousness experiences the future events in terms of an ongoing flux. In this case every element of the flux carries with it open horizons of empty anticipations referring to *following* experiences, which may or may not fulfill what was anticipated. These following events are then known – if this term is here admissible at all – merely in terms of likelihood, and all the seer's statements relating to them are hypothetical ones. Or on the other hand we may assume that the seer experiences future events as if they had already occurred. They are no longer in flux, no longer carry along empty anticipations; they *have* happened, or at least the seer experiences them as having happened. Then his veridical statements relating to them have a categorical and not a hypothetical character. An "if ... then" statement could at best refer to the explanation of the meaning of events experienced in such a way, not to their occurrence.

Neither assumption, however, explains what motivates Tiresias to select this and that particular moment of the future rather than any other as his point of vantage in order to become the chronicler or historiographer of events now still to come but experienced by him in terms of an ongoing present or of an irretrievable past. Moreover, neither assumption explains why

Tiresias' knowledge of the future, as in the case of his forecast
of Odysseus' homecoming, is either fragmentary or heterogeneous
and what determines the gaps or the heterogeneity of his knowledge. We ordinary human beings are motivated in our selections
by our biographical circumstances and by our situation within
the world. Tiresias' knowledge of the future is, however, supposed
to be independent of his present and past experiences. The famous
demon of Laplace is free from the seer's predicament. Knowing
in full the state of the universe at a given moment, knowing also
in full the laws governing this universe, the demon has a complete
and homogeneous knowledge of any future state. Tiresias is
neither a Laplacian demon nor an ordinary human being. He is a
human being upon whom the gods have inflicted the gift of
seercraft.

II

But enough of Tiresias and his dubious gift. I have analyzed
his fictitious consciousness not alone with the purpose of showing
that the assumption of a perfect knowledge of future events by a
finite mind leads to unsoluble inconsistencies. My main concern
was to prepare the ground for the description of certain features
of the manner in which the common-sense thinking of ordinary
men, leading their everyday life among their fellow-men, anticipates things to come. Thus, for the time being, problems of
scientific prediction are intentionally disregarded. We have to
deal with the world in which each of us carries on the business
of living, in which each has to find his bearings and come to terms
with things and men. It is the *Lebenswelt*, as Husserl called it,
the structures of which he was starting to investigate in his last
writings.

In order to apply our analysis of Tiresias' consciousness to the
common-sense knowledge of future events, it may be useful to
enumerate briefly three of the major differences between the
situation of man within the *Lebenswelt* and that of the seer. In
the first place, man in everyday life interprets his past, present,
and future in terms of the preorganized stock of knowledge he
has at hand at any moment of his existence. Tiresias' visions of
things to come are independent of his pre-experiences. Second,

Tiresias is a mere unconcerned onlooker of the future events he envisions. Man, in daily life, is eminently interested in what he anticipates. He has to be prepared to meet or to avoid the anticipated events; he has to come to terms with them, either by enduring what is imposed upon him or, if it is within his power, by influencing their course. Thus his anticipations are determinative for his plans, projects, and motives. They are relevant to him, and he experiences these relevances in terms of his hopes and fears. Finally, Tiresias' visions are events within his private world, and as such are inaccessible to others. His knowledge of things to come is by no means related to the knowledge other people have. The *Lebenswelt* of man is from the outset socialized, one world common to all.

A word of elaboration regarding this last point: my stock of knowledge at hand does not consist exclusively of experiences lived through directly and originarily by me. The greater portion of it is rather socially derived: it consists, that is, of experiences lived through directly and originarily by my fellow-men, who communicated them to me. Hence I assume – or better, I take it for granted in the practice of everyday life – that other people's knowledge at hand is to some extent congruent with mine, and that this holds good not only with respect to knowledge of the world of nature, common to all of us, but also with respect to knowledge of the social and cultural world I am living in.

This congruency enables me, especially as regards the social world, to anticipate future events in such a reliable way that I am inclined to state that I "know" what will happen. I "know" that tomorrow will be Friday, that people in the United States will file their income-tax returns on or before April 15, that every year the total of retail sales in New York during the month of December will be higher than during August, that in the first week of November 1964 a person born in the United States not later than 1934, most probably a white male, will be elected President of the United States. Closer analysis shows that the validity of anticipations of this kind is founded on the assumption that some or all of my fellow-men will find in their stock of knowledge at hand typically similar elements, and that these will determine the motives of their action.

Unfortunately, the socialized structure of our knowledge of the

Lebenswelt cannot be investigated within the frame of this paper. Such an analysis would require a rather detailed discussion of the various dimensions of the social world and the social distribution of knowledge conditioned by them. Instead of embarking on such an enterprise, I propose to devote the remainder of this paper to the first two problems mentioned: that of the role of our stock of knowledge at hand in forming anticipations of future events and that of man's interest in his anticipations.

III

Man in daily life, as I have said, finds at any given moment a stock of knowledge at hand that serves him as a scheme of interpretation of his past and present experiences and also determines his anticipations of things to come. This stock of knowledge has its particular history. It has been constituted in and by previous experiencing activities of our consciousness, the outcome of which has now become our habitual possession. Husserl, in describing the constituting process that is here involved, speaks graphically of the "sedimentation" of meaning.

On the other hand, this stock of knowledge at hand is by no means homogeneous, but shows a particular structure. I have already alluded to William James' distinction between "knowledge about" and "knowledge of acquaintance." There is a relatively small kernel of knowledge that is clear, distinct, and consistent in itself. This kernel is surrounded by zones of various gradations of vagueness, obscurity, and ambiguity. There follow zones of things just taken for granted, blind beliefs, bare suppositions, mere guesswork, zones in which it will do merely to "put one's trust." And finally, there are regions of our complete ignorance. To investigate all the details of structurization would far surpass the scope of this paper. I have to restrict myself to pointing out in a highly sketchy way a few features.

First, let us consider what determines the structurization of the stock of knowledge at a particular Now. A preliminary answer is that it is the system of our practical or theoretical interest at this specific moment which determines not only what is problematic and what can remain unquestioned but also what has to be known and with what degree of clarity and precision it has to be known in order to solve the emergent problem. In other words, it is the particular problem we are concerned with that subdivides our stock of knowledge at hand into layers of different relevance for its solution and thus establishes the borderlines of the various zones of our knowledge just mentioned, zones of distinctness and vagueness, of clarity and obscurity, of precision and ambiguity. Here is the root of the pragmatistic interpretation of the nature of our knowledge, the relative validity of which has to be recognized even by those who reject the other tenets of pragmatism, especially its theory of truth. To be sure, even within the restricted limits of common-sense knowledge of everyday life, the reference to "interests," "problems," "relevances" is not a sufficient explanation. All these terms are merely headings of highly complicated subject matters for further research.

Secondly, it must be emphasized that the stock of knowledge is in a continual flux, and changes from any Now to the next one not only in its range but also in its structure. It is clear that any supervening experience enlarges and enriches it. By reference to the stock of knowledge at hand at that particular Now, the actually emerging experience is found to be a "familiar" one if it is related by a "synthesis of recognition" to a previous experience in the modes of "sameness," "likeness," "similarity," "analogy," and the like. The emerging experience may, for example, be conceived as a pre-experienced "same which recurs" or as a pre-experienced "same but modified" or as of a type similar to a pre-experienced one, and so on. Or the emergent experience is found to be "strange" if it cannot be referred, at least as to its type, to pre-experiences at hand. In both cases it is the stock of knowledge at hand that serves as the scheme of interpretation for the actually emergent experience. This reference to already experienced acts presupposes memory and all of its functions, such as retention, recollection, recognition.

It is with good reason that I have just referred to the typicality of our experiences. As Husserl, to whose basic investigations the present view owes so much, has convincingly shown, all forms of recognition and identification, even of real objects of the outer world, are based on a *generalized* knowledge of the *type* of these objects or of the *typical* style in which they manifest themselves.

Strictly speaking, each experience is unique, and even the same experience that recurs is not the same, because it recurs. It is a recurrent sameness, and as such it is experienced in a different context and with different adumbrations. If I recognize this particular cherry tree in my garden as the same tree I saw yesterday, although in another light and with another shade of color, this is possible merely because I know the typical way in which this unique object appears in its surroundings. And the type "this particular cherry tree" refers to the pre-experienced types "cherry trees in general," "trees," "plants," "objects of the outer world." Each of these types has its typical style of being experienced, and the knowledge of this typical style is itself an element of our stock of knowledge at hand. The same holds good for the relations in which the objects stand to one another, for events and occurrences and their mutual relations, and so on. In other words, we experience the world from the outset not as a "blooming, buzzing confusion" of sensory data, or as a set of individual insulated objects without relation to one another, or as isolated events that could be detached from their context, but in its structurization according to types and typical relations of types.

At this point in the discussion it is important to realize that our actual experiences are not referred to our past experiences by retentions and recollections alone. Any experience refers likewise to the future. It carries along protentions of occurrences expected to follow immediately – they are so called by Husserl as a counterpart to retentions – and anticipations of temporally more distant events with which the present experience is expected to be related. In common-sense thinking these anticipations and expectations follow basically the typical structures that have held good so far for our past experiences and are incorporated in our stock of knowledge at hand.

Husserl handled this problem in investigating the underlying idealizations and formalizations that make anticipations in daily life possible at all. He has convincingly proved that idealizations and formalizations are by no means restricted to the realm of scientific thinking, but pervade also our common-sense experiences of the *Lebenswelt*. He calls them the idealization of "and so forth and so on" (*und so weiter*) and – its subjective correlate – the idealization of "I-can-do-it-again" (*ich kann immer wieder*).

The former idealization implies the assumption, *valid until counter-evidence appears*, that what has been proved to be adequate knowledge so far will also in the future stand the test. The latter idealization implies the assumption, *valid until counter-evidence appears*, that, in similar circumstances, I may bring about by my action a state of affairs similar to that I succeeded in producing by a previous similar action. In other words, these idealizations imply the assumption that the basic structure of the world as I know it, and therewith the type and style of my experiencing it and of my acting within it, will remain unchanged – unchanged, that is, until further notice.

Nevertheless – and again Husserl has pointed this out with utmost clarity – our protentions and anticipations of things to come are essentially empty references to the open horizons and may be fulfilled by the future occurrences or may, as he graphically puts it, "explode." In other words, any experience carries its own horizon of indeterminacy (perhaps an indeterminacy that is to a certain extent determinable), which refers to future experiences. How is this insight compatible with the basic idealization of "and so forth" and "I can do it again"?

I venture to propose two answers, for neither of which Husserl is responsible. First, our anticipations and expectations refer not to the future occurrences in their uniqueness and their unique setting within a unique context, but to occurrences of such and such a type typically placed in a typical constellation. The structurization of our stock of knowledge at hand in terms of types is at the foundation of the aforementioned idealizations. Yet because of their very typicality our anticipations are necessarily more or less empty, and this emptiness will be filled in by exactly those features of the event, once it is actualized, that make it a unique individual occurrence.

Secondly, we have to consider that, as stated before, not only the range but also the structurization of our stock of knowledge at hand changes continually. The emergence of a supervening experience results by necessity in a change, be it ever so small, of our prevailing interests and therewith of our system of relevances. It is this system of relevances, however, that determines the structurization of the stock of knowledge at hand, and divides it into zones of various degrees of clarity and distinctness. Any shift in the system of relevances dislocates these layers and redistributes our knowledge. Some elements that belonged previously to the marginal zones enter the central domain of optimal clarity and distinctness; others are removed therefrom to the zones of increasing vagueness. Moreover, it is the system of relevances that determines the system of types under which our stock of knowledge at hand is organized. With the shift of my prevailing interests, therefore, the types valid at the moment of anticipating will also have changed when the anticipated event occurs and becomes an actual element of my vivid present.

Using the terms *in their strictest meaning* we may therefore say paradoxically that in the common-sense thinking of everyday life whatever occurs could not have been expected precisely as it occurs, and that whatever has been expected to occur will never occur as it has been expected. This is not in contradiction of the fact that for many useful purposes we may and we do in everyday life correctly anticipate things to come. Closer analysis shows that in such cases we are interested merely in the typicality of the future events. It may be said that an occurring event was expected if what really happens corresponds in its typicality with the typicalities at hand in our stock of knowledge at the time of our anticipating its occurrence. The important point to be emphasized, however, is the fact that merely in hindsight – *ex eventu* – does an occurrence turn out to have been expected or unexpected. Used in the present tense the statement "I expect" has an entirely different meaning. All anticipations in the common-sense thinking of daily life are made *modo potentiali*, in terms of chance. It is likely, presumable, conceivable, imaginable that "something of this or that type" will occur. Thus all anticipations refer in the mode of chance to the typicality of future events, and carry with them open horizons that may or may not be fulfilled when the anticipated event occurs in its uniqueness – provided it occurs at all – and becomes itself an element of our stock of knowledge then at hand. And again, this discrepancy between our expectations and their fulfillment or non-fulfillment by the anticipated facts is itself an element of our stock of knowledge at hand and has itself a particular cognitive style.

Although it is impossible to deal within the frame of the present paper with the problem of scientific prediction, it might

clarify the issue under scrutiny just to state why scientific prediction *is* possible. The system of verified and tested propositions
accepted in the corpus of the particular science may be regarded
as the stock of scientific knowledge at hand. This knowledge, in
contrast to that of everyday life, is homogeneous, in so far as the
methods and rules of scientific procedure determine, at least
ideally, the scientific interests, that is, the conditions of selecting
and stating the problems, the types of constructs to be used for
this purpose, the system of relevances, dependent on them, the
degree of clarity, distinctness, and consistency of scientific knowledge, and the criteria according to which a problem has to be
regarded as solved; the latter include the rules of verification or
falsification. Nevertheless, all modern philosophers of science
agree that the system of science is of a hypothetical nature, and
that scientific certainty – like all empirical certainty – is, in
Husserl's formulation, "certainty until further notice" (*Gewiss-
heit bis auf Widerruf*).

IV

The foregoing analysis of the dependency of our common-sense
anticipations upon the stock of knowledge at hand has already
referred to the prevailing interest that determines the structurization of our knowledge. I find myself at any moment of my
existence within the *Lebenswelt* in a biographically determined
situation. To this situation belong not only my position in space,
time, and society, but also my experience that some of the elements of my *Lebenswelt* are imposed upon me, while others are
either within my control or capable of being brought within my
control and therefore modifiable. Thus the ontological structure
of the universe is imposed upon me and constitutes the frame of
all my possible spontaneous activities. Within this framework
I have to find my bearings and I have to come to terms with its
elements. For instance, the causal relations of the objective world
are subjectively experienced as possible means for possible ends,
as obstacles or supports for the spontaneous activities of my
thinking and doing. They are experienced as contexts of interests,
as a hierarchy of problems to be solved, as systems of projects
and their inherent performabilities.

This is the reason why I am vitally interested in anticipating the things to come in the sector of the world that is imposed upon me and escapes my control. I am a mere onlooker of the ongoing happenings herein, but my very existence depends on these happenings. Hence my anticipations concerning events in the world beyond my control are codetermined by my hopes and fears. They are framed, in common-sense thinking, not only in the potential but also in the optative mode.

A special problem as to the anticipations of future events originates, however, in the sphere of human action. For the purpose of this paper the term "action" shall designate human conduct as an ongoing process that is devised by the actor in advance, that is, based on a preconceived project. The term "act" shall designate the outcome of this ongoing process, that is, the accomplished action or the state of affairs brought about by it. All projecting consists in an anticipation of future conduct by way of phantasying. It is, to use Dewey's pregnant description of deliberation, "a dramatic rehearsal in imagination." Yet projecting is more than mere phantasying. Projecting is motivated phantasying, motivated by the anticipated supervening intention of carrying out the project. The practicability of carrying out the projected action within the imposed frame of reality of the *Lebenswelt* is an essential characteristic of the project. This refers, however, to our stock of knowledge at hand at the time of projecting. Performability of the projected action means that according to my present knowledge at hand the projected action, at least as to its type, would have been feasible if the action had occurred in the past.

The project is in still another respect related to the stock of knowledge at hand. This becomes clear when we examine whether it is the future ongoing process of action, as it will roll on phase by phase, or the outcome of this future action, the act as having been accomplished, which is anticipated in phantasying or projecting. It can easily be seen that the latter, the act that will have been accomplished, is the starting point of all of our projecting. I have to visualize the state of affairs to be brought about by my future action before I can draft the single steps of my future acting from which that state of affairs will result. Metaphorically speaking, I have to have some idea of the structure to be erected before I can draft the blueprints. Thus in order to project my future action as it will roll on I have to place myself in my phantasy at a future time when this action will already have been accomplished, when the resulting act will already have been materialized. Only then may I reconstruct the single steps that *will have* brought forth this future act. What is thus anticipated in the project is, in the terminology proposed, not the future action, but the future act, and it is anticipated in the future perfect tense, *modo futuri exacti*.

Now as pointed out before, I base my projecting of the forthcoming act in the future perfect tense on my experiences of previously performed acts typically similar to the projected one. These pre-experiences are elements of my stock of knowledge at hand at the time of projecting. But that knowledge must needs be different from the stock of knowledge I shall have at hand when the now merely projected act will have been materialized. By then I shall have grown older and, if nothing else has changed, at least the experiences I shall have had while carrying out the project will have enlarged and restructurized my stock of knowledge. In other words, projecting, like any other anticipation of future events, carries along empty horizons that will be filled in merely by the materialization of the anticipated event; hence for the actor the meaning of the projected act must necessarily differ from the meaning of the accomplished one. Projecting (and still more, carrying out the project) is thus founded on the stock of knowledge at hand, with its particular structurization, at the time of projecting.

On the other hand, the project once constituted modifies this structure decisively: the goal to be attained, the act to be accomplished, the problem to be solved becomes the dominating interest and selects what is and what is not relevant at this particular moment. It has to be added that neither this dominating interest nor the projecting in which it originates is isolated. Both are elements of *systems* of projects, interests, goals to be attained, problems to be solved, arranged in a hierarchy of preferences and interdependent in many respects. In ordinary language I call these systems my plans, plans for the hour or for the day, for work or for leisure, for life. These plans, themselves in continuous flux, determine the interests presently in focus and hence the structurization of the stock of knowledge at hand.

This double relationship between the project and the stock of knowledge – on the one hand the reference to my experiences of previously performed acts that I can perform again, on the other hand the reference of the project to my systems of hierarchically organized interest – has a highly important additional function. I have spoken, very loosely, of the particular moment of time, the Now, at which the stock of knowledge is at hand. But in truth this Now is not an instant. It is what William James and George H. Mead have called a specious present, containing elements of the past and the future. Projecting unifies this specious present and delimits its borderline. As far as the past is concerned, the limits of the specious present are determined by the remotest past experience, sedimented and preserved in that section of knowledge at hand that is still relevant to the present projecting. As far as the future is concerned, the limits of the specious present are determined by the span of the projects presently conceived, that is, by the temporally remotest acts still anticipated *modo futuri exacti*.

As long as we succeed, within this unified and delimited realm of the specious present, in keeping our projects consistent and compatible both with one another and with the stock of knowledge at hand, there exists a reasonable chance that our future action will conform, at least in type, to our project as anticipated *modo futuri exacti*. Such a chance will, however, be a subjective one; that is, it will exist merely for me, the actor, in the form of reasonable likelihood, and there is no warranty whatever that this subjective chance – chance for me – will coincide with objective probability, calculable in mathematical terms.

V

These much too cursory remarks have shown, I hope, that in common-sense thinking our knowledge of future events consists in subjective anticipations that are founded in our experiences of past events as organized in our stock of knowledge at hand. We have seen that we have to distinguish between events that will occur without our interference and those to be brought about by our actions. The former refer to the preconstituted typicalities and their system, as we find them at hand in our stock of knowledge. Under the idealization of "and so forth and so on" we take it for granted, until counter-evidence appears, that anticipated events will partake of the same typicalities. The latter are anticipated as if they had already materialized, since our project refers *modo futuri exacti* not to our future on-going actions but to the acts that will have been the outcome of such actions.

Thus we are brought back to the problem of Tiresias. Is it possible to have knowledge of future events otherwise than in terms of anticipated hindsight? Are we in the role of mere spectators, are we the makers of future events, or are we retroverted historians? In common-sense thinking we must refer to our pre-experiences and to our specious present, which connects our expectations of things to come with our experiences of things that have been. As regards future events that we are unable to influence, we may anticipate their course merely by assuming that, as a rule, what has held good in the past will hold good for the future. Otherwise – except for Tiresias, who does not refer what he envisions to his stock of knowledge at hand – we cannot expect any event of whose typicality we have had no pre-experience. Unable to control what is imposed upon us, we are mere observers of what is going to happen, but we are observers governed by hopes and fears. Like the spectator at the theater, we do our best to make sense of what we have lived through so far, and remain confident that the author of the onrolling drama will reveal its meaning at the end. This end itself is undisclosed to our knowledge. Though it may be hoped for by our religious or metaphysical faith, it is not known to us.

In the realm of future events that we assume can be influenced by our actions, we consider ourselves the makers of these events. Actually, what we preconceive in the projection of our action is an anticipated state of affairs that we imagine as having been materialized in the past. Nevertheless, in projecting our actions into the future, we are not merely retroverted historians. We are historians if we look from any Now back to our past experiences, and interpret them according to our stock of knowledge now at hand. But there is nothing open and empty in our past experiences. What was therein formerly anticipated has or has not been fulfilled. In projecting, on the other hand, we know that what we anticipate carries along open horizons. Once materialized, the state of affairs brought forth by our actions will necessarily have quite other aspects than those projected. In this case foresight is not distinguished from hindsight by the dimension of time in which we place the event. In both eventualities we look at the event as having occurred: in hindsight as having really occurred in the past; in foresight as having become quasi-existent in an anticipated past. What constitutes the decisive difference is the bare fact that genuine hindsight does not leave anything open and undetermined. The past is irrevocable and irretrievable. Foresight, as anticipated hindsight, depends on the stock of our knowledge at hand before the event, and therefore leaves open what will be irrevocably fulfilled merely by the occurrence of the anticipated event itself.

Tiresias does not have this problem. He does not act, does not interfere, does not hope and fear. He has immediate and originary knowledge of future events (if a consciousness of such a structure is thinkable at all). We, who have not received the gift of seercraft from the gods, do not have such knowledge. We do not even know what to wish and what to pray for. Let me, in concluding, explain how this is meant.

Among the apocryphal works of Plato there is a dialogue, the so-called Second Alcibiades, that was probably written by a member of the Academy in the third century B. C. Though the dialogue is apocryphal, the style a poor imitation, the spirit is truly Platonic. Socrates is in the temple of Zeus. Alcibiades comes to pray. Socrates brings up the question: how do we know what we should pray for? A man may without knowing it implore great evils for himself, believing he is asking for the good, especially if the gods are in the mood to grant whatever he may request. The dialogue turns around this question, and Socrates offers as a last word of his wisdom a prayer by an old Pythagorean poet:

King Zeus, grant us good whether prayed for or unsought by us
But that which we ask amiss, do thou avert.

INDEX

WITHDRAWN

142.7 S396c 1966
v.2
Schutz, Alfred,
 1899-1959.
Collected papers.

    1962-66.

DATE DUE

GAYLORD   PRINTED IN U.S.A.